THE QUIET
ASSASSIN

ALSO BY THOMAS KIRKWOOD

THE SVALBARD PASSAGE (WITH GEIR FINNE)

THE QUIET ASSASSIN

A NOVEL

BY THOMAS KIRKWOOD

DONALD I. FINE, INC. • NEW YORK

Published in the United States of America by Donald I. Fine, Inc. and in Canada by Fitzhenry & Whiteside, Ltd.

Library of Congress Catalogue Card Number: 84-073451
ISBN: 0-917657-14-4
Manufactured in the United States of America

This book is printed on acid free paper. The paper in this book meets the guidelines for permanence and durability of the Committee on Production Guidelines for Book Longevity of the Council on Library Resources.

For Nancy

I would like to thank Dr. Jan F. Kreider, Dr. James Tharp, Dr. R. Stanley Brenton and Timothy Fox for technical advice in areas where my knowledge is thin, and Molly LeClair for ongoing editorial assistance.

I am especially beholden to Nancy Kirkwood, who nurtured this story from start to finish with ample encouragment and a fine critical eye.

What follows is the account of a woman, Käte Frassek, whose courage and perseverance were legendary, whose honesty in that murky area between private and public life remained undiluted through years of deprivation, whose humanity was never tainted by the bitter trials of her calling...a woman who nonetheless became an assassin. How does one pronounce ethical judgment on such a life? Better that task be left to the biographers and historians. And to you, the reader, should you be so predisposed.

PART I

CHAPTER ONE

A chill November fog settled over Berlin. In the Western Sector, it softened the blues and reds of the dazzling neon lights and muffled the strident din of traffic. The great city became more gentle to behold, as though its rough edges had been smoothed away. But in the East, the fog spread like a dark blanket over lifeless gray squares and boulevards. The gloom, already pervasive, deepened.

Käte stood at the window, her shawl pulled tightly around her shoulders. A streetcar clanked by four stories below, lighting up the rails that stretched across the uneven cobblestones. Mist swirled in the dim orange lamplights and transformed the tavern sign on the corner into a smudge. Vopo troops from the nearby casern marched over the cold sheen of the sidewalk, their ranks as straight as the row of leafless chestnut trees lining their path.

It began to rain. At first it was only a drizzle, but it soon fell in great silvery sheets, lashing the drab facades of the buildings and sending the few late-night pedestrians scrambling for shelter. The wind howled down from the Baltic across the sandy plains of northern Pomerania.

11

It tore holes in the fog and swept it away. Käte could see the bright glow of West Berlin reflected in the sagging overcast . . . West Berlin, an island surrounded on all sides by a police state . . . an island she hoped to reach when her work in the East was finished.

Where is Ursula? she wondered nervously. The Chekhov play was out at ten. She should be here by now. Had something gone wrong? Had the message failed to reach her in West Berlin? Had she perhaps gone off on vacation?

The sight of a woman Käte's age briskly rounding the corner in front of the tavern put an end to her speculation. She scolded herself for worrying: Ursula Landau did not take vacations in November, nor did she fail to show up when Käte needed her. Smiling to herself, she hurried into the kitchen to fetch the cakes and coffee.

At the door, Käte helped Ursula out of her stylish raincoat and placed her umbrella in the wooden stand. The weather had been bad in Berlin that fall, abnormally bad.

"Are you all right?" asked Ursula, examining her friend with concern. "You look so pale."

"I'm fine," said Käte. "Come and sit down. I've made us some coffee. How was Chekhov?"

"Splendid, really." She paused, holding the coffee cup to her lips. The rain hammered the window in staccato bursts. "I've been so worried about you since your message came. What is it? Is something wrong?"

"On the contrary. I have happy news. Karl and I are going to try to escape—"

"Oh, God, I—"

"Don't worry about us. It will of course be with Clayton's help. There are some fairly safe ways to get out if one has his kind of money to spend."

Ursula stared at her, shocked. "Yes, he's told me as much. But why now, in the middle of the police crackdown your Hannah Mühlendorff has caused? Wouldn't it be better to wait?"

"Ursula, calm down. We'll be all right."

"Yes . . . yes, I'm sure it will work out. Oh, Käte, Clay must be absolutely euphoric. It's really all he's wanted since he met you. How is he taking the news?"

Käte averted her eyes. "He doesn't know yet. That's why I needed

12

you to come. I've got to see him soon. Now that I've made up my mind to go, the waiting has become unbearable."

"Oh, I can imagine! He's in the States right now, but he's returning to Berlin soon. He left word at the bank. The twenty-second, I believe. Do you want me to telephone him in Colorado?"

"Thanks, Ursula. That would be great." She thought for a moment. "He'll be back in West Berlin on the twenty-second?"

"That's what he wrote."

"Good. Perhaps he could cross over on the twenty-third. Would you ask him to meet me in the Zentralfriedhof that evening? I'll wait for him from seven to eight."

"The cemetery?"

"Yes. My late so-called husband Heinz-Albert is buried there, as you know. And Professor Kirstein, whom Clayton once worked with, has joined the ranks. It gives us both nice excuses if we're questioned."

"Let's hope you're not. Shall I break the news to him?"

Käte's brief flicker of a smile vanished. Tension sharpened the tiny lines around her eyes. "It won't be necessary. He'll understand..."

"Käte, what is it? You're frightened, aren't you?" Ursula hurried behind her chair and put an arm around her shoulders. "I know it must be terrible. Everything is so *frightening* here. Just looking at all those policemen makes me shiver. But don't worry. You're going to make it. Käte, remember what fun we had before the Wall went up?"

"That was a long time ago."

"I know, darling. But we're hardly old ladies. When you get out, there's so much we're going to do."

"Yes... yes. Thank you for being so kind."

They talked quietly for another half hour and embraced at the door as Ursula prepared to leave.

"There's one more little detail," Käte said quietly. "I'd like you to ask Clayton to wear a navy blue Rodier blazer when he comes. Size 42-L. It's very important."

"Käte! Have you lost your mind? Why start smuggling now? People get caught all the time, you could jeopardize your escape. This is—"

"Please. I'm not able to explain—"

"But, Käte, what do you have here that's worth risking your freedom for? You just can't—"

13

"Please just do as I ask and don't think me insane. Clayton will understand. I'll be out soon. And when I am, I'll be the old me again. I promise."

Ursula hugged her with tears in her eyes. "I know you will. I'll tell him. Good-bye, Käte. Be brave."

She hurried down the unheated staircase and out into the cold wet night. In forty minutes she had passed through the checkpoint in the Friedrichstrasse railway station and was on her way back to West Berlin via subway.

On the afternoon of November 23, Käte left work early. She walked alone through the main entrance of VEB Elektro-Apparate-Werke, the giant electronics firm where she had been employed as an engineer for twelve years. It was an odd sensation to cover the short distance to the overhead railway station at Treptower Park without being an anonymous drop in the great stream of workers with whom she otherwise came and went.

She glanced back over her shoulder. The soot-blackened plant seemed to her bigger and uglier than usual, the huge red billboard in front proclaiming solidarity with the Soviet Union an even greater eyesore. She quickened her pace.

The S-Bahn, the urban commuter train, was almost empty. Two Vopo lieutenants in riding boots stood at the back of the car, automatic weapons slung casually over their shoulders. They looked her over— not as a potential criminal ... how could they know who she really was, what she planned to do ... but as a very attractive woman. She ignored them. All her life they had been part of the daily environment, as common as postmen and streetcar conductors. You learned how to behave around them, displaying neither interest nor hostility. It had become harder these last years not to look at them, though. They wore the same uniform as her son, Karl. She often found herself wondering whether he was the only secret enemy of the state among them. She would know the answer soon...

The train clattered over the bridge spanning the river Spree. An industrial moonscape stretched out to either side along the banks. She gazed at the dismal factories, the rusty barges, the heaps of coal and gravel, the towering smokestacks belching their feculence into the leaden sky. She permitted herself no dreams of a different world that began just a few bends downriver, a world in which she and Karl and Clayton could live the life they all wanted. Such dreams promised too much, tended to divert her from her mission...

When she reached her small fourth-story flat in the Pankow quarter of East Berlin, the day was rapidly fading. A chill lay in the room. She blew the cinders in the old stove to life and placed a coal brick on the embers.

In the kitchen she put water on to boil and straightened her soft blond hair in the pantry mirror. From the closet she took her sewing basket and an elegant navy blue blazer, size 42-L. She laid both on the sofa, admiring the jacket while she waited for the water to heat up. One-thousand-eight-hundred West German marks at the most exclusive Intershop in East Berlin—and worth every penny of it, she thought. What a wonderful gift it would have made; what a shame to turn it into a piece of dangerous baggage for the man she loved.

The coal stove, hot at last, groaned and popped. Her mug of bitter coffee sent up tiny wisps of steam. The last steely light of the afternoon slanted across her fingers as she worked with delicate precision on the blazer.

Through a large opening in the back, she probed beneath the silk lining for an internal seam she had not used. Finding one, she slit the stitches carefully. From her sewing kit she took a long, narrow strip of weightless nylon that was numbered and covered with fine, scarcely visible handwriting. She placed it between two layers of separated wool fabric and expertly closed the seam, using the same holes as the original thread. A thorough check on the outside of the blazer revealed no hint of tampering.

As darkness fell, the last nylon scrap was in place. She closed the incision in the jacket lining like a surgeon completing a long operation. The tedious work was at last finished. And none too soon. If General-oberst Heinrich Bülow, head of the Vopo—the East German People's Police—was to die as planned, that jacket had to go out with Clayton tonight.

CHAPTER T WO

Käte and Clay: a love that had begun more than twenty years ago. At the time, Clay was an exchange student in West Berlin. It was the daughter of his German host family, Ursula Landau, who conspired to send him East; she whom he would alternately curse and thank for the rest of his days...

They had been sailing her little red sunfish on the Wannsee all morning. Now they sat in the elegant enclosure of a waterfront cafe, drinking beer and eating sandwiches. Berlin was still new to him, and he was admiring most everything: the chic waitress, the green and white umbrella over their table, the ingenious latchlike lid on the beer bottles.

"Look over there," said Ursula, squinting into the summer haze. The year was 1963, the month, July.

Clay gazed at the wooded horizon beyond the lake.

"Don't you see those towers nestled among the trees?"

"I think so."

"Clayton, those are the watchtowers along the East German border. That's where the good life stops. You as an American are permitted to cross over for a day. Any desire to see what's on the other side?"

"I don't know. I've heard it's depressing."

"It's also reality, Clayton. I'd like you to go."

"I don't care much for that reality. West Berlin is more my style."

"Clayton, I'm asking you to do me a favor. My best friend lives over there. I haven't seen her since the Wall went up. We West Berliners aren't allowed to cross. She's depressed, I can tell from her letters."

"I'd be depressed, too. What does she look like?"

Ursula laughed. "I think you'd better stick to Lenore and the other girls I bring around. She's married."

"Married? How old is she?"

"Eighteen."

"My God! Is she a masochist?"

"I don't know, Clayton. Perhaps you can provide some answers. She wrote that he was an older man—much older. She's so full of life. It isn't like her to get tied up with someone like that. Her letter sounded like a funeral announcement. Clayton, please. Will you go see her for me?"

"All *right*. When?"

"Tomorrow."

West Berlin's U-Bahn Number Six is one of the divided city's many oddities. On its long journey from Tegel in the north to Altmariendorf in the south this modern subway passes beneath the downtown of East Berlin. The dilapidated stations in the Communist Sector have been permanently closed; the Number Six noses through their cavernous interiors like an intruder. On the cracked platforms are no waiting passengers, only occasional Vopo guards standing in the shadows with their automatic rifles.

There is, however, one point beneath East Berlin where the Number Six stops and opens its doors—the Friedrichstrasse station in the heart of the Communist capital. Like Checkpoint Charlie, it is a regular border crossing, only it offers visitors from the West immediate access to the S-Bahn trains operating behind the Wall.

Following Ursula's instructions, Clay got off the subway when it shook to a stop beside the faded FRIEDRICHSTRASSE sign. Haunted by the image of those dark, defunct stations through which the U-Bahn had just carried him, he kicked at the un-Germanlike heap of wrappers and cigarette butts on the platform. What must go through the heads of those Vopo guards? he wondered. How could they stand to spend their days in the subterranean gloom watching the bright subway cars roll to the West? His inclination was to feel sorry for them.

He glanced at the round clock hanging above the platform: 8:03 A.M. Better get moving, get this unpleasant mission over with. He walked through the exit and found himself face-to-face with a uniformed official behind a glass window. "Passport!" said the man, snapping his fingers. He studied the document carefully, then examined Clay's face for a full minute.

"Move ahead," he ordered, gesturing toward the far wall. Electrically operated doors opened with a loud bang, and Clay moved forward to another window. The scenery was better. A young woman, pretty except for the scowl on her face, prepared his one-day entrance visa and exchanged the obligatory five West marks into East marks. He decided to warm her up with his broad American smile. She glared back at him with contempt before yanking her head in the direction of the metal doors. *"Next!"*

"Nein," he heard her growl at someone else as he slunk off through the curtained exit. "Of course you can't change more than five marks here. This is a *border*, not a bank. Next!"

He pushed his way through the shabbily dressed crowds to the S-Bahn ticket window. "One ticket one way and one back..."

"Destination?"

"Heinersdorf."

By mistake he placed a West German mark on the revolving tray. The fat woman official, fiftyish and dressed in a sloppy blue uniform, fixed on him the same contemptuous stare the others had given off. *"What's that?* You are in the German Democratic Republic, the DDR. Here you use *our* currency."

"Terribly sorry," he muttered, dropping a feather-light East mark into the tray. His change and ticket whirled toward him like a round-house punch. "One more thing," he said, trying not to sound intimidated, "Could you please tell me which train goes to Heinersdorf?"

"Eh?"

"You see, this is my first visit to East Berlin—"

"*East* Berlin! This is not *East* Berlin. This is *Berlin*, capital of the German Democratic Republic!"

"Terribly sorry. I won't make that mistake again. Which train did you say went to Heinersdorf?"

"Go to information."

"But you must know which train it is. Look at the line over there."

"Information is not my job. What if everyone asked for information? *Next!*"

The enormous woman behind him bulldozed forward like a panzer, bumping him aside. Two Vopos who had been milling around nearby caught his attention. He walked up to them. Policemen, even unpleasant ones, usually liked to give information. It seemed to make them feel important. He would try. An hour wasted in line was an extra hour he would have to spend in a country he was rapidly coming to hate. "Gentlemen . . . officers . . . would you please tell me which train I take to Heinersdorf?"

The Vopos looked him over like human rubbish they were considering for extermination. One of them exhaled cigarette smoke into his face. The other gestured with his thumb toward the information booth and hoisted his automatic rifle higher on his shoulder. In their uniforms and high riding boots, they reminded Clay of Nazis.

"Thanks," he said, trudging off toward the line. The station was filthy and run-down. Decay hung in the air, intangible but real as rifle fire. Everywhere he turned he met more hostility. Why? He wasn't a Russian. He wasn't responsible for these people's misery.

At half-past nine he finally boarded the S-Bahn. The doors hissed shut and it clattered and lurched out of the station. In spite of the sunny weather, the city was a paragon of ugliness; a peculiar but nice phrase, he thought and almost smiled to himself. Out his left window was a massive dome, blackened and half-collapsed, the bones of its tired steel skeleton looming like a reminder of death above the gray Stalinist-style apartment complexes. Antiquated factories belched thick smoke. War ruins peppered scraggly, overgrown lots. At one point the train swung close to the Wall, affording him a view of the hodgepodge brick and cinder-block barrier. He could see the barbed wire along its top, the no-man's-land he knew contained mines, the dogs on runs,

20

the abandoned buildings nearby with their windows boarded up, the signs proclaiming the *Zonengrenze* with warnings against entry, the watchtowers manned by armed Vopos.

If he had not known it before, he knew it now: he was definitely on the wrong side of the tracks...or rather Wall...He would not come back here—not ever. He would make this visit, it was too late to turn around. But if Ursula expected him to while away his entire afternoon in this place, he'd have to disappoint her.

The house, like the others around it, was brown stucco. There was a garden in front and in the ceramic window boxes were geraniums. He had to force himself to knock.

A woman with the face of a bulldog opened. *"Bitte?"*

"Käte..." stuttered Clay. "Is Käte home?"

"Who are you?"

"I've come from the West. I'm a friend of..."

"Frau Frassek is unavailable. Leave your name, I will tell her you called."

He felt relieved in a way. At least he had an excuse for a quick exit. But he was also angry. It wasn't his practice to let everyone he met trample him. "Look, I've come a long way. At least tell her I'm here. I'll wait."

The voice, muffled by doors and walls, was fresh and very feminine. "Who is it, Frau Arburg?"

The housekeeper glared at Clay, then reluctantly ushered him into the vestibule. "It's a young man from the West," she bellowed. "He says he's someone's friend."

"I live with Ursula Landau's parents," called Clay up the staircase, pleased with himself for besting the old hag. "I'm an American exchange student."

"Wonderful," said Käte. "I'll finish my bath and be right down. Frau Arburg, make Herr..."

"Bentley, Clayton Bentley." He could hear her bathwater splash and imagined her lifting a naked leg to kick open the bathroom door.

"Make Herr Bentley a cup of coffee."

"How about a beer instead?" called Clay while the housekeeper looked on angrily.

21

"At ten-thirty in the morning?" answered Käte. "I don't know about you Americans. Frau Arburg, serve our guest a beer and make him a ham sandwich as well. I won't be a minute."

Clay followed the bulldog into the kitchen. She slammed a glass and bottle of beer with a hinged lid on the table and turned to the manual slicer to cut some bread.

He was eating his fat *Schinkenbrot* to the silent company of Frau Arburg when Käte swept into the room. He dropped the sandwich and stood, scarcely able to swallow. She extended her hand. "I'm delighted and honored, Clayton Bentley, that you've taken the trouble to come."

"The pleasure's mine, *all* mine." He had not been properly prepared for what he saw. She was young, as Ursula had said, but she carried herself with the elegant self-assurance of a much older, experienced woman. She was thin, of medium height, with full breasts and lovely blue eyes. Her blond hair, still wet from the bath, was piled casually atop her head. He traced the lines of her exquisite body beneath her light print dress, probing gently with his imagination. Whatever the ills of East Germany, he was suddenly willing to forgive and forget.

"So you live with those Landaus. They're marvelous people, aren't they?"

"That they are. Ursula sends her special regards."

Käte looked away. "It's been so long since I've seen her." A shadow passed over her pretty face, and Clay could see it cost her considerable effort to drive it away. "I don't want to be sad today," she said. "I want you to tell me everything, all the news from over there. Frau Arburg, when is Heinz-Albert expected home?"

"Not until after dinner, *gnädige* Frau."

"Good." She put her hand through Clay's arm as though they had known each other for years. "We'll take an excursion into the country. I get out into nature so rarely. It's one of the few things the government hasn't spoiled."

"*Gnädige* Frau, Herr Commissioner Frassek will be displeased."

"He won't know, will he, Frau Arburg? Unless you tell him, of course. See that you keep silent. Now come with me, Clayton. You like to walk, no?"

"I love to."

She pulled him by the hand through the living room, where the heavy oak furniture seemed more the housekeeper's style than hers. Frau Arburg followed for a few steps, looking on, scandalized, as Käte pushed open the heavy front door with a groan. Outside, she took off running. She laughed when Clay caught up to her, and was briefly her real age.

"Who is Commissioner Frassek?" asked Clay, a little out of breath.

"Shhh. We won't speak of him today. He's a dreadful boor. Unfortunately he's also my husband...I married him because I believed he could help my brother..."

Clay's heart sank. He had been praying for an error in communications, hoping she was not married after all. She certainly did not *seem* married.

They returned on foot to the S-Bahn station where he had gotten off, sat across from two thoroughly bored Vopos on the outbound train and rode to the end of the line. Clay worried they might be venturing beyond the city limits of Berlin—strictly prohibited by his visa—but he said nothing. A spectacular female was transforming the police state into paradise before his eyes, and he did not want to interrupt the magic.

Käte ducked into a shop and came out with a net full of cheeses and beer bottles. She handed it to him to carry, then took him once more by the arm. They strolled down a tree-lined country lane until they came to a wrought iron pedestrian bridge that arched over a railyard. Clay made her stop to watch when they were partway across. Below, dozens of giant steam locomotives puffed under the bright noon sun, proud beasts of another age on display in a veritable rural museum.

"My grandfather used to take me to the station when I was a kid," he said. "We'd watch a few of the expresses steam in and then go drink hot chocolate in the restaurant. It's really sad. Railroads have all but died out in the States."

"You can get your fill here," said Käte with a smile. "I spend half my life being shaken to death on the S-Bahn. Did you come in through the Friedrichstrasse station?"

"Yes. The employees weren't very friendly."

"I suppose that's true. I don't notice anymore, but I remember complaining earlier. You get used to almost anything. I'll be taking the

S there every day this fall. I'm starting out at Humboldt University."

"Maybe you can find another way to go. What's your major field going to be?"

"Engineering. I wanted to study literature, but that's not allowed if you've got any scientific talent at all. The political leadership here stresses technical education, as you probably know."

Smells from the farmland ringing the metropolis wafted in on the light breeze; the tarnished copper spire of a medieval church rose from the nearby horizon. Clay imagined himself for a moment in quaint preindustrial Germany, a land of poets and thinkers. He was charmed by the rustic vistas all around him and, of course, by Käte. He wanted to pull her close, wanted to forget the guards in the U-Bahn stations, the officials with their icy inhuman stares, the awful woman at the ticket window. "Will you be happy studying engineering?"

She stopped in her tracks and looked directly into his eyes. "Clayton, there's something you should know about me. I don't think about being happy. I've... I've known too much. My mother. My father. Now Rolf."

"Rolf? Your brother?"

"Yes. They killed him." Just like that, an announcement, scary in the practiced control with which she said it. "He opposed the government, they killed him. It's not so unusual. So don't talk to me about happiness... that's a subject for children."

Now he put his arm around her, and she waited several moments before removing it. "I'm sorry," he said.

"I shouldn't have told you ... It's not been easy lately."

"I understand," said Clay. But he didn't, really. How could he? He was a young American who knew nothing about death or midnight police interrogations.

The road was now little more than a rutted dirt path. It meandered through several tiny farming villages and sank into vast rustling fields. An old peasant approached, shooing a team of oxen.

Clay and Käte scurried up an embankment hand in hand, walked through the straight rows of wheat to a thicket of poplar trees until they reached an unfarmed swath of meadow on top of a gentle rise.

Far away, across a sea of fields and villages, they could see the gray skyline of Berlin. It was warm, nearly hot, and the smells of earth and

24

hay were strong. When the wind hit them just right it brought a whiff of pine from the forests.

Käte kicked off her sandals. She lay back on an elbow, shook out her damp hair, lifted her face to the sun. Clay watched her from the corner of his eye. The breeze caught her dress and slid it halfway up her thighs. She reclined on both elbows and did nothing to cover her legs.

He opened a beer and looked away, confused. What the hell was he supposed to do? She was driving him wild, stretched out like that beside him with her dress nearly up to her panties. Who was she, anyway? She claimed to hate her husband. She was eighteen years old. She said she was unhappy. Did she want him, or was this some Eastern version of the cock-tease? No . . . why was he so slow to learn? It was nothing more than a simple European lack of modesty. He remembered how he had almost drowned three weeks ago when Ursula had changed into her bathing suit right on the Wannsee beach. Germany. What a riddle. What a mind-boggling mélange of good and bad.

Käte seemed unaware of his agony. She told him about her schooldays in the West and reminisced about happier times. Then, placing a hand on his, she described the day the Wall was begun. That had been two years earlier, in 1961. Throughout the Soviet Sector, people were forced to decide on very short notice whether to leave everything they had— family, friends, possessions, careers, homes—in order to flee. With her connections and friendships, she would have much preferred to slip across the border during those last chaotic days. But her mother was ill and Rolf was deeply involved in the underground. Neither would consent to go with her, and she was unwilling to abandon them.

"And now?" asked Clay. "You must be very bitter . . . are you in the resistance?"

She smiled. "Why don't we get off the subject of East Germany. It's a wretched place. Tell me about yourself, Clayton. What do you do in the States? What brought you to Berlin?" She rolled on her stomach in the grass, crossed her ankles and kicked up her feet behind her.

What was he to say? His desire for her was rising again, and his overtaxed German was getting worse by the minute. Was he supposed to talk about his life? What the hell could he say that wouldn't shame and embarrass him? Should he tell her that he was rich, that his trust at the Chemical Bank, worth several million, had passed into his name on his twenty-first birthday? Or that he had gone to the best schools America had to offer, had done well, had always felt that life wasn't much of a problem and—at least until today—had never had much sympathy with those who did?

Käte...the East. In the course of one brief day he had been pushed far beyond the limits of his meager awareness. How did one explain such an experience? He couldn't. He was horny as a bull and hopelessly afloat in a world he no longer understood. He had lived in a hermetically sealed bubble all these years. He was a prisoner, too, confined in a musty cell of puerile beliefs and even prejudices. "Me?" he said, deflated. "Oh, there isn't much to tell. I'm just an average guy out to see a little of the world."

What drivel poured from his shiny American mouth! He felt so naive, so...*impoverished*. Why was this wonderful person bothering to listen? Why didn't she get up and walk off? He must somehow convey to her a sense of what he was. Well, what was he? "I'm going to be a doctor," he said. "Well, I guess I am. That's what I'm doing now, studying premed. But...you see...none of the things like you've been through have ever happened to me—"

Käte rolled on her side and was closer to him. "Be grateful for that. It's wonderful you're planning to be a doctor. My father was a doctor..." She ran her fingers through the grass. "Clayton, I'm so happy you came to see me. It's been like receiving a gift. It's the first nice thing that's happened to me for many months." She found his hand and squeezed. "Hold me," she whispered. "Would you mind terribly holding me?"

He tried to look at the situation with some objective distance. Was she, by chance, trying to involve him in a scheme to get her out of East Germany? Was she an agent for the Stasi, the secret police his friends in West Berlin had warned him about? Or did she simply mean what she said? Suddenly he didn't care. He took her in his arms and held her tight, brushing his lips across her cheek. She seemed to tremble. Was he kidding himself, or was she for real? Maybe he should ask her straight out to make love. Be direct with German women—that's what Ursula had told him. He found her lips, kissed her, pulled back and looked into her eyes. She smiled at him, tenderly and without the

26

slightest embarrassment. He kissed her again, felt the last vestiges of his self-control begin to dissolve. "Forgive me," he heard himself say, "but I want to make love to you. Am I getting out of line?"

"Clayton," she sighed, pulling away. "Clayton, after all that I've been through, do you think I would deny myself a moment of happiness? From the second I saw you sitting there with Frau Arburg, I knew I wanted you."

Not taking her eyes from him, she draped her leg over his thigh. The hot wind of the afternoon had dried her hair and now blew it provocatively about. He felt as though he were falling into a dangerous abyss, but if so at least lured by unimaginable pleasures. Slowly, he thought, slowly...

Her dress billowed with the next gust. She did nothing with it, continued to look at him. He smoothed the light material down over her legs, took her in his arms and kissed her for a long time. He felt the contours of her superb body against him—her breasts, her legs, her sex. He buried his face in her hair. "Käte..." he whispered.

She fell back free of him and slipped out of her clothes. The wind carried her dress away. She helped him undo his jeans while he lifted his cotton shirt over his head. He struggled to prolong his passion and lay with her for what seemed a bittersweet eternity, not yet coupled but entwined in a soft embrace...

Later, when she begged him to enter her, the wind had ceased. He could hear the ever-so-faint laboring of the steam locomotives in the railway yard they had passed. And he could hear Käte. She talked to him in a low, sweet voice until her rapid breathing swallowed her words. Then suddenly she clutched him and whispered something in his ear he didn't understand. She moaned, cried out, moving so violently beneath him that he could stand it no longer...

They had rolled to the edge of the clearing. She snared her dress with a raised foot and let it fall on his stomach. He spread it over them. And with her head on his chest she began to cry, quietly. He caressed her hair and back, and as he did he knew his carefree, empty life in the West could no longer interest or satisfy him.

CHAPTER THREE

Käte's plot to assassinate Bülow was the last stage in an intricate revolutionary scheme she had begun to piece together not long after meeting Clay. All through the harsh winter months of 1964 she would lay awake at night, watching the dim glow of the coal stove as she struggled to find a new and more effective device for fighting the autocratic, suffocating police rule. Then, one night in April, she hit on it. Three weeks later, as spring came to northern Europe, she went to see Wilhelm Jahn...

Near the Weissensee on the outskirts of East Berlin, an overgrown path twisted through the foliage behind a small gardener's cottage. The path led to a clearing, where rows of fine wooden birdhouses hung from the lower branches of great oak trees. The gardener who occupied the cottage was ill, and he no longer looked after his birds. But the birds still came, drawn home, perhaps, by the memory of better times.

Käte pushed a wisp of her blond hair from her forehead and glanced at her watch. She knew Jahn was near, waiting to show himself. She did not object to his caution. It was why he was alive, and why her brother Rolf was dead.

She had known Wilhelm Jahn for many years, and had always been fond of him. He was a chemistry teacher at the local secondary school, a soft-spoken man of thirty with intelligent brown eyes and thinning hair. Had Rolf not confided in her during one of his monumental drunks, she would never have suspected that this modest academic was an important figure in East Germany's fledgling underground.

He appeared in the clearing without a sound. "Good day, Käte," he said, extending his hand.

"Good day, Wilhelm." She brushed off a faded green bench and pulled him down by the arm. "I have a proposition to make to you." She didn't smile when she said it.

Jahn jabbed his wire-rimmed glasses into place with his thumb and studied her. "I think I know what it is . . . Käte, I can't take you in. Not yet. Your brother's murder is too recent. You must give yourself another year to cool down. Besides, you're too young and the work is too dangerous—"

"I don't want to go to work for you. What I want is a collaboration you will find . . . irresistible."

"Oh?"

"The people of this country are crippled with fear, Wilhelm. They don't trust the underground. Until you have mass support you'll get no further than Rolf. I can provide you with a tool that will have a chance to revolutionize the people—not just a few courageous souls like yourself, but the ordinary men and women of the DDR."

"A magical tool? And what might it be?"

"Stories."

"Stories?"

"Yes. Tales of resistance, set in the Nazi past. Allegories, of course. You have printing presses, don't you?"

"Presses, we've got. But you're not going to revolutionize anyone with stories—"

"I believe you'll change your mind. I want you to forget that I'm Rolf's little sister. From now on think of me as Hannah Mühlendorff. That's the name I've taken for myself as an underground writer. I've already begun. I'm writing about a family named the von Ettingers, a very brave family that lived during the Hitler years. The head of the family, General von Ettinger, has always been a loyal military man, but when the Jews are brutalized during the *Kristallnacht* he has a rude awakening. He announces in a dramatic speech to his family that he has made his choice—he's going to oppose the beast. He discovers, to his relief, that his wife, daughter and three sons all share his feelings. That night the family concludes a pact that will change German history. They agree to become a tiny resistance cell whose objective is the assassination of top-level Nazis... But, Wilhelm, the real goal of my assassins is not to kill a few evil men. It's to stir up mass popular opposition to the police state. The von Ettingers know that in order to succeed they must make the assassinations into rousing mass events. They decide that the best way to do this is to announce each assassination in advance in hundreds of thousands of leaflets. The leaflets will identify the 'condemned' Nazi, discuss his crimes and predict how he will die. With the entire population waiting, the assassins will strike. Try to imagine the reaction each time new leaflets flutter from church steeples and factory roofs all over Germany. With your help my stories about the von Ettingers will come down just like those leaflets. The stories can give the people of this sad land something to *rally* around. Our citizens will start off by cheering the anti-fascists Hannah Mühlendorff has written about. But it won't be long until they're cheering Hannah Mühlendorff herself—and you, all of you, the men and women of the underground who have risked so much."

Jahn looked at her, impressed. "Go on. I'm listening."

Käte was tense with excitement. "I will write twenty, thirty, forty of these stories. In each one the von Ettingers will predict the death, and then dispose of some rotten Nazi. Then, Wilhelm, when you and I agree the East German people are ready—and I realize this might take years—I will write one final story. This last one will be set in the present. The victim will not be some fictitious Nazi but one of our own oppressors, the worst East German official we can find. My story will explain the reasons this man must die and predict the way his death sentence will be carried out. The story, with your help, will come down all over the DDR. And then we shall actually kill him. If we succeed at this we'll have the people behind us. The days of vicious police rule in this country will be numbered—"

Jahn took hold of her arm. "Käte, it's something we can work with ...it's the device we've needed and not been able to come up with."

31

And then he was abruptly glum. "But this work of the resistance writer isn't for you. I'll find someone else to—"

"*No.* You must let me at least try."

"Shhh. Keep your voice down. I'm sorry for this, but before we met I had some of my people check on you. You and that American friend of yours are being watched by the Stasi—"

"Do you really believe I haven't noticed. That relationship is coming to an end. It's a decision I've not easily made these last weeks. But I *have* made it. You know that I'm not naive enough to start on a career as Hannah Mühlendorff while I am involved with a foreigner. The affair is over, I swear this to you. It has to be. I've already set the date to tell him—next Thursday. I *am* going to do what I've spelled out today, even if it means working with another underground group..."

She felt sick to her stomach and split in half by pain, as she did whenever she thought of the coming break with Clay. Their love had grown into something far more serious than she had expected. Whenever he stayed away more than a couple of days she would find herself hungry with longing. And when he would finally appear, waiting for her with his broad smile and dark curly hair outside the vaulted lecture hall at the university, she would feel a relief and excitement that left her weak. They would give each other the signal and rush along separate routes to Helene's flat above the cigar store, where they would make love until it was all they could do to climb out of bed. Clay would open his packages, prepare a spread of Western delicacies while he regaled her with perfect imitations of border guards, then take her once more—for the road, he would say. Their passion for one another was so pure, and explosive, she knew it could never die. No matter what. And when he would leave, she would stand at the window and watch him cross the dark square on his way to the Friedrichstrasse station, afraid that each time he disappeared around the corner he would not return...

And now she was ending it—and with that she felt numb. Nothing, not even Jahn's tight embrace, could make her feel she was anything but horribly, totally alone on this earth.

"You love him, don't you, Käte?"

"Yes. But I refuse to give into that until I've done what I must do. I know myself, Wilhelm. There is only one way for me—"

"Käte, dear Käte. Go West, I'll arrange your escape. Make your meeting with him a happy one. He wants you too, doesn't he?"

She struggled against tears. "He talks marriage. He's already looking into buying my way out. If only he would *stop*. He doesn't know what it does to me inside."

"Go, Käte. They took your father. Your mother died as a result. They took your brother Rolf. You've sacrificed much more than your share. Go, with my admiration for the plan you've devised and with my heartfelt best wishes—"

She dug her nails into his arm. "Wilhelm, I'm *not* going anywhere. Besides, there's something that will help me . . . I'm pregnant. I'll at least be able to keep a part of him, and that fool I married will never know the child belongs to someone else. I'm strong, Wilhelm. Stronger than you think. You and I *are* going to work together. Six months from this Saturday you will find the first Hannah Mühlendorff story in that birdhouse up there—the fourth one from the left with the hinged roof. Every three months after that you'll find a sequel. Print them, distribute them. Don't worry about the Stasi following me to you. We'll see each other only when we are ready to move to the final story, the one set in the present that will predict the death of one of our leaders. Then there will be much to coordinate. We will have to kill him—and get me out of the country as well. But until then, you have your job and I have mine. No one in the world but you knows who Hannah Mühlendorff is. Which is how it must remain. I intend to work quietly, very quietly. Go on now, Wilhelm. I know you're busy. And don't look at me that way. I'm not a child, and I'm not the emotional wreck you take me for. I'm your friend and *partner.*"

With those words, she kissed him on the cheek, stood and walked down the tangled path without looking back.

On Thursday Clay rode the "Six" unsuspectingly toward his impending breakup with Käte. He was happy. He'd at last reached an agreement with an organization in West Berlin he was confident could smuggle her out. She had always said she wouldn't go—at least not for a while—but when he presented her with the concrete possibility he was sure she would change her mind. It was time for her to come out . . . he'd been commuting across the damn Wall for nearly eleven months now.

33

He completed his border formalities without incident, crossed the Alexanderplatz on foot and pushed his way into the crowded cafe where he was to meet her. She was nowhere in sight. He ordered a round of pilsner and schnapps, drinking like a native as he watched the entrance.

But it was Käte's friend, Helene, who finally appeared. Clay rushed to her side. "Is something wrong?"

"No, I don't believe so. She's waiting for you at the railway yard near Heinersdorf. She said you would know where it is."...

He found her sitting on a black pile of cinders, her arms wrapped around her knees. He pulled her to her feet and hugged her, but she was limp as a rag doll. "Käte, what is it?"

With her head solemnly bowed, she took his hand and led him among the tracks. A steam locomotive approached through the haze, and he felt almost as though he must pull her out of its path. While the cars rumbled by, she began to speak. "It must end, Clayton. You mustn't ask me why. You and I can't go on, I can't explain, I'm sorry—"

"What the *hell* are you talking about? I've got a surprise for you. You can *leave*, Käte."

She ran behind a caboose and disappeared into a maze of tracks and freight cars. When he caught up to her, she turned away. He grabbed her by the arm and shook her. "Käte. Tell me what's going *on*."

"You've got to leave me," she said, out of breath. "I'm *not* in danger. Heinz-Albert has *not* discovered us. I'd be lying if I told you that. It's something else I can't discuss with you... please, don't torment me, Clayton. Or yourself. It's over, it has to be—"

She let herself down on a coupling between two boxcars. He stood over her. "It's someone else?"

"Come," she said, her voice suddenly warm. "Come here." She put her arms around his neck, pulled him close and kissed him. "It is not ... believe that, at least. Clayton, this has nothing to do with you. But it's something in my life that has to be done. I'm sorry..." God, she thought, what an understatement. But how could she risk the plan, or him if he knew of it ...?

Two railway workers came in their direction, staring curiously. He jerked her to her feet and hurried off with her. He dragged her up the thorny embankment along the tracks and kissed her when they were hidden in the bushes, as though trying to wipe out what he couldn't

34

accept. "You can't do this to me, Käte. To us. You're coming out of this dungeon—"

"Clayton, stop. Forget me. Go home and finish your university. Make a life for yourself..."

And then they were making love, arguing, crying until his midnight exit deadline. By the time he left, he was an exhausted, confused and wounded man. He packed his things and moved out of Ursula's house, arriving in Princeton the next week.

Käte was more accustomed to pain than he, and she now had an obsession that at least helped her ignore her pain. She gave her agony over to Hannah Mühlendorff, who was learning how to fashion such things into a weapon more powerful than tanks.

As it turned out, it would be nineteen years until Käte and Clayton saw each other again...

CHAPTER FOUR

In October of 1981 East Germany was once more plunged into turmoil. The latest story in the ongoing saga of the von Ettinger family had just appeared, and people were reading it wherever they could: beneath the amber streetlights, in the long lines at the food stores, on the crowded commuter trains.

Vopos scurried about like confused bird dogs, ripping the forbidden pages from anybody they could catch. They were not making arrests; they had long ago learned the futility of trying to throw an entire nation in jail. But they did not hesitate to use their truncheons, and more than a few skulls were cracked. People grew angry at this ugly police violence, but they were still frightened... and a long way from open defiance.

In East Berlin the hubbub was particularly severe. Hoping to avoid it, Karl Frassek took the long way to the S-Bahn station, wandering into the deserted expanses of Treptower Park. Clouds skirted across the moon. The trees, almost leafless now, stretched like gnarled hands into the milky sky. Dew glistened on his shoes and on the neat arcs of lawn illuminated by the path lights. In the shadows along the shrubbery, fog hovered in weird formations near the ground. It was cold. He drew

37

up the collar of his jacket and thrust his hands into his pockets. Stopping beside a park bench, he listened for the owl that was reputed to come live in the park every fall.

He was on his way to visit his mother. It made him sad to think how little they saw of each other since Coach Grundig had moved him to the special training dormitory. They used to take the train up to the Baltic on Sundays and spend the day walking among the barren dunes. But now Sundays were like all other days. He trained and trained and trained.

He knew he shouldn't complain. Every time he threw the discus, it seemed to soar a little farther. He was only seventeen and far from his prime, but he was so good that he was all but assured a spot on his country's 1984 Olympic team. That, for him, was the key. As soon as he got to Los Angeles, he would defect. But until that far-off day, much remained to be done.

He thought for a moment he heard the owl, but he soon realized it was the distant cry of a steam whistle. Perhaps it came from the giant VEB-Elecktro plant on the other side of the park where his mother had worked as long as he could remember.

He pulled his own hidden copy of the new Mühlendorff story out of his pants and began to read in the beam of his miniature flashlight. It was another brilliant tale, he could tell from the beginning. But he could not go on. Why should he read about the police state? He lived in one and knew every gruesome detail. Why should he think about insurrection? The problem for him was to keep the lid on his anger for another three years so he didn't land in prison before he could get out. Ah, but they were marvelous, inspiring stories. He agreed in principle with the thesis too. One should fight oppression. But he had already let his youth slip away. Was he supposed to sacrifice his adult years as well? Anyway, he wasn't in the same situation as the von Ettinger family. He had an escape for himself, and his mother.

He folded the pages and laced them through the slats of the bench so that someone else would find them in the morning. There were never enough of the stories to go around, and it had become a tradition in the DDR to make sure one's copy reached others.

He walked deeper into the park, veering left to avoid the massive Soviet War Memorial. His mother was not going to be happy with the news he was bringing her. The Vopo Academy in Berlin had recruited him. They had even brought in the head of the People's Police himself, Generaloberst Heinrich Bülow, to help make their pitch. Everyone knew the police loved to count the up-and-coming young athletes among their ranks. If you joined, they made life easy for you. You had plenty of time to train, a secure profession when your competitive years were over and access to special favors. Karl hated the police. But if his defection plan were going to succeed he would need one very special favor: a foreign travel visa for his mother in 1984. The authorities rarely extended such visas to sole remaining family members of traveling athletes. But if you were with the Vopo, exceptions were not unheard of.

He hated to upset her. He wished he could tell her the real reason that he was joining. But he didn't dare. If she knew about the defection plan in advance, she might get cold feet, might inadvertently say something...

When he arrived outside her apartment building a steady drizzle had begun to fall. He buzzed beside her name at the street-level entrance. When he got no response he used his own key to let himself in. He bounded up the unheated staircase to the fourth-floor flat they had shared until last year and buzzed again at her door. Nothing. He had strong nerves, but as he twisted the key in the lock he could feel his heart beating in his throat.

"Mother," he called, stepping inside. The small living room was chilly. He touched the coal stove. It had gone out. He knew she rose early to get to her job before the crush. Maybe she had turned in. He walked to the bedroom door and tapped. Not a sound. "Mother," he called again. "It's me, Karl."

He knew she was not in bed as soon as he opened the door... the curtains were not drawn and lights from the building across the street glittered in the mist on the window. It was raining hard now, and he listened to the drops beat a noisy rhythm on the glass. He wasn't really worried about her. She went to the theater or a concert from time to time during the week. It was just those first moments when he got no response to his buzzing and knocking. They were so close, mother and son. If something ever happened to her...

39

He cursed himself for neglecting to bring an umbrella. He had planned to have his mother call Coach Grundig and explain that her son would be spending the night. It was the only way to get around the ten o'clock dorm curfew the old martinet imposed. But his mother might not be here by ten, and explanatory calls *after* the curfew the coach did not accept. He glanced at his watch: 9:15. He'd better get back.

The umbrella first. He would have plenty to worry about if he showed up with wet, cold muscles. He could hear the bear growling at him already: "What? You let that golden arm of yours get soaked? Too bad you haven't got the same thing upstairs you've got in those muscles, Frassek. What's wrong with you? Trying to let your country down? Do I have to surround you with baby-sitters?"

He searched in the hall closet. The umbrella stand was empty. His mother would no doubt have listened to the weather forecast and gone out prepared. He found one of Heinz-Albert's bulky wool sweaters. The old man had been dead for three years. His mother, expert seamstress that she was, must have been saving the wool to refashion it into something else. He tried it on. Not a bad fit, but half a sheep wasn't going to do much good if he didn't have an umbrella.

He walked into his old bedroom and found it full of Käte's books and boxes. Perhaps the closet. He opened to the smell of mothballs and groped his way through the stored clothing. To his surprise his hand landed on the U-shaped handle of one of his old umbrellas. Pleased with himself, he backed out, dresses and slips draped over his head and something wrapped around his ankle. He kicked to free himself of the bothersome tentacle and launched a sewing basket ten feet into the room. Spools, needles, thimbles and buttons flew in all directions. He cursed out loud and brought a standing light to the disaster area to make sure he found everything.

He sat on the floor, did several of the hamstring stretches Grundig liked, then began to refill the basket. A few rumpled pieces of paper peeking from a side pocket caught his eye. Curious, he pulled them out.

Shock. On the pages, scribbled in Käte's own hand, was a draft of what was unmistakably the sequel to that day's Hannah Mühlendorff story. Incredible. He thought of his gentle, apolitical... or so he thought... mother, remembered her in a hundred innocuous poses:

40

making tea for him in the kitchen after school; smarting at some nasty adolescent thing he had said; politely consenting on the phone to work overtime at VEB-Elektro. What was *she* doing transcribing early drafts of the Mühlendorff stories? Did this mean she actually knew the notorious and elusive resistance writer?

His head began to spin. Wasn't there in the very first paragraph of these scrawlings he was holding an uncommon metaphor, or pun, his mother had used with him just a couple of weeks ago? "The birds of prey...prayers can't save them..." What had she been talking about ...? God, could it *be*...?

He was so caught up in his outrageous thoughts that he did not hear her enter the apartment.

Käte hung her raincoat and placed her umbrella in the stand. When she saw his wet jacket on the doorknob she walked directly to his old room, where bright light shown beneath the door. "Karl?" She gasped as she opened the door. "Karl, what are you *doing?*"

He looked up at her startled, then got to his feet, waving the pages. "Mother...what in God's name—"

"Karl. I should..." She became silent, then went to him, without a word, and hugged him long and tight. "Karl, you must forgive me. This is my secret. I've kept it from you because it's too dangerous. It's been bad, darling, living with the knowledge that if they catch me your life will be ruined too—"

He pushed her gently from him, looked at her, shook his head back and forth. "My God...you're *her,* aren't you? You are really her."

Käte nodded, forced a smile. "There are times I wish I weren't."

"Mother, I'm so proud of you. I don't know what to say. Do you have any idea what you've accomplished? Who you *are*...? Millions of people..." He shook his head, still not able to take it in.

"Karl, I'm a wretched, selfish woman. I've put you, my own son, in an impossible position. I should have told you the truth when you were young. I should have gotten you to the West earlier. But I just couldn't bring myself to tell you. I knew you wanted to stay here, you've worked so hard to be a part of the Olympic effort and...and, to be truthful, I didn't want to be without you. Selfish..."

He smiled, still shaking his head. "I always imagined Hannah Mühlendorff to be a tough, older woman. Someone who would sit with a bunch of hard-core revolutionaries in damp cellars smoking cheap cigarettes. Excuse me, mother...this is going to take some getting used to."

"Listen to me, Karl. I've given you a horrible jolt and you're not paying attention. You must leave the DDR. For my sake and yours. I'll come join you in the West as soon as I'm able. I have the contacts to smuggle you out. There's still time to get yourself on some other country's Olympic team. I spoke with Grundig the other day. He says you've already set a DDR record in practice—"

"Grundig! I'd forgotten him completely. Will you call him for me and tell him where I am? He's a stickler about that new dorm curfew—"

"Of course, and I'll also prepare us something good and warm to drink. Autumn is here, isn't it? Why don't you get the stove going and make yourself comfortable. Now that you know this much about me, I suppose the time has come to tell you the rest."

The stove came slowly to life, groaning and creaking as the hot iron expanded. Rain pounded the windows, driven by a gusty northeast wind that seemed to be growing stronger.

"I was young then," Käte said, "not much older than you are now. And stubborn. You've asked me several times why I married Heinz-Albert. It turned out to be a mistake, but my brother was in the Stasi prison in Berlin-Lichtenberg—you know, the Normannenstrasse facility where the really bad offenders end up. He'd taken on the whole system by himself and lost, of course. Heinz-Albert wanted very much to take a pretty young wife. He promised me he would use his influence to get Rolf out. I was warned that he had no influence to speak of... it was a last gamble, and it failed."

"Well, at least you got *me* out of the old fool."

Käte slid closer to her son and took his face in her hands. "Darling, I don't know how you will take this. I'm grateful, I suppose, that you were not fond of him...Heinz-Albert was not your father..."

"What?"

"Karl..."

"Yes...? For God's sake...who *is* my father?"

42

"An American."

"What?"

"A man named Clayton Bentley. A man I loved very much. A man I still love. I guess I will for the rest of my life." She poured another measure of rum in his tea, then drank it herself.

"Where is he? Did he leave you? I'll break his neck if he hurt you—"

"Karl, I ended it when I decided to become Hannah Mühlendorff. It was pretty bad ... I don't know how I survived those first months. But I was determined, oh, God, yes. They robbed me of my whole family. I couldn't have been happy in the West if I'd simply turned my back on their atrocities. And then you came along ... which took so much of the hurt away. I saw Clay in you ..."

"I always wondered why I could throw the discus so far. I remember you helping father—I suppose I should say Heinz-Albert—lift his own five-kilo suitcase onto the train. Is this Bentley still alive?"

"Do you remember Ursula Landau-Kettering? She's come over from the Western Sector to visit me a few times since the restrictions have been lifted."

"Yes?"

"She's kept in contact with him. He's become a rather famous medical doctor. He lives in the United States, is married and has no children."

"You're forgetting, mother."

Käte smiled. "So I am."

"What's he like?"

"I'll let him surprise you. Would you like to go to him?"

"Maybe. When you decide to leave the DDR."

"Karl, you must go right away. I can't leave until my work here is finished—"

"What do you mean? You've done this for how long, written your stories? Fifteen, twenty years? You've made everyone see what kind of society we live in. You've drawn the issues as clear as they can be drawn. If the people don't like the police state, they should overthrow it. Your work is finished, it seems to me."

"I'm afraid there's more."

"What?"

43

"Karl, my role in the DDR is identical to the role of the von Ettingers in my story. I am the catalyst. I am the one who has to supply the spark—"

"But you've already *done* all you can."

"There's more, darling. I haven't worked all these years merely to make the issues clear. The time is coming when I shall move to a more ...concrete form of resistance."

"No more secrets."

"No. Soon...when I feel people are ready, I plan to write a story set in the DDR. In the *present*, not in the past. In this story I'm going to predict the assassination of a particularly horrible party official. Then, Karl, with the help of the underground...well, I'm going to kill him. Please—don't interrupt. When I see things have finally gotten off to a good start, the people are ready to *act*, I'll be ready to go West. I'll have done my part, what I set out to do. And I'm sure the underground will be more than willing to smuggle me out. It would be bad for morale if Hannah Mühlendorff were caught—"

"God...you're incredible..."

"Now, precious, knowing what you do, you must leave. I'll have Ursula contact your real father. I'm sure he'll help. But go on with your life as usual for the moment. It will take a few days to arrange for your escape."

Karl opened the curtains now on a grimy pink dawn. "I've made a decision, mother," he said. "Two decisions, actually."

Käte looked up from the stove, where she was preparing coffee. They were both exhausted from hours of arguing. "And?"

"I'm not going West without you. If you want to give up this... this final action of yours and let the underground smuggle you out with me, I'll go with you. Otherwise, I stay."

She ran to him and hugged him. "Karl, please, no. You're all the family I've got—"

"Mother, remember that my family is the same size as yours. I am not going to leave you, and that is final. You'd better sit down. I'll finish making the coffee. And there's something else I have to tell you. A little secret of my own."

Käte let herself down in a chair beside the kitchen table, watched the water in the pot come to a boil. Karl took down the can of bitter ersatz.

"So what is this secret, Karl? I have the impression you've contrived some elaborate lie to justify your stubbornness."

"Not true. You'll be able to check out everything I'm about to tell you. And I don't need to justify my stubbornness. It's inherited."

"That was mean." But she had to smile.

"Mother, the reason I originally came here last evening was to tell you I'm going to be enrolled in the Vopo Academy."

"In the name of—"

"It's not what you think. They wanted me badly enough to put me under a lot of pressure. But that's not why I agreed. Do you really believe my obsession with the discus is just athletic? Do you see me as another muscle-bound idiot working for the glory of the party? Mother, I've been planning to defect for years. That's what all this is about. The Eighty Four Olympics were to be my ticket to freedom. My joining the Vopo was yours. Generaloberst Heinrich Bülow himself interviewed me. He liked me, even promised me a job on his personal staff when I graduated. Are you beginning to understand? To get you an exit visa to watch me at the Games, I needed some friends in the police. Give it to me, mother. I've made a damned good start." He handed her a cup of coffee and stooped to kiss her on the forehead.

"I had no idea," she said. "We've been two ships passing in the night, haven't we, darling?"

"Two ships of the same navy, at least ... This is the part you're not going to like—my second decision."

"Karl..."

"Hannah Mühlendorff builds her entire movement around a family resistance cell. You must approve of the concept."

"I don't. It's strictly a literary device. Karl—"

"Mother, we *are* that family cell you've been writing about. You *and* me."

"What are you talking about?" Knowing only too well.

"You don't really expect me to sit it out while you take all the risks. Remember what you told me last night about the man who was so totally opposed to letting you do the stories? Remember how you said to him that he had no right to keep you out of the movement? It's now

45

seventeen years later. I am in the position you were in when you made your decision to fight. If we don't leave the DDR together, I am going to join you—"

"Karl, you will *not* be involved in this..."

"Just listen, dear mother. Bülow was impressed with me. I could tell. In a couple of years or so I'll be a trusted member of his staff. He's the symbolic type you're looking for, *nicht wahr?* We needn't go into his public record. Everyone in the DDR is terrified of him. He's the right choice, and I am going to be in a position to kill him. Your chances of getting the job done will be a thousand times better with me in on it. We'll let your resistance friends help. We'll let them set up our route of escape for us. But the act itself... we'll do it ourselves."

Käte put her head down in her arms and cried softly. "What have I done? My God, what have I done?"

"You, mother, have done too much alone. Now pull yourself together and get ready. We both have a few shocks to get over. When we do, I think you'll find we'll work just fine together."

"Karl," she whispered, reaching for his sleeve. "Karl, darling, you must change your mind..."

But he did not. When he was eighteen years old he enrolled in the Vopo Academy in Berlin. As he had hoped, his good mind and physical prowess continued to attract the attention of Generaloberst Heinrich Bülow. Two years later, Karl was exactly where he wanted to be.

And thus was the Frassek resistance cell born. It was smaller than the von Ettingers' by more than half. But in courage and cunning it was every bit an equal.

CHAPTER FIVE

"Clayton," said Ursula. "I got your message and I'm delighted." She was telephoning him from West Berlin. He sat in a lounge chair on his redwood deck in the hills above Boulder, Colorado, a drink in one hand, his cordless receiver in the other. It was July again; July of 1983.

"It's always good to get back to Europe," he said.

"Clayton, would you and Elizabeth consider staying with us? I've discussed it with Michael and—"

"Elizabeth is no more. I'm on my own again."

"Oh, Clayton, I'm sorry."

"I'm not. I should have run when I found out her mother was chairman of the Michigan Republican Party."

"My, Clayton, but you've become crotchety in your old age. I doubt very much the problem was Elizabeth or her mother. You know as well as I you've been incapable of loving anyone since Käte. I tell you, you're going to die a bitter old man if you don't face up to that."

"Goddamn it, will you drop this crazy theory of yours. You're talking about something that happened twenty years ago—"

"I see you've been keeping track. Clayton, listen to me. Why do you insist on torturing yourself? You're divorced now—it should have come long ago, in my humble opinion. Apparently you feel the same. You're rich, you're a famous doctor. Heinz-Albert is long gone. What's stopping you?"

He looked east across the endless plains, east toward Europe and Berlin. "Have you seen her recently?"

"Yes."

"Well?"

"She's still beautiful, Clayton, stunningly so. But she's sad. She loves you. Don't you understand?"

"The hell she does. A woman doesn't spend a year making someone crazy about her and then smash it all. Not if she loves him."

"There's a reason she did it. I don't understand it either, but I know it has to be something important. Very. Clayton, when your name came up last time I was with her, she burst into tears." Silence. "Yes, she came completely unglued. I've not seen her like that in years. Go to her. Michael told me you would be doing some exchange work in the East..."

"That's right, the medical faculty at Humboldt University wants me to help them design a new children's anesthesiology program. I suppose it's less embarrassing for them than bringing in a West German."

"Clayton, you're full of it. East Germans don't make a habit of recruiting Americans. How did this arrangement come about?"

"I suggested it to a professor I know. Kirstein. But I'm not going to be with her. It's just the memories, Ursula. That's all. I think it was the last time I can say I was really happy. East Berlin—a damn strange place to be happy, if you think about it..."

He went to find her on the last day of his scheduled stay in the East. He had not been able to bring himself to go earlier, but now that he had made the decision to see her his emotions ticked like a time bomb beneath his hide. It was rush hour when he reached the gates of the VEB Elektro complex. When he first spotted her across six lanes of traffic he thought his mind was playing tricks on him. But then she glanced in his direction, and he knew it was Käte. Käte.

He actually shouted her name, and stepped from the curb, causing a black Wartburg to slam on its brakes. She hadn't seen or heard him in the tumult, and she began to walk north. He continued into the street, waving frantically. The traffic roared around him. He cursed the motorists. A salvo of blaring horns pounded at his temples. A tram blasted him with its shrill warning bell. He stopped so close to the clattering coaches he could feel the wind and smell the friction of worn parts. It ground to a halt before it was all the way past him, blocking his route. He ran behind it, where hordes of sweaty workers were getting on and off. He plowed ahead, using his elbows German-style. But when he reached the far sidewalk, she was gone.

He paused, scanned the crowds, then spotted her blond head just as she disappeared into a side street. He ran to the corner where she had turned, but again she was gone. Sweat poured into his eyes. His heart pounded. He did not know if he could generate the courage to come for her again.

He groped like a stricken man for support, found the corner of a building and slumped against it. All around him rose the gray facades of the city, scarred from the shrapnel and machine-gun blasts of past battles. Clay saw in them the reflection of his own life. Wiping his forehead with his sleeve, he prepared to return to his hotel.

He had not taken five steps when she came out of a bakery door several yards in front of him. She was carrying a loaf of bread, and when she saw him, she let it fall to the pavement. She went to him with only a little cry, went into his arms. "Clay..."

He pressed his lips to hers before she could finish his name, pulled her close and felt her incomparable body come to life underneath her light summer dress. "Happy anniversary," he whispered. "Twenty years. Long goddamn years."

She pulled free. "Clayton. We mustn't be seen in public, we must go separately. Come to my apartment. Grimmelsweg 8 in Pankow. Make sure you're not followed. And hurry. Please *hurry*."

"Shhh..."
"But Clayton—"
"Shhh..." His hands had already found their way beneath her dress. He hooked her panties with his fingers, dropped to the floor and slid them down her legs.

A summer shower had passed. Dappled light from the sun on the rain-splotched window made patterns on his hands. Still on his knees, he twisted and pulled the curtains to.

"Let's go to the bedroom."

"No." He rose slowly, kissing her thighs, her perfect legs. It was the same Käte, as though untouched by the years. She smiled, reaching behind her neck to undo her buttons. He lifted her dress over her head, and he took her standing.

He had forgotten how good it was; had forced himself to forget. She came with her legs laced around his back, her sounds ringing in his ears. He felt as though he could go on forever, as though all the times he should have made love to her these last decades had accumulated like some sort of sexual compound interest.

He took her again on the sofa. She lay on her back. He knelt above her and lifted her buttocks to him. As she moved, she let her ankles come to rest on his shoulders. So much he had pushed from his mind ...how her face in that burning instant held the passion of a whole lifetime.

Following her into the bedroom—she had at last insisted—he wrapped his arms around her from behind and toppled with her on to the bed. She laughed, a playful laugh that seemed to float through vacant time from a soft green meadow near Heinersdorf.

"Can you again?" she asked.

He did not answer, did not have to.

"I love you, Käte," he told her afterward.

"Oh, Clayton, I love you too. It hasn't diminished, not even a little. I knew it wouldn't."

"And people say time heals?"

"People who haven't really loved. Hold me tight."

He stroked her back as he whispered to her. "Käte, you must tell me now. You realize that, don't you?"

She sat up and turned away from him. He took her chin and forced her to look him in the eyes. "Käte, you *are* going to tell me. I mean it. And then you're going to leave this horrible place and come home with me. We love each other. If twenty years of separation doesn't prove—"

She stood up and started to walked away. "I'm sorry, my love. I cannot tell you yet."

"Käte." He got to his feet and seized her by the wrist. "I swear to God, I won't leave this apartment until I have *all* the answers. Let them come arrest me, you won't get me out of here yourself. Listen to me. Listen to *reason.* I've got connections. I've been working with the Humboldt University medical faculty. They like me and they're an influential lot. It'll cost, but who cares? I'll have you West in one week."

"Let go, Clayton. You're hurting me."

"Käte, for Christ's sake." He released her and watched, bewildered, as she hurried into the bathroom. The lock clicked and bathwater began to run.

"Käte, god*damn* you," he called out. "Open the damn door. You love me, goddamn you. I'm not twenty-one this time. You love me and I'm taking you with me. I don't care if I have to give you a general anesthetic and ship you to Boulder in a box. Where's the beer?"

"Clayton—"

"Shut up, and don't come out until you're ready to tell me everything. *Everything,* hear me?"

He rummaged around in her closet, found a short pink kimono and tied it around his waist, using the sleeves as a belt. In the kitchen he opened the refrigerator door and pulled out a half-liter bottle of pilsner. And waited.

Three-quarters of an hour later she had still not appeared. He tried to envision the outside of the apartment building. No balconies, no fire escapes—of that he was positive. It would be impossible for her to get out, but he might have a long wait. He really should call Professor Kirstein and report himself taken with a bad case of the stomach flu. Kirstein was giving him a farewell party later that evening and it was important to stay on the influential old man's good side. It looked as though he would need his help—very soon.

He tightened the kimono and walked to the phone, but before he could pick up the receiver a Vopo, in full-parade dress, opened the apartment door. Clay glared at him, thinking that Käte had found a way to signal down to the street. Well, he would show her he meant business. He would put up one hell of a fight before they dragged him off. He would rather have her at the prison door pleading for his release then go West without her. There were going to be no more goddamn broken hearts, no more nights spent in futile, frustrated speculation.

He backed up, straightening the crumpled pink garment over his private parts. The young policeman did not seem overly aggressive. He posed his automatic rifle and glanced at the pile of clothes the lovers had abandoned in the living room. "Consenting adults, I assume?"

"What the hell do you want?" Clay said, feeling ridiculous. The Vopo did not answer. He walked to the clothes, picked up the American passport that had fallen onto the rug and leafed through it. "Interesting," he said, tossing it onto the sofa. He shed his heavy uniform coat and white gloves, sat briefly to tug off his high riding boots. "Hot," he said, walking toward the refrigerator.

Clay circled like a cornered animal, staring at this intruder. "Look you. Don't you have any respect for people's privacy? Is it public policy in this goddamned dictatorship of yours to walk in on intimacies and drink everyone's beer. Get *out* of there."

Karl ignored him, took up a bottle and opened the hinged top. "Why don't you change into something a little less ... laughable?" he said, sitting down at the table.

"To hell with you. If you want to drag me out of here I'll go like this. Let your countrymen see what pigs you are."

"I wouldn't want the neighbors to see you in that garb ... father."

"Father? I'm about as far from a father as one can get—"

Karl smiled. "Well, then, if you're not going to change, why don't you join me? I see you've already opened your third bottle."

"What are you doing here? I demand to know—"

"I've come to visit mother. I presume you've done the same. I have a key to her apartment. I'm sorry if I startled you. I've imagined our first meeting many times, but, I confess, never quite like this."

Clay pulled up a chair and glared at the intruder through the thicket of beer bottles. "Who the hell are you? A relation of Frau Frassek?"

"And of yourself, sir." A ghost of a smile spread across Karl's face: it was a great relief to discover he was fond of the man who had sired him. "Don't be so blind." He brushed his long brown hair from his forehead and fished out his Vopo identification. He pointed at the official-looking document. "Date of birth, you see it right here. November 1964. Where were you in March of that year? I think we both know." He pulled back his sleeve, as if he had not already offered proof enough, and made a fist. His discus thrower's arm bulged. Then he tapped Clay's big muscular chest. "You must have seen Heinz-Albert at some time. These muscles aren't his. They're yours, sir. We're trained in anatomy. It's evident to me right off."

"*Holy Jesus.* You mean to tell me I've got a son? A goddamn East German policeman as a son? Come here, boy." He examined Karl's arms, his eyes and jaw, turned his left hand backside up. "God... see that big knuckle you've got there? It's my grandfather's. You've *stolen* it from my grandfather. I used to ask him when I was a kid what that knot on his hand was for. Know what he'd say? 'To thump kids on the head who ask too many questions.' When... when did you learn about this?"

"I've known for some time. Mother told me."

"Nice of her. Why the hell didn't she tell me?" He got to his feet, nearly losing his loincloth. "What the hell has that woman been up to? She ruins my life and doesn't even tell me I have a son. I'm sorry... son. You'll see me in better form one of these days. What's your name? I've got a son who's a goddamn East German Vopo and I don't even know his goddamn name."

"Karl, father."

"Well... well, Karl. Delighted. I'd give you a hug if this pink thing would stay up and you weren't wearing that Nazi uniform. You and I and your mother are going to have a little talk tonight if we can get her out of the bathroom. I think I'm owed a few explanations, Karl, and I intend to get them."

"I think you will, father. Mother can be on the quiet side."

"Quiet. She's a damn mute. Now excuse me while I dress. And leave your buddies at the goddamn barracks, if you don't mind."

Clay, that July evening, once more learned the meaning of shock. But when he crossed into the West, he was not empty-handed. He was the third person—after Jahn and Karl—to learn the identity of Hannah Mühlendorff. And he had one up on the rest of them: she had, by God, agreed to marry him when her work was finished. Yes, he knew about that too, knew about Karl's position as Bülow's bodyguard and their incredibly risky assassination plan. He didn't like it; he was terrified for them. Yet he hadn't tried to talk them out of it. He had gotten to know Käte's determination a little too well twenty years before. He agreed not to visit them in the East again; agreed because he knew how dangerous it could be for them. But he attached one condition to his promise: that they should contact him through Ursula the minute they got into trouble and needed him to do something—*anything*. The future loomed damned scary, uncertain. But as long as there was hope they might get out, well, it no longer seemed quite so black.

CHAPTER SIX

The party chairman was no fool. He could see that Hannah Mühlendorff was beginning to have a dangerous influence on his once-timid subjects. And the home front wasn't his only worry: if he let things go much further he would have the Soviet leadership to contend with. It was time to throw every resource at his disposal into the search for this troublemaker.

He called an emergency session of his Politburo and fired the head of the Stasi, the secret police, which had until now borne primary responsibility for Mühlendorff's capture. He named a new Stasi chief on the spot: Ulrich Kammer, a soft-spoken man whose brilliance not even his enemies questioned. In addition, he gave Generaloberst Heinrich Bülow, head of the seventy-five-thousand-man People's Police, an ultimatum: either catch her within three months or go the way of the previous Stasi boss.

In this fashion the party chairman established a rivalry between the new man at Staatssicherheit and the seven-year veteran at the Volkspolizei. Perhaps "competition" was frowned upon in the official dogma, but there were times when it helped...

The barbed wire on top of the station wall looped in rusty coils through the patchy autumn fog. The wall surrounded a large rectangular field lined with row after row of tanks draped in canvas. The station house did not look like much. It was a drab four-story building of sooty brick, distinguished from other Vopo stations only by the loathsome rumors that clung to it like maggots to a corpse. This was Bouchestrasse 236, the address to which Generaloberst Bülow had recently transferred his headquarters.

Bülow sat behind his desk, the smoke from his Cuban cigar forming whorls in front of his face. He was studying the collection of Mühlendorff stories his investigative teams had assembled for him. Some of the stories were two decades old, which gave Bülow secret pleasure. If he pulled off in three months what the Stasi had been unable to do in twenty years, his star would once more be on the rise.

He flipped through a random sample of material. The pages were stained and tattered from the hands of many readers—too many. Diverse print faces stared up at him, including the old Germanic script. The presses responsible for printing the stories were obviously ancient. But was it really possible that not a single one of these presses operated in some other capacity that could be traced?

His specialist in linking the printed word to its source assured him this was so. Who, then, grumbled Bülow to himself, was printing these abominations? People with old broken-down presses in their basements, presses retired half a century ago? Or a tight group of dissidents who stockpiled the old machines somewhere and used first one, then another, to throw the police off the track? Well, he was going to find out. He had already initiated a search-and-shadow policy toward foreigners entering the DDR. This should tell him soon if there was Western involvement. And he was extending his tentacles deep into the East German literary community. He had a couple of advantages over the Stasi. He had five times the manpower, and the faces of his people working in undercover positions were new. He would get her, no question about it. The only thing that worried him was the party chairman's deadline.

He glanced at his calendar. A man he was grooming as an informer in literary circles, the celebrated young poet Jürgen Adelbert, was reporting to him after lunch. Which made him feel good. With the proper ministration of carrot and stick—perhaps a bit more stick in the case of cocky little Adelbert—he was likely to uncover some very interesting leads.

Bülow returned to the Mühlendorff stories . . . An SS general, home from the Russian front, was to appear as a local celebrity at a Christmas party given by the elders of his town. The day before, leaflets describing the general's role in the death camps had turned up all over town. The leaflets predicted his assassination "at, around or because of the party." The general, paralyzed by fear, stayed home, sending word to the gathering that he was ill. The next day, new leaflets appeared, accusing him of "cowardice, a quality as prevalent as brutality among the swaggering fools who lead us." Hitler himself heard of the incident and ordered the general shot for "disgracing the SS, the *Vaterland* and me personally with his shameful display of Jewish pusillanimity."

"The von Ettingers," continued Hannah Mühlendorff, "were delighted. The Nazis, brawny and brainless, had themselves carried out the will of the resistance! The family cell had achieved a new level of effectiveness in its struggle against the beast."

Bülow slammed down the story in disgust. The binding split and the pages, like the leaflets of Hannah Mühlendorff's resisters, fluttered lazily to the floor.

What was wrong with people for being affected by such trash? No self-respecting German officer, Nazi or otherwise, would ever behave in such a fashion. You appear at the party, obviously. You meet the challenge head-on. You reveal the resistance for what it is: the feeble and desperate work of losers. Those idiots who devoured Mühlendorff's lies with such delight would soon learn the truth. When he had her, he would expose her to the world for what she was. It would take a gigantic showcase trial, a masterpiece in the orchestration of popular sentiment. But what a lesson for the people. He could smell the promotion to come.

Bülow, speaking loudly on the phone, affected not to notice Jürgen Adelbert's presence. Which gave the poet a chance to study the man and his environment, to catalog sensory impressions for a poem he was planning to write. There was certainly no lack of subject matter.

The Vopo chief, Adelbert could see, had one of those volatile faces that expressed extremes. He could be charming; and terrifying. The two Bülows alternated before his eyes in the course of the phone conversation. His features, taken individually, were rather unattractive. But the generaloberst was handsome in a rough, military sort of way. Adelbert watched him pace back and forth, holding the receiver away from his ear when the person on the other end of the line spoke. His body was remarkable; it would require at least two stanzas.

The poet shifted the weight of his delicate frame from one foot to the other and ran his fingers through his curly blond hair. He could not pinpoint the reason that the generaloberst, even when motionless, appeared to be charging forward. Was it his enormous barrel chest that seemed ready to burst from the confines of his tight-fitting uniform? Was it his large gray head, supported by his bull shoulders without the visible aid of a neck? In part, yes. But there was something else. Ah, yes. Now he had it. The generaloberst, in spite of his two-hundred-twenty solid pounds, had no ass. None at all.

The room, too, was a poet's delight. On one wall hung the grizzled head of a wild boar, on another wall a vast weapons collection, on the third photographs in black and white of the generaloberst on horseback. The desk was of dark, heavy wood, and at its center sat the remains of the chief's lunch—a little mustard, a smear of uneaten potato salad and a huge white sausage that seemed right at home, a repugnant creature, alive and throbbing to the metabolism of its master.

Bülow hung up. "Afternoon, Adelbert," he boomed, approaching.

"Good afternoon, sir." The poet left his limp hand at the mercy of the generaloberst's crushing grip.

They took their seats across from each other at the desk, peering over the weisswurst. "Well," said Bülow, his face friendly and his tone all carrot. "Tell me what you've been able to find out."

"Comrade generaloberst, I've made discreet inquiries throughout the whole circuit. Everyone has read the stories, of course. Who hasn't?"

"Well, yes, no great crime in reading them." He nodded at his own collection. "Stupid stories, rubbish. But no great crime in reading them. What else, Adelbert? I understand you're not going to get to the author right off. But who prints them? Who passes them out? You must have some clues."

58

The poet tensed. This was the moment he had been dreading. "Comrade generaloberst, I promised you to do my best and I have. But I was not able to uncover anything. Please believe me. The literati are as curious as you about this whole Mühlendorff process. But they are also in the dark. We know nothing, sir, and that is the truth."

Bülow's facial expression underwent a transition. He glared menacingly at his guest. It was vermin like this, he thought, who were infecting the youth of the DDR. How could a little runt scribbling something called a "modern poetry of the senses" attract anything but scorn? At least you could understand what Hannah Mühlendorff was writing about. He just did not get it. This feathery little snip was the rage of the entire younger generation. And from the reports of his undercover people, Adelbert was quite a hit with the women, too.

Bülow imagined the poet's slight body, naked and childlike, stretched out on a writhing heap of young females. It just didn't make sense. That man, if you could call him such, resembled a faggot. Why did the young women of the country swarm around him like bitches in heat? This was the sort of decay that was supposed to infect capitalism. And the eggheads on the Central Committee let Adelbert continue!

Well, the little twerp wasn't dealing with the Central Committee any longer. If he wanted to continue—continue to write, continue to *live*—he was going to have to help the Vopo find Hannah Mühlendorff. The carrot had not worked. It was time for the stick.

"Adelbert, you act like this is a meeting in a cafe with one of your poet friends. You seem to have forgotten you're dealing with the head of the East German People's Police. You're going to talk. See that sausage? I was saving it for you. My people tell me you're a strict vegetarian. Is this correct?"

"Comrade generaloberst, I—"

"Shut up and eat," Bülow said, rolling the sausage toward the poet with his pencil. "Perhaps a little pork fat is what you need to lubricate your vocal cords."

Adelbert, fighting not to appear squeamish, picked up the weisswurst and returned it to Bülow's tray. "No. I won't eat it."

"I order you to eat it *now*. I can't see why your type man should have trouble with a weenie."

"Comrade generaloberst, I do not appreciate the implication that I am a homosexual. I am not. I am a normal healthy male who has chosen to be a vegetarian. I'll gladly clean up the grease slick your sausage left on your desk, but I will not eat it."

"Tough words, Adelbert. But only words. I've known a lot of big talkers in my professional life. Heroes of the word, I call them. But what happens when you take away their words? Are they still heroes, Adelbert, or were they all talk?"

Bülow pushed his intercom button: "Send up Leutnant Frassek."

"I'm sorry, comrade generaloberst, but this is the leutnant's day off."

"Very well. Send me the new boys. All of them."

He skewered the sausage with his pencil and twirled it under the poet's nose. "We'll see if your eating habits change in the basement."

"Where are we going, sir?"

"The White Room," answered Bülow, jovial again.

Adelbert waited two levels beneath the ground floor in a dank, dimly lit corridor. Moisture was heavy in the air, an invisible fog. It condensed in dark splotches along the vaulted concrete ceiling and entered his lungs with an unpleasant bite.

The White Room. It was rumored Bülow was not only a tough chief, but also a psychopath. The White Room was said to be his personal chamber for torture and execution. Adelbert had a hard time believing this. The party chairman, while no saint, was certainly not a barbarian. He would not condone such practices among his top officials. The rumors, sure. They were helpful in keeping the people frightened— and in making cowards such as himself talk. He was already trembling. Thank God he did not know anything. How sad it would be if these primitive police methods could make him betray a very noble woman. Thank God he had no idea who she was.

He tried to imagine himself in more agreeable surroundings. What a fabulous wine cellar this would make. He conjured up the image, and in his mind's eye the dreary walls were suddenly lined with row upon row of green bottles. Bright, cheerful labels identified the various selections. Most of the wines were from Bulgaria and Yugoslavia. They probably didn't taste great but they were a far cry better than nothing. And over there? Ah, magnificent. Over there were the French wines, Chateau this and Chateau that. Even the names were enticing. And the

Italian section warmed the heart. How wonderfully those Chianti bottles snuggled into their wicker baskets.

He looked at the four guards, who stood two to either side, and smiled. Are they really so frightening? They're mere children. Look at the baby skin on this one's cheeks—soft, rosy, dusted with fine down. And that one. Why, he still has the gangly limbs and pimpled skin of adolescence. If you set him lose with a beautiful and willing woman he'd bury his face in his arms and scream for his mother. Children, mere children...

Footsteps approached through the cold gloom, menacing footsteps ...no, don't think of them that way...clumsy footsteps. Yes, that was much better. And whom were they bearing toward him? Why, the generaloberst himself, tilted forward as though he must constantly run to keep his massive chest from pulling him over. God, how old Grosz would have loved this one. The great Prussian general, unable to turn his head from side to side because he has no neck, so blind to the world that he carries in place of his elegant walking stick a lowly *weisswurst*. The poet had almost stopped shaking when Bülow reached him.

"That little door to your left, Adelbert. See it?"

"Barely, sir. It's a trifle dark down here." The wine cellar of his imagination vanished. The guards turned from children into snarling watchdogs. Bülow was no longer ridiculous but terrifying. Fear, cold as the subterranean air, washed over him.

"Dark, Adelbert? You don't know what dark is. Wachtmeister... open up for our guest."

A small rectangle of black emerged behind the steel door, which swung open on well-oiled hinges. The door itself was thick as a safe and, with its felt lining, appeared capable of a hermetic seal. Bülow pitched the sausage into the opening. The time lag between the throw and the splat announced that the room was large.

Lucky the generaloberst doesn't know of my claustrophobia, thought Adelbert, his breathing already rapid and shallow. Jesus God in heaven, what are they going to do to me?

"What are you waiting for?" Bülow said.

"You want...me...to go in?"

"I didn't open it for myself, Adelbert. I know what's inside. Go on, go on." He laughed—low, guttural. "Explore to your heart's delight.

I'll be thinking about you. And when I return, I strongly suggest you have found and eaten your dinner." He shoved the trembling poet into the darkness and slammed the door.

Compose yourself, thought Adelbert, landing on his hands and knees. The floor beneath him was oddly smooth. Don't panic. I live by my imagination. Imagine something comforting. Speak, fantasy.

But his imagination, for the first time in all his twenty-four years, was dead. He held his breath. His claustrophobia shrank the blackness until he felt the pressure of the ceiling, floor and walls push the breath from his lungs. He gagged and wretched, unable to inhale, thought he must certainly die.

Then, suddenly, he was crying. Tears streamed down his face. He could breathe again. He sat up. God, what have I done to deserve this? I've tried my entire life—from cowardice perhaps, but no matter— tried to stay within the rules of this wretched land. I've cooperated with the authorities and even tried to believe some of their crap about this being a more humane form of society. Well, it's time to look reality in the eye. This is a police state, a goddamned police state. And now it's got *me* between its jaws.

Furious in spite of his terror, he leaped to his feet, only to come crashing down as his head slammed against the low ceiling. The claustrophobia returned for a moment, choking off his breath. But a new sense of defiance was burning inside him, freeing him from his fear.

Still on his rear end, he slid rapidly to the right, assuring himself that the walls would not crush him. Such blackness he had never experienced. His eyes had still made no progress toward adjusting.

Fifteen, perhaps twenty feet from where he had begun he found a wall and examined it with his fingers. Tile, just like the floor. He stood this time very slowly, and touched the five-foot ceiling. Also tile. A tile room. It reminded him of an operating room. He noticed an antiseptic smell unlike the mustiness of the corridor. Ether? A lethal gas? No. Bülow would not let him off so easily. It must be some industrial disinfectant, something they use to clean the tile. But why clean the tile?

Explore, don't think. He pushed along the wall until his hand brushed an object on the floor. He drew back, heart pounding. A snake? No, wrong texture. Gingerly, he touched it again, ran his hand along it. A silly garden hose. He followed it to the wall and found a tap, then followed it in the other direction to its end. The floor seemed to slant here—quite steeply, in fact. He continued in the direction of the incline until he came to a hole several inches in diameter. A drain. If he could locate that sausage, he could get rid of it. *Bülow might kill me, but he isn't going to make me eat that repulsive weisswurst.*

He set out on his hands and knees, probing the tile floor with anxious fingers. On his second sweep of the room his hand landed on the thick sausage. Clutching it triumphantly, he returned to the drain.

There's probably a grate down there, he thought, plunging a hand into the hole. At elbow depth he encountered a cold, slippery, gooey substance he couldn't identify, and yanked his arm out in horror. But he was like any man driven by a higher purpose: no obstacle was too great for him. Don't think, he told himself, you've felt worse. Doesn't matter what it is. Dig through it, find the grate, pull it up. Parting the horrid stuff, he hit what he was looking for. The grate refused to come out, but the holes were large—large enough to shove the sausage through bit by bit if he pushed with all his strength. Then he would wash himself off with the hose and take whatever he had coming...

Ah, excellent. A little more of this gook aside, a little more still. There. Good. Push, push, push. There she goes. The skin is splitting, the inside is coming out, mixing with that other slime, going through the holes...

Blinding lights came on. Bülow came through the door, leaning farther forward than usual because of the low ceiling. He stared at the poet in disgust.

Adelbert, who was straddling the drain, looked up, blinded by the sudden glare.

"You can see it better now," roared the generaloberst. "The White Room. Do you like it?" He tapped against the wall with his knuckles. "Thin tile, Adelbert. Breaks easily. That was important in designing the room. Wood and plasterboard in back. We don't want any ricochets in here."

Adelbert's vision slowly adjusted to the bright light. He saw Bülow hunched above him, saw the rows of high-intensity lights and the nozzle of the infrared camera in the ceiling. The place was a nightmare of dazzling white sterility, as terrifying to him as gargoyles to his ancestors.

63

"We had to shoot an enemy of the state in here just a few hours ago. Look at yourself, Adelbert. *Look at yourself.*"

Realization of what was in the drain struck the poet at the same instant he saw his blood-stained hands and trousers. For a split second he sat stunned and motionless. Then, mouth agape, he began to slide backward across the slippery tile, his arms and legs floundering wildly until cramps brought him to a halt. An involuntary scream escaped from the depths of his modern soul, followed by the contents of his stomach. He grew faint, but the muses refused to deliver him into unconsciousness. "Not rumors," he muttered. "Not rumors... true."

Bülow, presently in command of the hose, directed a blast of icy water onto the poet's face. Then, like a conscientious janitor, the generaloberst began hosing the mess on the floor toward the drain. Adelbert, head in arms, sobbed violently. Bülow went to him, patted him on the shoulder like a father, bestowed on him a compassionate smile. "I assume you'll work with me now," he said.

"Yes," choked Adelbert. "Yes."

"Good, my boy, very good. They tell me you're something of a genius. It would be a shame to see the best part of you follow that sausage down the drain."

CHAPTER SEVEN

It was a beautiful autumn day, brisk but not cold. The sky was blue for a change, and a light breeze kicked up the fallen leaves. The smell of burning wood made Käte think of long morning walks to school when she was a young girl. She remembered how the first hints of winter had always filled her with excitement and foreboding. She felt these things now; and knew why.

She did not walk all the way to Wilhelm Jahn's bungalow but stopped two blocks shy around the corner. She played with the red-and-white package in her hands and ruffled the bow on top. Inside was a beautiful leather-bound edition of Rilke's early poems. The book was not inscribed, and contained no material other than the poems. It was her signal to him that a meeting was imperative.

Waiting beneath a street sign, she scrutinized the passersby. Soon a small girl in Sunday dress came shuffling toward her through the leaves. Käte bent down and spoke to her: "You look pretty as a picture today."

The girl flushed and pushed a foot through a pile of leaves.

"Tell me, honey. Do you know by any chance where Herr Jahn lives?"

The child looked up with big eyes. "Of course. Everyone knows where *he* lives. *He's* a teacher."

"I've got a nice surprise for him, but I don't want him to know who it's from. How would you like to deliver it?"

"I know who you are. You're his girlfriend, aren't you?"

"Well...just tell him it's from a very good friend. Run along now. It will make Herr Jahn happy."

"All right," said the child. "Since you're his girlfriend, I'll take it for you." Käte placed the package in her outstretched hands. The girl admired it, smelled the paper to see if she could guess what was inside, then skipped off with a smile. They waved to each other as the youngest resistance messenger rounded the corner and disappeared.

Käte walked quickly to Amalienstrasse, where she left the sidewalk for the familiar path tunneling through the thicket. Thorny bushes, all dark brown branches and nasty spikes, clawed at her coat and kerchief. Giant oaks swayed above her, the last shriveled leaves of summer trembling from their bows. Ivy was everywhere—green ivy that climbed up the tree trunks, red ivy that wove in and out of the untended trellises, brown ivy that crackled wearily underfoot. She came to the widening where the wooden birdhouses, warped and paintless, hung from the lower branches. She took a seat on the old bench and waited.

Bluejays swooped down amid the falling leaves, squawking and squabbling. A brown spotted head appeared in the round hole of the birdhouse where she left her stories. The little bird glanced about nervously, then ducked back inside.

Käte closed her eyes and inhaled the wonderful mixture of fall fragrances. She could pick out the acrid odor of coal, the pungent odor of burning leaves, the fresh scent of pine that the wind carried from the great forests beyond the city. The smells of decay were particularly strong—of leaves and compost and distant fallow fields, all rushing to decompose before the winter freeze.

She longed to shed her constant, gnawing fear, to watch the birds playing in the thicket without a thought in her head, to absorb the peacefulness of nature into her very soul. And she worried she would never have the chance.

Wilhelm Jahn silently appeared. He looked the same after twenty-one years—slight of build and dressed in a synthetic leather jacket and black stocking cap. But when he pulled the cap off she could see the passing of time: his head was as barren as the coal heaps along the river Spree. He ran to her and took her in his arms. "Käte, how often I've wanted to break our pact and see you..."

"And I you, Wilhelm." She took his hand and tugged him down on the bench beside her. The steam from their warm embrace covered the lenses of his wire-rimmed glasses. He took them off and wiped them on his trousers.

"Wilhelm, I don't know how to thank you properly. I—"

"Stop it, Käte. It's I who owe you the thanks. All through the dismal seventies you, and you alone, kept the dream of liberation alive in our people. It makes me cringe to think I once tried to deny you the chance. As you know, the ferment in Eastern Europe is finally spilling across our borders. Because of you, and your work, we in the underground don't have to begin again from scratch."

She allowed a smile. "Then let's call it a collaboration. Wilhelm, there is so much to discuss and so little time. We should get down to business."

"Regrettably, Käte. It's sad ours must remain a friendship of telepathy."

"Wilhelm, Generaloberst Heinrich Bülow is coming to VEB-Elektro, my place of employment, on December ninth. He is going to present an award to the firm in the People's Auditorium with the entire work force present. And the ceremony is going to be carried *live* on national television."

"Käte—"

"I haven't finished. Karl, my son, the child I was pregnant with when we last spoke, is one of Bülow's bodyguards. The man we have been stalking is coming to *us*. We can kill him. We need you to get us out."

The resistance leader shook his head. "With each new story...my admiration for you has grown. And now you tell me that you actually *have* a family resistance cell like the von Ettingers. You are a remarkable woman—"

"You flatter me too much. The family cell was never my intention. Things just worked out that way. But what about it, Wilhelm? Can you get us out?"

Jahn stretched out his stocking cap and pulled it over his shining dome. "I was afraid when you contacted me that the opportunity would come now..."

"Afraid? What do you mean?"

"The presses are down."

"What? You haven't had a problem with the presses for two decades ... Wilhelm, you're not getting cold feet, are you? Or is it because you don't want Karl and me to be involved in an assassination—?"

"Please, Käte, let me explain. Years ago I made a decision—a bad one, perhaps—to put all our printing facilities in one spot. There was a tiny brewery in a village outside Leipzig. The owner, an old man, became the new state director following nationalization. But no one from Central Planning in Berlin was interested in a business as small as his. The brewery went on as before, a tiny family enterprise different only in name. Boxes, crates and supplies came and left uninspected. The old man's only employees were his two sons—also 'ours.' We put our old presses—all of them out of service since before World War I— in the basement. That's where all those ancient, intriguing print faces for your stories have come from. Until now this arrangement has worked well ... the Stasi and Vopo are as baffled today just as they were when we began ... Unfortunately the old man died last year. I almost didn't get your last story printed. You see, the sons have been losing their nerve. And now, with the crackdown, they're just plain scared. I can't force them. They know more than they should. If they went to the police ... well, we're in the process of moving the presses right now. As you can imagine, it's not an easy job. They must go piece by piece to our new location halfway across the country. I understand how you feel, Käte. Your opportunity would have been perfect. But I'm afraid we are going to have to wait—"

"I'm sorry, Wilhelm, but I don't believe I *can*. I'm near the breaking point." She turned away, feeling sick. She was faced with an awful choice.

"Käte—"

"Listen," she interrupted, "let me ask you something. If I were somehow able to deliver the stories predicting Bülow's death to the brewery, would you be able to distribute them as usual?"

"Of course. I'd send the two sons on a vacation to Hungary and proceed as though nothing had changed. But, Käte, your question is academic. I can assure you there is no possibility of having the stories printed anywhere in the DDR. You are talking about the most explosive piece of literature to come along in the last—"

"I'm talking about having them printed in the West and smuggled in."

Jahn looked at her, stunned. "You have the means to do that?"

"Yes."

"Kate, do you realize that the professional border runner you would have to hire to drive the stories in would cost you a million West marks? Not to mention the printing..."

"Money is no obstacle."

"The American?"

"Yes. Karl's father, and my fiancé. He knows the truth. I had to tell him two years ago to keep him from coming back. He's been wanting to help and he's rich—very rich. If you can give me the names of some trustworthy DDR expatriates in the West—"

"There's one man in particular, Horst von Oldenburg in Munich. He was with us for ten years before we had to get him out."

"And he would be willing to help with the secret printing of the stories, help get them hidden in some sort of legitimate transport coming East?"

"More than willing." There was a note of excitement in Wilhelm's voice, the first in a long time. "Something else, Käte. The brewery receives weekly shipments of barley from a Western company named Ferkel Grains. If I'm not mistaken, they have a branch in Munich."

"What about our escape? I know things are difficult at the borders now."

"It's been waiting for you for nearly twelve years. What worries me, though, is getting your story to the American. All outgoing mail is censored, as you know. And with the new policies at the crossings, the Westerners who used to take out information for us have understandably stopped showing their faces. My organization is stronger than ever internally but our links to the outside are nonexistent. I'll have to recruit someone for the job and inform him, of course, of what he's carrying—"

"*No*, Wilhelm, not at this critical point. An opportunity like this

69

will not come round again in our lifetimes. We mustn't have any weak links in the chain. I'll see that he receives the material and the correct instructions."

"If you're sure..."

"Yes, I am..." Or as sure as she could ever be.

He nodded, glanced at his watch. "Käte, I've got to go. An important meeting. But I must see you again. There is preparation you will need for your escape, and I'll want to know the details of your plan so that we can coordinate our efforts at the plant... When is a good time?"

"Next Sunday at five P.M. Same place."

"Käte, I think you're magnificent—"

"Only stubborn, Wilhelm. Until next week, then."

She watched him walk briskly out of sight. The tiny bird was again peering through the round hole in the birdhouse. Alone with that frail creature and the great towering oaks, Käte was finally struck with the full realization of what she had done. She had amended her plan in a way that required Clayton's near total involvement. She'd never dreamed she could be capable of such...selfishness. Of using the man she loved this way. And yet it had come so naturally, as though she had had it in the back of her mind all along.

PART II

CHAPTER EIGHT

The subway screeched to a stop in the Friedrichstrasse station beneath East Berlin. In his new Rodier blazer, Clay got off and walked with several other disembarking passengers up the long narrow hallway to the checkpoint. There were no lines; few Westerners were visiting the Communist capital these days.

He glanced around the dreary rooms and filthy corridors, musing over how little the facility had changed since his first unforgettable crossing when he'd met Käte. The East Germans had a bizarre talent for letting all public buildings deteriorate to a uniform level of squalor, a level they then maintained with Teutonic precision. He hoped he would never again have to confront this unseemly synthesis of sloth and Prussianism, hoped this would be his last and conclusive visit to the East.

The person in front of him moved away from the window, leaving him face-to-face with the border official. The official inspected his passport, then examined him coldly — the standard procedure, to which Clay paid no attention. "Herr Bentley, what is your purpose in visiting Berlin, capital of the German Democratic Republic?"

"Herr *doktor,* if you don't mind." Stick it to these sticklers for titles.

"'Doktor' stands nowhere written in your papers. Purpose of your visit, Herr *doktor?*"

"Tourism."

"Could you be more specific, *bitte.*"

"Citizens of signatory nations to the Four Powers Agreement aren't required to be specific."

The official conferred with his colleague. "Yes. New policy."

Clay guessed this type of harassment had something to do with heightened tensions inside the DDR. He also rightly suspected Käte was to blame, and felt proud that she had the power to goad these Neanderthals. What an upset her stories and their impact must be to them, the voice of justice hidden in the entrails of their rotten system...

"Hurry up," snapped the official. "If you are not prepared to reveal the purpose of your visit, you will be denied entry."

Clay wished he didn't have to submit to the tyrant behind the glass. It was his unpleasantly acquired insight that you received decent treatment from Germans in uniform—West Germans, Swiss Germans, Austrian Germans, Volga Germans, Sudeten Germans and, above all, East Germans—only if you stood your ground. As usual, he was itching for an argument. But today he could hardly afford to indulge himself... far too much was at stake. He said, "I am going to attend a play at the Brecht Theater, the Berliner Ensemble. I want to buy my ticket ahead of time, then have dinner—"

"Where?"

"I haven't given it much thought."

"We must know. New policy."

"All right. The Restaurant Moskau. If you have a menu, I'll tell you what I intend to eat."

The official glared at him. "Offending a public employee in the German Democratic Republic is a crime."

Again, Clay had to suppress his urge to fight back. "Excuse me, *no* offense intended."

The official scribbled a note on his pad and pushed the slip through a slit in the wall behind him. "Next," he barked out, though there was no one waiting.

74

* * *

Before Clay reached the Berliner Ensemble, he knew he was being followed. He hadn't seen anyone yet; hadn't bothered to look. It was a kind of sixth sense he had developed as a young man during his months of frequent crossings.

Back then, he had been followed half a dozen times, which simply postponed his seeing Käte for two or three days. But tonight's meeting could not wait. The strange business with the blazer convinced him that something crucial was up. Something that couldn't wait.

When he joined the line behind the ticket counter he was already piecing together a complicated plan. He gazed casually around the ornate interior of the theater, observing the others who had come to purchase their tickets well in advance. It was just four o'clock; the workday in East Berlin was not yet over. Most of those in line were youngsters, housewives and old people. There were also a few Westerners like himself. The one person who did not belong to any of these groups was a man of about fifty several places behind Clay in line who looked and dressed like an East German of humble means.

The man had a curved spine and steeply slumping shoulders, making him appear to huddle around his large belly. He wore a weathered top hat and drab brown overcoat that splayed awkwardly at the bottom—the work, from what Clay could determine, of an unusually broad posterior. The man's eyes darted from floor to wall to floor like those of an embarrassed schoolboy. He looked hapless, but Clay knew this might be part of his act.

"Yes, *mein* Herr?" asked the harried woman at the ticket counter.

"Tonight's offering," said Clay in a voice too soft to be heard by the man behind him, "I'm not familiar with it. *Blaue Pferde auf rotem Gras—Blue Horses on Red Grass*. Is it about horses?"

"No, *mein* Herr. It is about revolutionary politics."

"Well, just between you and me, is it any good? Politics and theater don't usually mix too well."

"It has been very favorably reviewed in our press."

"Would you suggest it even for an apolitical such as myself?"

"Of course."

75

Clay intended to irritate her and was beginning to succeed. He wanted to push her near the boiling point so that she would be less than cooperative if the man in the overcoat behind him arrived with too many questions, the kind that could provoke suspicions about him.

"*Mein* Herr, if you don't mind! I sell tickets. I can't make decisions for you. Now what do you wish? We still have a wide selection of seats."

He had been studying the theater plan affixed to the counter. "I'll hold you personally responsible if I don't like it. Give me a left mezzanine seat close to the stage, please. Yes, fine. And one other seat where a late entrance will not disturb."

She looked at him.

"I have a colleague I wish to invite. He works till seven-thirty..."

"Very well. Second balcony rear. Thirty-two marks, please."

He paid, careful to plant his body between the transaction and the man in the line. He slipped his change and the balcony ticket into his wallet, then walked along the line to the exit, studying his mezzanine ticket all the way. Once outside, he assured himself he was not being watched, defaced the ticket and tossed it into a trash container. While he was waiting for a taxi, the pear-shaped man came out of the theater, bought a newspaper and loitered nearby.

At the Restaurant Moskau, Clay ate a sauce-smothered German meal with vague Slavic pretensions and worked out the last details of his scheme. He paid his check, stuffed his sugar wrappers in the grounds of turkish coffee at the bottom of his cup and visited the upstairs toilet. From a slightly cracked window he could see his new companion pacing on the sidewalk below. He returned to the Berliner Ensemble on foot, his cheeks stinging in the damp wind. His tail came in not far behind, visibly out of breath.

The house lights dimmed. Ushers scurried about, ordering stragglers to take their seats. The tail seemed relieved, complacent. Clay decided the girl at the ticket window had been persuaded to give him the number of his, Clay's, mezzanine seat. So far, so good.

Clay slipped unnoticed into the men's room. When he reemerged, the lobby was empty, cleared like a quarantined area by the autocratic ushers. He bounded up the staircase with his topcoat over his arm, reaching the second balcony just as the curtain rose. He dug the balcony ticket from his wallet and allowed himself to be seated, ignoring the usher's whispered lecture on the unspeakable rudeness of a late arrival at the Brecht Theater.

Two minutes after seven. She would wait for him until eight. Absorb as much of the set as possible—costumes, props, lighting. Käte would know the play. She knew everything there was to know about literature and drama. She could fill him in on the details later. He would be able to *prove* at the border that he had been here. The main thing now was to get to Käte unfollowed. It was a long way to the Zentralfriedhof. He had to hurry.

He surveyed the great semicircular sweep of seats on the mezzanine below. Somewhere in that vast crowd was his tail, no doubt trying, like himself, to formulate his next move.

Suddenly the man, his shape unmistakable even in the penumbra, stood and walked to the aisle. Clay smiled: he was leaving. He waited a couple of minutes, then got up and hurried past the grumbling usher who had seated him. He felt a rush of exhilaration as he raced down the long marble staircase, but his first view of the lobby brought him to a jarring stop: the tail stood at the ticket counter, hunched low over a telephone.

Clay ducked behind a pillar, glanced at his watch: no time to spare. He was trying to figure out which of many routes Käte would take from the cemetery back to her apartment when the tail hung up the phone and reentered the mezzanine. Now. He descended the stairs with what he hoped resembled calm authority, held his breath as he passed the doors leading into the mezzanine and disappeared into the dark alleys of East Berlin.

He found her standing in the shadows near Heinz-Albert's gravestone. "Keep walking," she whispered as he approached. "There's a patrol out tonight. Don't say a word. Go to Professor Kirstein's grave. I'm all right. I'll meet you at the eastern corner of the Prenzlauer Berg Volkspark after you've paid your respects. *Go.* They're due to pass again any minute."

The rhythmic clacking of boots echoed in the distance as he walked by her without turning his head. He was a hundred feet away when they reached her. "*Guten abend,*" he heard one of the Vopos say. Her reply was muffled, credibly that of a woman in mourning for her husband. He continued toward the newer section of the cemetery where he assumed Kirstein was buried. The patrol left Käte and came up behind him, the beams of their flashlights jumping at his feet.

"*Guten abend,*" said the same voice that had addressed Käte. Clay turned and looked at the head Vopo.

"*Guten abend.*"

"Out for a stroll?"

The half dozen policemen examined Clay with their lights.

"If you don't mind...I've recently lost a dear friend."

"A little late to visit a grave, not so?"

"I'm within visiting hours. Perhaps you could help me. His name was Kirstein, Doktor..."

"You'll have to go to information in the morning. We're officers, not *auskunftsbeamten.*"

"In that case I'll continue my search."

"You have forty minutes. The cemetery closes at twenty-one o'clock."

"I know. Good evening, officers."

It took him fifteen precious minutes to locate Kirstein's grave. He squatted in front of it and placed a hand on his forehead. When he stood he could see a single Vopo through the trees, left behind, no doubt, to check on his story.

He met up with the patrol again on the way out. The Vopo who had watched him must have reported favorably, because the group leader was not interested enough even to respond. He and his colleagues were focused like persistent hunting dogs on two long-haired youths who had just arrived at the northern entrance...

In five minutes Clay was aboard a tram, in twenty at his destination— a seedy park in the old working-class district of the city. He wandered among the bushes and leafless trees, watching the sky. There was snow on the way, he could feel it in his bones...

"Over here," she whispered. He looked toward the voice, saw only night.

"Where?"

"Here. To your left. In the pines."

They embraced properly this time, but he broke off quickly. "We've got to be brief," he said.

She apparently assumed nothing was wrong. No reason to tell her yet. "Yes, we must," she said. "We'll be together soon, my love."

"I'm glad you sent for me."

"Darling, I shouldn't have..."

"Enough of that."

"I feel guilty involving you, but I've done it."

"It's what I wanted... Why the jacket? Hide the story?"

"Yes."

"What happened?"

"It's maddening. No trouble with the presses for twenty years, and suddenly the people housing them have gotten frightened. But Bülow is coming to VEB-Elektro... I couldn't pass up the opportunity—"

"I understand. Are you wearing the jacket under that thing?"

"Yes." She slipped off her long black overcoat and took off the blazer. "Rodier, size 42-L. You followed my instructions, I hope."

"Did you doubt it? I'm neurotically precise, even more so when not practicing medicine, where I'm supposed to know what I'm doing." He took off his overcoat. They swapped blazers, put their heavy coats back on. "My lovely Käte, I wish I could see you better. I'm afraid we're growing old. The clothes used to come off, even in winter."

"They will again very soon. Very soon. Hold me just for a moment."

He did, so long that he had trouble prying himself away. "When is ...when is it supposed to happen?" He mocked himself for the euphemism. He wasn't as tough as she was... Käte had lived with the notion of assassination for so long she could take it for granted. It was part of her. After all, she'd lived with it for twenty years. He couldn't even say the word—the tough American...

"When?" he repeated.

"The ninth of December."

"Jesus! And Karl will be one of the bodyguards?"

"Yes."

"What's... the plan?"

"I'm not sure I should tell you, but it helps to share it. I'm human too... We're going to create some commotion in the auditorium where he'll be speaking—blank bullets, we hope. When his bodyguards, including Karl, knock Bülow to the floor to protect him, Karl will give him a lethal injection. Bülow will seem to die of a heart attack."

"Which drug do you plan to use?" This was his turf now.

"I don't know yet. The important thing is the story. It signals the act. The two must go together. We must have it printed in absolute secrecy in the West and then smuggled back in."

"What size truck will I need to make the delivery?"

"Clayton! I'm not asking *that* of you. After tonight you must *never come here again*. There's a man in Munich who used to work with our underground. His name is Horst von Oldenburg. You go to him. We've already got a plan for returning the printed stories to the DDR. The brewery where the presses are set up receives weekly shipments of barley from Ferkel Grains in the West..."

"I thought the people around the presses had gotten frightened."

"They're being sent to Hungary on vacation. The team that usually distributes the stories will be waiting for the barley shipment. What you and von Oldenburg must do is find out which branch of Ferkel Grains—there's one in Munich, one in Regensburg and one in Würzburg—is to send the barley to the Scholler Brewery in Laucha the week of December second. Jahn—my underground friend—asks you to cancel the order. He says von Oldenburg will know how to get all the forged documents needed to bring in a similar load with the stories hidden inside the truck. Clayton, all of this is going to cost a lot of money. You'll have to hire someone with impeccable credentials to drive the truck in..."

"Money is cheap. What you're doing has no price... all right, Horst von Oldenburg in Munich. The Scholler Brewery in Laucha. Where the hell is Laucha?"

"Near Dresden. Your driver is to use the Mellrichstadt crossing. Jahn says it's the least thorough."

"Anything else?"

"We'll be coming up in West Berlin sometime on the ninth. The Reinickendorfer subway station—"

"How are you going to get on that subway? You should see the Friedrichstrasse facility now, machine guns all over the place."

"Jahn won't tell me yet. In any case, he figures the Stasi will be active on the other side after the assassination. You must pick us up immediately and take us to hide out somewhere."

"I can arrange it. What else?"

"That's all of it, Clayton." She hugged him, tight as she could. "Please don't get searched tonight. They won't search you, will they?"

Suddenly the cool, precise Hannah had become a frightened woman, worried for the man she'd loved all her adult life. He hated to add to the anxiety, but it was necessary...

"Käte, I wouldn't tell you this if I didn't need some information... I was followed—"

"Oh, God. Then you mustn't cross with that—"

"Calm down, it's not as bad as it sounds. The man they put on me was fairly inept. But I have to hurry. I want to join the post-theater crowd at the Opera Cafe, make a little scene so I'm noticed, hang on to my receipt. As long as I can convince them I was at the play, nothing will go wrong."

"But you can't cross tonight with that jacket! I won't permit it—"

"Käte. Things are very tight. They're denying entry to Americans now. I know it's against the law, but if they don't want you in, they've got the means to keep you out. I'll be all right. I'm not a complete idiot, you know. Let me do my job...I've got to hurry now. Tell me about *Blaue Pferde auf rotem Gras*."

"Clayton..."

"*Tell* me. I'm leaving in five minutes with the story. I'll be all right. I'm a friend of the East German State...Christ, I designed their whole children's anesthesiology program. I've probably saved a hundred of their kids in the last two years..."

She kept silent for a long moment, then spoke very quietly. "At least it's not the kind of play a person could very well describe without seeing it. It's a sort of potpourri of songs, aphorisms, letters, talk among young people—all excerpts from documents of the twenties. They're supposed to make up a day in the life of Lenin."

"It sounds awful."

"This is no time to be a critic...now listen carefully. All of these songs and sayings are from what's called the stormy, hard, magnificent period of the Russian Revolution. They're supposed to stir us up, make us draw comparisons with the present, shame us into moving into the bright socialist future." She gave a compact sketch of the plot, characters, props and costumes. Clay made her repeat the parts he couldn't remember.

"I'm glad I missed it," he said, and forced a smile. "Feel better?"

81

"I suppose so. It's time for me to get out of this country. I'm beginning to lose my nerve."

"It's been *time* for twenty-two years . . . I just hope this Jahn character is as resourceful as he claims. Oh, I amost forgot. I need twenty marks."

"Twenty marks?"

"Yes. I've bought one ticket to the theater I didn't use, one I did. If they demand a currency accounting . . . it's complicated, I'll explain later."

She took her wallet from her purse. They leaned over the small roll of bills, straining to see in the darkness. "Here's one," she said. "Go on, now. I think your idea of making a scene at the Opera Cafe is all right. But don't get yourself arrested. Be careful, darling. Karl will be able to tell me if . . . if you've made it—"

"I'll make it. And, Käte, about those drugs. I'll send a few pediatric syringes full of concentrated curare along with the stories. I'll make the stuff dense enough so that a simple subcutaneous injection will do. Karl won't even have to hit a vein."

"Curare? The old Indian poison?"

"Yes. We use it in small dosages in my work. There will be an apparent heart attack, I assure you. Now, what will Karl be wearing?"

"Parade dress."

"White gloves?"

"Yes."

"I'll design a device that will allow him"—*him?* he was talking about his son, *their* son—"to carry the syringe beneath his glove . . . It shouldn't be difficult. We'll make it so that he can inject through the glove without taking it off. We'll get it done and get both of you out of here. It's only a few more days . . ."

They spent their last moments holding tight to each other, and they parted without words.

CHAPTER NINE

"*What?*" Bülow was not upset without reason. He stared at the boar's head on his wall as he spoke into the phone. "You put a tail on him and *still* lost him?"

"But, sir, it was hardly my fault—"

"Look, comrade major, let's get one thing straight here and now. *Whatever* happens at Friedrichstrasse is your fault. If you want it otherwise, I'll put someone else in charge."

Major Solberg, who loved his new underground facility in the Friedrichstrasse station as much as Bülow loved the White Room, shuddered at the thought. "No, comrade generaloberst, I don't want that. I was trying to explain—"

"Then *do* it."

"I've got forty new people here because of the crackdown, and most of them haven't had more than a few days training in surveillance techniques. There's no substitute for experience. This man, Forsch, has been—"

"*Get to the point.*"

"When the American came through, comrade generaloberst, Wachtmeister Forsch was the only man we had left. We asked the visitor the standard questions. He objected mildly, then answered. He said he was going to the Berliner Ensemble to buy his ticket in advance, then having dinner at the Restaurant Moskau before the play. Forsch listened from behind the partition and left with him. The bad news came an hour ago—"

"An *hour*. I told you to inform me *at once* when anyone slipped his tail. Why did you wait, major?"

"Well, sir, I called you when it happened, so technically I didn't wait. Your staff . . . they said you had left word not to be interrupted under any circumstances. I left the message you just responded to."

"Continue, damn it."

"Yes, sir . . . We got our first call from Forsch around seven-fifteen. He reported that the man had followed his itinerary—bought a ticket for the play, gone to dinner, had even appeared in the lobby of the theater just before curtain call. But he did not show up in the seat he had purchased a ticket for. We sent Forsch back into the theater and told him to watch the rest of the play and carefully screen those leaving at the end of the performance. We had to assume the American was in the theater . . . somewhere. He had, after all, exactly followed his itinerary to that point. Evidently, though, he was not. Forsch's second call came after the play. No sign of the American at the exit—"

"*Enough*, Solberg. Who is this man? What do we know about him?"

"The name, sir, is Bentley, Doktor Richard Clayton Bentley. We've checked on him very thoroughly. Our computerized records show that he came over a good deal in the summer of nineteen eighty three. He was working at the time with the medical faculty at Humboldt University and living in West Berlin. We checked with Professor Rausch at the clinic. Everything seems to be in order. I'm waiting for the minister of public health—"

"Comrade major, I want you to hold him at the border when he shows up tonight. He is someone I'd like to have a personal chat with."

"Sir, after what Professor Rausch told us, I really—"

"And that moron who lost him, what was his name?"

"Forsch, sir."

"Round him up, too. I'll want him there when this Bentley arrives."

Bülow hung up and paced. A professional with legitimate ties to the outside...one of those slick, sophisticated types who never comes under suspicion. This could be the break he needed.

"A full report on my desk in one hour," he ordered his information chief, whom his call had interrupted at home in the act of servicing his neglected wife.

"But, sir, it will take me an hour just to get to the archives where the records from the precomputer days are stored. It might take weeks to check through that mountain of paper—"

"You'll work all night. I need that material. Get back to me as soon as you've got it."

Bülow hung up and stabbed the intercom button. "Who's my bodyguard tonight?"

"Klaustermeir, comrade generaloberst. He's waiting for you downstairs."

"Klaustermeir be damned. Get me Frassek."

"But, comrade generaloberst, Leutnant Frassek is not on duty tonight. He's participating in a track and field event in the morning. You yourself instructed him to—"

"You *heard* me. Get me Frassek. Dispatch search teams if you have to. He's working with me tonight."

The black Volga limousine sped through East Berlin toward the Friedrichstrasse station. Generaloberst Heinrich Bülow puffed on the stub of an expensive Cuban cigar. He felt uncomfortable in his dark business suit, as though he had left his rank hanging in the closet with his uniform. That was what he hated most about civilian dress...you couldn't tell Heinrich from Hans, or the party chairman from some plant foreman who had earned enough on the black market to buy himself the most expensive western cut at the Intershop.

But it was important he remain anonymous tonight. He was supposed to notify Stasi chief Kammer of all interrogations involving suspected foreign agents, and he didn't want word of his independent initiative getting back to his rival too soon. In a few days, when he had solved the Mühlendorff case, it would no longer matter...

"Something wrong, Frassek?" he boomed.

Karl suppressed a yawn. "Just tired, comrade generaloberst."

"Tired? You'd do well to stay away from the young ladies in these times of crisis. By the way, comrade leutnant, how are the young ones these days? As loose as the sluts on the other side?"

"Sir, I was at your house until three A.M. last night. I wouldn't know."

"After you left, Frassek? Don't tell me you went straight home to bed."

"That is exactly what I did. You realize, I believe, that I was required to report to the Bouchestrasse station at six A.M. this morning—which left me just an hour and a half to sleep—"

"Complaining about hours, comrade leutnant?"

"Yes, sir. I don't think I can give you my best work when I'm exhausted."

Bülow slapped his bodyguard on the leg with his left hand, which still clutched the cigar. Karl brushed the ashes from his uniform, bone-weary but careful not to show too much emotion.

"Look here," the generaloberst said, "I know what's bothering you. It's that *gottverdammte* track and field meet tomorrow. Forget the discus, Frassek. You'll spend another three years preparing for the Olympics and the politicians will wreck it again. You've got a brilliant career with us. That's what counts. Now toughen up. You don't see me falling apart."

"Allow me to point out, sir, that you were not in your office until noon."

"Frassek you're sounding more like that sorry faggot informer of mine every day. Pathetic . . . you and your entire generation."

Karl watched the dark apartment houses glide past the window. Fatigue scrambled his thoughts. He wished he had a dial to turn down the volume of Bülow's voice. "Faggot informer?" he said without interest.

"*Wake up.* I'm *talking* to you. That poet we recruited."

"I'm not aware of any poet working for us, sir."

"You should be. I told you last week Adelbert was ours. You must have been dreaming about the Olympics again."

"Jürgen Adelbert?"

"That's right."

"Comrade generaloberst, you never mentioned the name to me— Jürgen Adelbert I would have remembered. I know the name, sir. You hear it all the time on TV, see it in the papers. I haven't had time to read a single verse of his poetry. What's he working on?"

"What's he working on? What's everyone working on? Frassek, you're growing dumber by the hour. What are *we* working on tonight?"

"Comrade generaloberst, allow me respectfully to point out that five minutes ago you refused to tell me what we were working on tonight. I have no idea what you're doing, and I was dragged from my casern after one and a half hours of sleep in the last twenty-four. Klaustermeier was on duty tonight, an arrangement you yourself endorsed when I told you about my competition tomorrow."

Bülow, unpredictable as ever, smiled. "You'll win it anyway, Frassek. And even if you don't you will have lost for a good cause. Tonight we're doing something more important than sports."

"Oh?"

"We're breaking the Mühlendorff case. I thought you'd be honored to be a participant. I believe this character we're stopping at the border is her connection to the West." He dug into his briefcase and passed a file to Karl. "Driver, some light back here."

Karl fought to control his emotions as Bülow pressed close against him, whispering in sibilant growls. "Just take a look...a doctor, educated and respectable. Not the average scum who makes his living running contraband across the Wall. Someone with a cover good enough to let him work right under our noses. Mark my words, Frassek... this man has something to do with Hannah Mühlendorff..."

Karl read:

NAME: RICHARD CLAYTON BENTLEY
SEX: MALE
AGE: 44
HEIGHT: 6'2"
WEIGHT: 194
HAIR: BLACK
EYES: BLUE
DISTINGUISHING MARKS: NONE
PROFESSION: MEDICINE, SPECIALTY: ANESTHESIOLOGY
PLACE OF BIRTH: CLEVELAND, OHIO, USA
RESIDENT: BOULDER, COLORADO, USA
CITIZENSHIP: USA

Page after page of records followed. Each entry into and exit from East Berlin appeared on the computer printouts, accompanied by dates and hours. Two starred entries—occasions when he had been watched—bore references to attached addenda. Karl was somewhat relieved to find no mention of his father's visiting his mother's section of town.

There was a long official description of his work at Humboldt University, including several transcribed interviews between colleagues at the medical faculty and the Stasi. Karl leafed through these, resisting the temptation to read what his father's associates had said about him. All the while, his facial muscles remained relaxed. On occasion, he smiled or frowned, paused to reflect or gave an appreciative little nod.

Behind his artful facade, his mind raced dizzily ahead. How much did Bülow know? How much was he relying on his damned uncanny intuitive powers? He had to find out. Closing the folder, he looked directly at his boss. The generaloberst had just lighted another cigar and was staring out the window.

They turned into the Alexanderplatz. The modern television tower, the restored churches and monuments, the showcase hotels and restaurants formed an ostentatious island of glitter in the heart of the drab metropolis.

"For once the planners were on target," remarked Bülow. "Too much Western influence for my taste, but at least they finished on schedule. We might pull ahead after all... Done with that, Frassek?"

"Yes, sir."

"Driver, lights out."

From the blackness inside the limousine Bülow continued to gawk at the great meretricious square, the "Alex," the celebrated center of prewar Berlin. "Yes, indeed, Frassek, we might pull ahead after all. Do you realize our standard of living has gotten so high the Poles can't afford to come here? One way to keep them out, eh?"

Karl forced an affirmative smile. "What do you want with his man tonight, sir?"

Bülow yanked his big gray head around toward Karl. "Frassek, what makes a *great* investigator, not just a good one like Kammer, but a great one?"

"Intelligence," said Karl warily. "Perseverance, common sense, thoroughness. I don't see anything in these documents that stands out..."

Bülow eyed him with contempt. "Intuition, comrade leutnant, is what makes a great investigator. I've got it and Kammer does not. That is why I, and not the Stasi with all their computers, will solve our little Mühlendorff riddle."

"Where do these documents come in?"

"Frassek, don't ever have an ear exam. You'll upset the doctor when he sees light out the other side. What is *clear* from this folder is that Bentley has managed to spend as much time in Berlin as the best Western agents. He might have entered under half a dozen aliases as well. And all we have here are the computer records. Imagine what we'll find when we dig out the stuff that's eight or ten years old. This man has been around, he's a piece in the puzzle..."

The limousine stopped at a traffic light on the wide boulevard Unter den Linden. Frederick the Great, on his pedestal again after a thirty-year absence, announced the revival of Prussia, newly ordained ally of East German socialism. Bülow's face as he examined his young body-guard glowed amber in the halo of the signal.

Karl struggled against his worst thoughts. Was it possible that Bülow already knew that Clayton was his father and Hannah Mühlendorff's lover? Had the generaloberst brought Karl along to preside over a sadistic humiliation of his father or mother, and himself. Well, *that* would never happen...

He brushed his hand against the leather holster of his pistol. If Bülow did in fact know—and Karl was going to find out one way or another before they reached the station—he would shoot him, commandeer the limousine, then call Major Solberg at the crossing. *"The generaloberst, comrade major, after once more consulting all the information we have on Bentley has decided the case doesn't warrant his personal involvement... he's gone to bed...you are to interview Bentley carefully and report back in the morning...detain him only if you have compelling reasons. It seems that he is some sort of friend of our government after all..."*

Then he'd go to Käte and they'd find Wilhelm Jahn, scuttle their plan and let the resistance get them out of the country. It would be a disaster for Hannah Mühlendorf—but better than degradation, and death...

First, though, he had to find out how much Bülow actually knew, and how much was conjecture. And quickly. They were almost at the station.

Bülow's face flashed green, and the limousine lurched forward. "Comrade generaloberst," Karl said, "I'd appreciate it if you would explain to me why you suspect that this Bentley is connected to Mühlendorff. I agree we need to question him but—"

"He was followed tonight."

Karl's heart sank; his hand moved toward his revolver. "Then we do have something more incriminating than the material in the folder?"

"We do. He slipped his tail. Rather expertly, I'm told."

"Expertly? How do you know he wasn't being watched by one of Solberg's new recruits? From what I've heard, some of them are still getting lost on the way to work."

"What are you suggesting, comrade leutnant?"

Karl took a deep breath and braced for what he knew would follow. "With all due respect, comrade generaloberst, it appears to me that you are perhaps on a...a diversion? Would it not be better perhaps ...and I am aware of the pressure you are under, sir...I mean somewhat better for you and your charge to solve this difficult case...to collaborate a bit more closely with Kammer?"

Bülow erupted. His own anxiety showing, he grabbed Karl by the lapels and shook him. Karl was obliged to take hold of Bülow's thick wrists and wrench himself free. They glared at each other in the darkness, and Karl wanted to smile. Bülow's rage was the confirmation he needed...it meant at least that the generaloberst did not know who Clayton was. If he had, his response would have been calm, condescending, drenched in *schadenfreude*.

"I'm sorry, sir," said Karl. "You know I've always been a proponent of better interdepartmental cooperation. I did not mean to imply—"

"*Enough.* Tonight I'll teach you. In the meantime, Frassek, watch your step. Another remark like that and I'll have you busted down to the rank of wachtmeister. Hear me, Frassek? *Wachtmeister.* And you'll stay there for as long as I live."

Which won't be long, thought Karl, if only we can get through the night.

90

*   *   *

The limousine stopped at curbside in front of the station. Karl scanned the line of visitors waiting to have their papers examined before catching the U-Bahn to West Berlin. They stood in apprehensive little groups, huddled in capes and long coats, hats pulled low and hands thrust into pockets. Their breaths steamed up into the cold night.

These were prosperous, well-dressed people, within the bounds of the law on both sides of the Wall. But posed as they were in the dim orange glow of the overhead lights, they looked like a contingent of disoriented prisoners.

Karl thought of Hitler's Germany, the Germany he knew so well from his mother's stories. He imagined for a moment that he was watching a group of Jews waiting to be loaded aboard a freight train— destination unknown, papers marked for extermination. He clutched his automatic rifle with an odd sense of revulsion. Where did it all end, man's awful cruelty to his fellow man? Stiffly, he waited for the driver to open his door.

From the darkness he saw a man approaching the line with hurried steps. The man wore no gloves and blew into his hands to keep them warm. Nearer now, he came into focus. He was half a head taller than the others in line even though he was hatless. He had thick black hair and a confident bearing.

Karl looked away. His demeanor remained cool and businesslike, but he felt nauseated.

91

CHAPTER TEN

Wachtmeister Forsch drove his smoking Trabant unsteadily toward the station. With every bump the car rattled and groaned, but Forsch heard only the sloshing of beer in his belly.

What misery . . . of all the times to send for him, this was the absolute worst. He had lost the man he was supposed to watch. Then in his fear and confusion he had gone to the *kneipe* and gotten himself thoroughly drunk. How was he going to account for his bad performance while he was in his present state? Scenarios of doom tumbled through his alcohol-dimmed awareness . . .

Why had they brought him to Berlin in the first place? He was a classics teacher, not a policeman. Leipzig was his home, not Berlin. The recruiting committee had misled him. They had told him that all his years of conscientious informing on his students had prepared him well for the job. It was not so. The informing was required. Duty was duty. Everyone did it, every last one of his colleagues. Why hadn't they chosen someone else for this godawful post?

"You see, Herr Forsch," one of the uniformed officials had explained, "you, of all our candidates, are the only one without family. Therefore, you fit the job description perfectly. I'm afraid we must insist."

Garbage, he thought, swerving out of the path of oncoming headlights. He did have a family, a happy one, too. His family was the school where he had taught for two decades. Maybe tonight they would see their mistake, show some mercy just this once, send him back where he belonged. There was his heart condition, too, recently documented at his fall physical...

He hit a pothole so hard his bladder almost burst. Better pull over and relieve himself, he thought. Wouldn't want to walk in feeling like a water balloon. The Trabant sputtered to a stop at curbside and Forsch struggled out. The city rose dark and deserted around him. He unzipped his fly. In the same instant, he noticed a small sign on a post beside his car: *Halten Verboten*—No Stopping.

Forsch lived by signs. There were a lot of signs in East Germany, and for this he was grateful. They were guideposts which helped you discern the will of the authorities, helped you steer a course in life that would please those above. But for this particular sign he was not grateful. He would only be stopping for a brief moment. He pressed his eyelids together, trying to ignore it as he tottered over the curb. Which only made things worse. The sign flashed larger than life behind his lids, flashed like the lights of a Vopo squad car.

He concluded that he must be responsible. After all, the sign was there for some good purpose, even if it escaped him at the moment. Forsch did not believe in breaking the law. Where would civilization be if everyone broke the law? Where would *he* be if he broke the law and got caught? All he needed now was a permanent blemish in the secret police computer file. He tightened the flaccid muscles of his groin, determined to hold on until he could relieve himself legally.

He pulled into a parking spot near the Friedrichstrasse station just as the chimes of the Marienkirche struck midnight. The sign in front of him read: No Parking, 22:30–24:00. To be safe, he waited for the twelfth stroke of the chimes, then hurried inside the station through the public entrance, almost brushing shoulders with the man who had eluded him several hours earlier at the theater. Driven by the agony of his bladder, he plunged toward the door marked Authorized Personnel Only. He expected to find the Toilette sign inside, but encountered instead the withering stare of Generaloberst Heinrich Bülow.

Clay, last in line, watched in disbelief as the pear-shaped man rushed past without noticing him. Things were going a bit too smoothly, and this made him uneasy. He stepped up to currency control. Behind him, the doors leading into the dreary hall were shut and locked, so to remain until morning.

The official, a woman in her forties with rolls of fat extending to her wrists and ankles, studied his face with indifference. But when she saw the name on his passport, she could scarcely contain her joy. *"Moment,"* she commanded, waddling off toward the Authorized Personnel Only door.

The last of the visitors passed through the curtained passport-inspection cubicles, where impatient guards examined them and their papers. At five minutes after twelve the hall was empty. Clay buttressed himself against the currency-control podium and waited for the inevitable.

Soon two young Vopo guards arrived and whisked him past the inspection cubicles without explanation. They continued down the long sloping passageway which led to the U-Bahn trains.

"What's going on—?"

The young men did not answer. Far below, a train screeched to a stop. Its doors hissed open and shut, and it rumbled off toward the West.

Käte...he didn't see how she would ever get aboard that subway. The station was an impregnable armed fortress. He noticed things he had not noticed before: closed circuit television cameras, doors with one-way glass. There were probably a hundred Vopos with automatic weapons waiting for anyone foolish enough to attempt an escape. And if you did somehow manage to get aboard one of those trains, the controller in the central booth would simply shut off the power to the entire subway system, leaving you stranded beneath East Berlin. He wished now he had insisted on becoming involved in her escape. Maybe there was still time...

A little whirlwind charged down the passageway in the aftermath of the train's departure, kicking up cigarette butts, paper and dust. They stopped in front of an unmarked door which one of the men opened

95

with a key. Another dimly lit corridor snaked off in several labyrinthine curves, ending abruptly at an enormous metal portal with neither handle nor keyhole. A guard pushed the button on the wall.

"Yes?" A voice through the hidden speaker.

"Obermeister Kranz here. Code 34471. We have Herr Doktor Bentley."

"Take him to Room C and return to your posts."

The portal slid open electronically, exposing a very different sort of passageway. This one was brightly lit, with pristine white walls and aquamarine carpeting. They entered. Every several yards they passed painted metal doors, each displaying a single black letter. Typewriters clattered somewhere.

Farther into the strange underground building the air trembled with the nervous buzz of a high-voltage transformer. The smell of antiseptic grew more distinct. The door marked C was flung open and he was shoved inside. The door slammed behind him, leaving him alone in the darkness. Seconds later there was a flicker overhead. He leaned against the wall and watched the room take shape under erratic bursts of fluorescent lighting. In the center of the room was a standard dentist's chair. That alone—given the state of East German dentistry—should scare the hell out of most interrogees.

He was able to smile at his private joke, but there wasn't much solace in it. Attached to the chair were thick leather arm and leg straps. Draped over the right armrest was a tangle of electrical leads fitted with rubber finger cuffs. An interrogation light peered down from the double-elbow swivel where the dentist's light should have been, and a microphone on a retractable stalk hung beside it.

He studied the long stainless steel table beside the chair. It was bedecked with syringes, vials and scalpels, giving it the appearance of some crazed medical experimenter's workbench.

Small cameras dotted with tiny red and green lights followed his movements from the room's four corners. Obviously someone was watching him.

He gingerly tried out the dental chair—and the door flew open. He stared in shock as Karl marched into the room, his expression severe, cold.

"Stand *up*. Who gave you permission to sit?"

"Who gave me permission to stand until now?" shot back Clay. He knew he was on camera and he wanted to appear appropriately outraged. "What the hell are you doing with me, anyway? The last subway has left. I have obligations you are interfering—"

"Stand *up*," repeated Karl.

Clay got out of the steeply reclined chair and assumed a rather slovenly pose beside the neat stainless steel table with the drugs and instruments.

"I must advise you," Karl said in a voice so icy and impersonal it was difficult for Clay to believe it was his son's, "that you are under suspicion of espionage against the DDR. You are presently being taped and filmed. Anything you say or do will be taken into consideration at your trial."

"Espionage?" He could hardly restrain himself from embracing his son; his performance was impressive. He'd worry no more about their escape. If the underground could get Karl to the Friedrichstrasse station on such short notice, they had the clout to do the job... "And what do you think the DDR has that anyone would want to steal? The latest in dental technology, perhaps?" Carelessly he let himself down in the chair.

"Stand up," Karl barked like a Prussian drill sergeant. Before Clay could move, the slap exploded in his ear and sent echoes through his head. He felt woozy for a second, but he was alert enough to see the briefest glimmer of sympathy in his son's eyes. "Once more, stand up."

Clay got to his feet, swabbing a rivulet of blood from the corner of his mouth. He must tone it down a bit. Karl didn't know about his plan.

"I didn't realize we were taking this all so seriously." Clay rubbed the side of his head and nursed his bleeding lip with a handkerchief.

"I need some preliminary information before the others arrive. Describe your exact itinerary this evening. Everything you did from the time you entered Berlin until now. The omission of a single detail will be considered a crime against the state. Begin."

"Well, I don't want to commit crimes against your fine state. I changed two hundred West marks here at the station, then walked directly to the Berliner Ensemble. There I purchased a ticket for this evening's play—"

"Name of play?"

"*Blue Horses on Red Grass.*"

"Continue."

"From the theater, I took a cab to the Restaurant Moskau on Karl-Marx-Allee. I had an awful meal at an exorbitant price."

Better, thought Karl. Sarcastic, but not provocative enough to get him into serious trouble. "Drop the commentary and continue."

"You said you wanted everything. Don't my impressions count?"

"*Continue.*"

"I returned to the theater on foot—a digestive necessity. There I remained for many hours the prisoner of a very bad group of actors presenting a play that was, without exception, the worst piece of drama I have ever seen. Afterward I walked to the Opera Cafe, hoping to salvage the evening. Another failure. I had a row with a waiter who needed to be reminded who serves whom in a restaurant, almost choked on a dessicated slice of *kirschtorte* your people should have relegated to the ancient history museum, then returned here via Unter den Linden, surprised to see old Frederick back on his pedestal, surprised even more to see him riding *east*. I thought your enemies were in the other directions. You really should turn him around before the Russians get the wrong idea. I should add that the Alex is looking pretty good these days—except for that phallic TV tower—"

"*Enough!*" roared a voice through the overhead speaker. "Our TV tower is a model work. Give the leutnant your receipts from all the expenditures you mentioned. Hand over all currency in your possession as well. Dollars, West marks, East marks, any other money you are carrying on your person."

Clay dug in his pockets, pulled out wads of bills and crumpled receipts. He began to sort them.

"That will do," said Karl. "We will undertake a full accounting when the others arrive."

"Who are the others?"

"That does not concern you. But you are in trouble, serious trouble. The highest echelons of the Deutsche Volkspolizei have a special interest in your actions." Karl leaned close to him and stared into his eyes. "Highest, understood?"

Clay thought he did. It made sense, too. If his son was one of Bülow's bodyguards, the generaloberst might well be here in person. "May I sit now?"

"Yes." Karl had already begun to adjust the leather leg straps on the dental chair.

CHAPTER ELEVEN

"Well now, comrade generaloberst," said Major Solberg proudly, "how do you like our new facility?" They were walking down the long carpeted passageway toward Room C.

Bülow stopped in his tracks, forcing Solberg to turn around and retrace his steps as though he had dropped something.

"Goddamn it, major, will you quit walking in front of me. What the devil is wrong with you?"

"Sorry, sir. Overanxious for you to see our new interrogation room ...Well, how do you like the facility? Generaloberst Kammer called it the best persuading facility he had ever seen, even better than the Stasi shop in Lichtenberg."

Bülow jammed a finger fat as a *weisswurst* into the startled young major's chest. "Look here, Solberg, Kammer's opinion isn't the last word. If the party chairman hadn't insisted the Stasi design this place, I'd have done things differently. All of you young people are so infatuated with gadgets you can't see beyond your noses. I've got my own little facility at the Bouchestrasse station. It cost a hundredth what this hotel did. You think I have any less success with my White Room?"

"Well, sir—"

"Well, nothing. My people talk. As for this electronic bordello of yours, it's probably made us the laughingstock of Western intelligence."

"Sir! Comrade generaloberst! I beg to differ. Just yesterday we arrested a French agent and got confessions from him that—"

"Major," whispered Bülow, "if you're being taped by one of your hidden bugs, I'm going to make you listen to yourself. A French agent! I could have gotten the same material out of him by threatening to withhold his wine at dinner. You know why this facility was funded. What have you done so far to help in the capture of Mühlendorff?"

"Comrade generaloberst, sir! We've all been blocked there. According to Generaloberst Kammer, the Bouchestrasse has produced no leads either."

"Kammer is wrong again, Solberg. Because of my shop, I'm onto something important. If we fail here with Bentley—which we probably will—you and he will both accompany me to *my* White Room. There I'll show you what makes a criminal talk."

"I fear Doktor Bentley is not our man. The minister of health called back shortly before your arrival to request we handle this interrogation with kid gloves. It seems Bentley has made some very important contributions to the improvement of our health care system."

"Bad procedure, major. You are beginning with a presupposition of innocence that will cripple your investigation. We will assume he is guilty. The burden of proof is on him, not us."

"Yes, sir. But if he is not guilty, I hardly think it would be fair to blame this facility. The new features are—"

"You're more interested in technology than in catching Hannah Mühlendorff," Bülow told him, and in a way he was right.

Forsch bent over and held his stomach, sure that he would soon burst in earnest. Such internal pressure he had never felt . . . what in the name of God was he going to do? They hadn't let him utter a single word when he arrived—not about his bladder, not even about his newly discovered heart condition. They had ushered him into this vacant room without a door handle, let alone a toilet. He looked at the dazzling white walls. True, there was no sign that read Urinating on these

102

Walls Strictly *Verboten*, but one had to assume certain things, especially in a clean new room like this. After all, he wasn't a Gypsy or a Pole but a good upright Saxon.

Minutes passed like hours, the tumescence in his bladder throbbed and burned. Why had they put that No Stopping sign right where he had stopped? When would they come for him? It must happen soon.

Suddenly he had the terrible thought that they might leave him here until morning. Something inside him snapped. Every man has his limits, he told himself. He could only hope the carpet would disguise his incontinence. But the Vopo certainly wouldn't shoot him for something that human, even if it was a rather revolting thing for a forty-nine-year-old classics teacher to do.

He would offer to pay for the rug. He began to circle like an arthritic dog in search of a tree, unable to find a good spot. Arbitrarily, he settled on a corner and commenced to improvise.

He could not remain standing, that much was clear. The rug was short-haired, almost hard, and it would be truly unforgivable to splatter those fine walls. He would kneel. But was that really safe? Six liters of beer was a lot of liquid. The under-rug lake might rise up beneath his knees and wet his trousers. He had better hold himself in a push-up position, ready at the first hint of dampness under his palms to sidle left or right—

The door swung open, interrupting his strategy. "You will come with us," said Major Solberg. "On the double."

Clay took a deep breath as the three men entered. He could see right away that Bülow, in spite of his smile and well-tailored suit, had not come on a social call. Beside Bülow in the standard Vopo uniform stood a handsome young major who looked a trifle intimidated, and several steps back, as though waiting for a command before he positioned himself, fidgeted the man Clay had ditched at the theater. With his sunken chest and monumental ass, he looked rather like the Vopo chief's inverted image. And his eyes were so full of fright that Clay could not help feeling sorry for him.

Bülow clamped a cigar between his jaws, waited for Karl to light it, then moved closer to the dental chair Clay was strapped into. Karl and Solberg accompanied him, one to either side. They both seemed shocked by Bülow's first words: "Undo those goddamned straps and get him out of there."

"But, sir," protested the major, "that's the interrogation chair."

"That will be *my* chair," Bülow snapped.

"Impossible, sir. If the suspect is not seated where he is supposed to be, the angle of our cameras will be incorrect, we will not have use of our special high-intensity interrogation light, we will not be able to attach the electric—"

"Comrade major! I said to get him out of the chair. You've walked me around here long enough. I need a seat."

"We can have a chair sent..."

Bülow took a puff on his cigar and tapped a long smoking ash onto the spotless carpet. While Karl unbuckled the straps, Solberg commenced to search for an ashtray. Dear Lotte, his wife, who scrubbed the concrete stairs in front of their apartment daily, would understand his frustration. Bülow was an impossible relic from the past...even though Solberg prized his job with the Vopo he was going to have to take Kammer up on his offer and transfer to the Stasi. Working for such a Neanderthal was impossible. Lotte would surely agree when he told her about the ashes...

Clay rubbed his wrists and ankles. While getting to his feet he looked again at Forsch, who stood trembling, his back to the wall. As he watched Bülow settle into the dental chair, his anger began to intensify. There sat the archetypal Kraut bully, the human aberration that had caused so much unnecessary suffering over the centuries. The record spoke for itself: Prussian militarism, Kaiser Wilhelm's slaughters, the unequaled carnage of Hitler...and now the DDR, that ugly little police state in the center of Europe. Karl and Käte had made a good choice. He hoped he was up to helping them make it come true.

Bülow flicked his cigar again, this time littering the stainless steel medical table.

"Comrade," said Solberg—he was careful not to use Bülow's military title in front of a foreigner—"comrade, please, you must be careful that your ashes do not contaminate the medical instruments. We might wish at a later hour to let Doktor Deiss perform an orifice search—"

"Orifice search, my ass. Next time you invite me here, *comrade* major, make sure you're better prepared."

104

A train rumbled by, separated from them by earth and concrete—a night subway on its journey from one end of West Berlin to the other on its gloomy leg beneath East Berlin. The trains were no longer stopping at the Friedrichstrasse station, would not stop again until morning. When the rumbling subsided, a silence took over the room. Bülow, smiling again, slipped a Luger from his breast holster. He took a silencer from the leather pouch he carried in his pocket and screwed it in place.

"My father's," he explained. "My father, Doktor Bentley, was frankly not a good man. When I was growing up he was kommandant of the concentration camp at Sachsenhausen. He did not discriminate among his victims. He beat his children. No, Herr doktor, he was not a good man, but his weapon was the finest of its kind produced in Germany. It will still outperform any pistol manufactured in the East or the West..."

"If this is meant to frighten..."

"I haven't finished, Herr doktor. I am not like my father. I *do* discriminate. If you are innocent, you have nothing to fear."

"I don't believe we've been introduced," Clay said. "Who are you?"

"You will call me Hans. Now, Herr doktor, let me say a few words to explain. I know you people in America have a serious race problem. I understand you use some brutal methods to keep your black and Gypsy populations under control. You do have Gypsies over there, correct?"

Clay knew he must show no signs of weakness or subservience. He said, "If you're curious about our Gypsies, why don't you come visit us? I'm sure your government would have nothing against your vacationing in the West."

"True. Any citizen of the DDR is free to travel wherever he wishes. The Wall, as I think you know, is there to keep undesirables *out*. But why go to a sick country on vacation? We have everything we need right here within our own borders. Now, Herr doktor Bentley, let me return to what I was saying ... the state—yours and mine—must often use harsh methods in dealing with severe national problems. Your country's problem is race; ours is penetration by foreign agents and other seditious elements—"

"I find it offensive when a German speaks about race in my—"

"I don't care what you find. Perhaps you're Jewish, Bentley? Perhaps this name is actually *Bentburg?* That would explain your sensitivity on the race issue."

"What are you getting at?"

"That we cannot let our socialist order be undermined by vermin sent in from the outside; that we have no-nonsense methods for dealing with such elements."

"I don't think this concerns me. I'm a medical doctor. I believe in contributing my skills and knowledge, whenever, wherever they may help. I've worked with your own health care—"

"I know what you have done." Bülow ground out his cigar on the stainless steel table and shifted his great torso in the chair. "First, an accounting. Frassek, the receipts! Solberg, the border reports! Shove some of this medical crap off of here so we have working room."

The three men at once began with the calculations. Clay had reported 410 West German marks on entering East Berlin. He had paid a 5-mark visa fee and changed the obligatory 25 West marks into East marks upon crossing. At the bank upstairs in the main hall of the station he had changed an additional 200 West marks into East marks. This meant he should still have 180 West marks in his possession. Karl counted out the Western currency: 180.

Of his 225 disposable East marks he had reported and produced receipts for one ticket to the Berliner Ensemble, 12M; one taxi ride to the Restaurant Moskau, 4M; dinner at the Restaurant Moskau, 74M; *kirschtorte* and coffee at the Opera Cafe, 14M. The total of 104M should have left him with a balance of 121 East marks. On the table, however, lay only 100 East marks.

His heart nearly stopped. Had Käte given him the twenty marks *before* they had exchanged blazers? No, impossible . . . he rummaged through his pockets, blood beating at his temples. He was unprepared for such small but deadly slipups. Bülow stared at him. Karl stared at him. Solberg stared at him. Even Forsch, perplexed by how he had been duped, stared at him.

Clay worried he was beginning to show the first signs of panic when his fingers brushed against a soft paper wad in his rear trouser pocket. "And twenty, *meine* Herren," he said, smoothing the bill between his palms. The major snatched it away.

106

"What about the other mark?" demanded Solberg. But his question lacked conviction: Hannah Mühlendorff could hardly be financing her revolt on such paltry sums. Still, these were Germans *and* bureaucrats. More thorough than logical.

"A tip for the cabbie," answered Clay, who had actually used the money for several tram and S-Bahn rides across town. His answer rang as flat and spiritless as Solberg's question. This little incident with the currency had made him realize how close he, and Karl, and Käte were to a trap with no exit.

"Wachtmeister Forsch!" ordered Bülow. "Step forward."

Forsch shimmied toward the dental chair, a floundering heap of flesh moving as though his limbs were bound. "Sir . . . sir . . . forgive me, I must use the toilet before I speak—"

"Quiet. I'll not have a Vopo whining like a faggot in front of me. You'll hold your bladder until you've answered my questions." He picked up an oddly shaped probe from the medical table and tapped it like a tuning fork against his Luger. "How did you let Bentley get away?"

"I . . ." He pressed his lips together so tightly the skin around them grew as white as Solberg's walls. The unsightly lump of wattled tissue beneath his chin shook with a life of its own.

Bülow lurched upright in his chair, his scowl melting into a smile. Clay looked away in disgust. The bully was obviously enjoying the dismemberment of his defenseless victim.

"I . . . I . . ."

"You . . . you . . . wachtmeister, haven't you heard that egotism is frowned on in our new socialist order? I forbid you to use the pronoun 'I' again." Bülow once more tapped the Luger with the probe. "*Speak.*"

Forsch stiffened. "Yes, sir . . . followed him to the theater. Stood in line behind him, several places back, as we had been instructed by Comrade Leutnant Werner, bought my ticket—"

"You knew where he was sitting?"

"Yes, sir . . . had asked the young lady at the ticket window where Herr doktor had chosen to sit, had showed her my identification as we had been instructed by Comrade Leutnant Werner at the academy . . ."

He pulled out his wallet and displayed his Vopo ID, as though the gesture itself would placate the generaloberst. It had the opposite effect. Bülow kicked at Forsch's outstretched arm. The wallet skittered across the floor and landed at Clay's feet, Forsch's photograph looking up at him. Forsch turned to fetch his wallet.

"*Halt.*" Bülow grabbed the Luger, rubbed it, contemplated it. "*Please* continue, wachtmeister."

"Yes... got the information and purchased a seat nearby, then went outside. Herr doktor was waiting for a taxi. Waited too. Several taxis came at once. Instructed my driver to follow Herr doktor. After showing my identification, of course."

Forsch cast a wistful glance at his wallet. For a moment his rheumy eyes lingered on Clay. I'm sorry, Herr doktor, they seemed to say. I know you did nothing wrong, this is all my fault for failing to do my job.

"And what if only one taxi had come? Bentley would have been gone before you managed to lose him at the theater. Idiot. God help us if all schoolteachers are as stupid as you. Bentley, tell the rest. Entertain us, Bentley. It can't have been difficult to lose this lard-assed *narr.*"

Clay had no relish for what he was about to do... but this was a matter of survival—not only his own, but Käte's and Karl's and most of all her mission that he was now an important player in. Forsch had to be sacrificed, the poor miserable bastard... "Herr generaloberst..."

"*Generaloberst?* You were to call me Hans. Or did you forget?" A smile formed on his lips. "By the way, Bentley, how did you know my rank? Foreign agents know such things, medical doctors do not. This interrogation might end earlier than I expected. Tell me how you knew my rank."

Clay's mind went blank. Hadn't Forsch just called him by his title? Or had he doomed himself and his family with the careless utterance of a single word? He couldn't remember. Panic filled his throat like phlegm. There was no time to think any longer, take a chance... "Wachtmeister Forsch referred to you as comrade generaloberst. I was merely trying to extend a courtesy—"

"I don't recall that, Bentley. No, I don't recall that at all. *Forsch.* You're not fool enough to refer to me by my rank in the presence of a foreign agent, are you?"

Forsch, hopelessly flustered, blurted out, "No, comrade general-oberst."

"*Idiot.*" Bülow turned to Clay. "Bentley, you will continue to address me as Hans. Wachtmeister . . . stop that damn shaking. Now, Bentley, your version of what happened."

"Very well . . . Hans," said Clay, trying to block out any feeling. "I noticed Wachtmeister Forsch behind me even before I left the station. He hovered over me at the currency exchange in an obvious fashion—"

"Not true," sputtered Forsch. "Not true. Three steps back, minimum, just as Comrade Leutnant Werner—"

"*Shut up.* Bentley, continue."

"Yes. Well, I thought maybe he was a thief or black marketeer. I almost had to walk a circle around him to avoid bumping into him. I hurried north on Friedrichstrasse toward the theater. He trotted along behind me like a dog—"

"Not like a dog," said Bülow. "I am a lover of dogs. Be careful with your analogies. Continue."

Clay pushed ahead. Bülow was incredible . . . and incredibly dangerous . . . "At one point I passed an officer. I thought about stopping him to complain—"

"Not true," muttered Forsch. "Herr doktor is distorting . . ."

Clay went on, inwardly wincing at the sound of his victim—which is how he now thought of Forsch—of his victim's voice "We arrived at the Berliner Ensemble around four. He followed me into the line at the ticket counter. I didn't know what to expect, I became uneasy. I bought my ticket and caught a taxi, glad to be rid of him. You can imagine how I felt when I saw him hovering around on the sidewalk in front of the Restaurant Moskau."

"*Forsch.* Is that true? Were you *outside?*"

"Well, comrade . . . general . . . you see . . . I feared I had too little money to pay for dinner. The restaurant is said to be very expensive and, as you know, a wachtmeister's pay, in spite of the most generous benefits, is hardly—"

"What happened next, Bentley?"

"I walked back to the theater, realizing he knew I was going to the play and would try to follow me to my seat. We entered the main lobby just before seven. When he moved to the coat check I saw an opportunity to lose him. By now I had to assume he was interested in me for sexual reasons—"

"*Nooo,*" moaned Forsch. "He has no right to accuse me—"

"Continue, Bentley."

"How should I explain . . . ? I was afraid he would find me in the darkness and—"

"Start yanking your *schwanz?*"

"Yes, well, something on that order. Anyway, I made up my mind that if I couldn't shake him before the lights went out I'd skip the play entirely. I slipped out the main entrance and waited."

"So *this* is your alibi for not attending the theater? You disappoint me, Herr docktor. I imagined you bright enough to come with something more credible."

"I did attend, Hans. When I went back inside after the last curtain call I caught a glimpse of Wachtmeister Forsch from behind as he entered the mezzanine. Since my seat was in the second balcony I felt quite safe. If only I'd known he was an official we could have avoided this whole misunderstanding."

"Forsch . . . true or not? Was his seat in the second balcony?"

"No, sir. False, sir."

"Where *was* his seat, then?"

"Mezzanine left side, sir."

"Was he in his seat?"

"No, sir. That's where it happened. I was sure he had gone off and left the theater, even though he had said at the crossing he would attend the play. So I called here from the telephone at the ticket counter. Comrade Major Solberg told me to go back inside and wait, that I probably could not see Herr doktor in the dark. He instructed me to go to the exit shortly before the play ended and pick up Herr doktor again when he came out. But he did not come out. I called Comrade Major Solberg a second time and reported this, as we are required to do in our—"

"Your version, Bentley."

"First, my seat was not in the mezzanine but, as I said, in the second balcony."

"Not true, not true—"

"Tell me, wachtmeister," Bülow said. "How do you know Bentley's seat was in the mezzanine?"

"Yes, sir. Simple, sir. The ticket clerk, after I showed her my ID, became very helpful. She told me that the tall gentleman in the Western overcoat would be sitting in that seat."

"I'm sorry," Clay put in, "but I must take exception. There were several tall gentlemen in Western dress in line. The girl at the ticket counter was very rushed. I'm sure she gave the wachtmeister the location of some other Western visitor's seat."

Bülow glared at Forsch: "You mean to tell me you took a ticket clerk's word for where Bentley went instead of following him to his seat? Criminal negligence."

Forsch bowed his head, said nothing.

"Look, Bentley," Bülow said, "don't get the wrong impression from this man's incompetence. We *know* you left the theater early. We also know what you did when you were supposed to be in there appreciating our art. We know a lot more about you than you realize..."

"Sir," whispered Forsch, squinting as though he expected a barrage of blows to come down on him. "Sir, I swear to you the ticket clerk could not have made a mistake. There was no one in our line who looked anything like Herr doktor. Only kids and some fat women. I swear it. Now please, sir, please allow me to use the toilet for just one instant."

Bülow ignored the wachtmeister's request but he examined him intently. "Let's settle this. Where's Bentley's ticket stub?"

Solberg handed it to Bülow, who had once more reclined in his dental chair. "Sorry, Forsch," he said. "The ticket says second balcony, third row. It seems we're going to have to put you on trial. Or maybe it would be easier just to shoot you."

"Not *here*," said Solberg. "We have a special room for such procedures. Room E."

Forsch looked distractedly about as though he had not heard. "Comrade, sir. I swear to you. Herr doktor was not among those who left the theater."

Again, Bülow seemed ready to believe Forsch. He drummed idly on the metal table with a syringe. "Well, Bentley, how do you account for this discrepancy? Another outright lie the watchmeister is telling?"

"No, I don't believe he tells outright lies. What happened this evening was not really his fault. If I'd known he was an official of—"

"You will refrain from judging my men, *klar?* Now, why weren't you among those leaving the theater?"

"I was. I stayed upstairs and chatted with a young couple about the architecture of the ensemble until the lights went out. On the way downstairs I again saw Wachtmeister Forsch from behind. He was going into the men's room. The beer in Berlin is very good, but it runs right through you."

Forsch, who had indeed made one quick trip to the men's room before leaving the theater, sank into a funereal gloom. In a last desperate spasm, he called out, "Ask him about the play. I'll bet he knows nothing about it. Ask him!"

"I'll allow you this one final request," said Bülow. "What was it called?"

"Blue Horses on Red Grass," Forsch said.

"You've seen it, major?"

"Yes, sir."

"You, Frassek?"

"Yes, sir."

"Go ahead, Bentley."

Clay began in his most pedantic German, drawing out each syllable and giving each word the same intonation. The soporific content of the play, presented in a droning monologue, soon exhausted Bülow's patience. "Well, men, has he seen it?"

"I would say that he has, sir," answered Solberg.

"Frassek?"

"I agree with Comrade Major Solberg's judgment."

"Solberg, all cameras and recording devices *off.*" Bülow then sent the Luger tumbling through the air toward Karl, who caught it.

"Shoot him," said the generaloberst matter-of-factly. "He is a disgrace to this organization, to this country, to manhood in general. It would be wasteful to squander time and resources on a legal process when the verdict is already clear."

Solberg looked away, unable to watch his Room C being used this way. Clay shut his eyes, again reminding himself that Forsch had to die to save his son. They all waited for the muted cough of the Luger.

But Karl did not fire . . . he would not do Bülow's murderous work . . . He lodged the safety into position—Bülow, in a typical gesture, had clicked it off before tossing the pistol—and placed the Luger on Solberg's aquamarine carpet. He took a deep breath, felt the pressure of his breast holster against his ribs . . . If necessary, Bülow would have to go tonight . . .

The generaloberst approached him in smoldering silence. Karl took a step forward to meet him. The three dumbstruck spectators looked on. Suddenly Bülow broke into a hoarse, guttural laugh.

"So, Frassek, not yet man enough to kill? It's a rite of passage you've got to go through." His laughter trailed off. "You'll go through it tonight. Pick up my pistol and carry out your orders. We've more important things to do. Bentley has our top billing, not this rodent. Get the job done, or Forsch won't be the only accident reported in tomorrow's paper. *Now* Frassek."

Bülow's words were followed by a shriek. Forsch, hands clutched to his chest as his ailing heart at last gave out, staggered forward. In the throes of death, the old teacher suddenly came to life.

"PISS," he yelled out, raising both fists above his head. "PISS . . . ON . . . GENERALOBERST . . ." And with those words he let go of his bladder. A torrent filled his trousers and gushed from his pantlegs. He continued to stagger toward Bülow. "SCHWEINE . . . .*HUND* . . . PISS . . . ON . . . YOU . . ."

Bülow stooped to grab up the Luger. But before he could act, Forsch collapsed in the lake of his incontinence. Gone from his expression, as earlier from his words, was any hint of servility or fear. A calm now lay over his features, a hint of dignity.

"All cleaning units to Room C," ordered Solberg into the intercom.

"Call in Deiss," ordered Bülow. "Before we move to Bouchestrasse we'll give Bentley your orifice search. And, major, while we've got him undressed, we will go through every thread of his clothing. Who is the best man for this?"

"Doktor Seifert," answered Solberg. "And you will be pleased to know his lab is right here in my facility."

Solberg was positively beaming.

The call crackled through the speakers at twenty minutes after eight in the morning. "Major? Major Solberg? This is Doktor Seifert. Are you in?"

Solberg stood and flipped a switch. Bülow hoisted himself upright. Karl got to his feet. Clay pretended to sleep.

"Major Solberg speaking. Sorry you had to come in, Herr Doktor Seifert. I understand the weather has changed."

"Yes, well, what can I do for you, major?"

"We have some clothing we wish you to examine."

"I trust you haven't allowed any of your amateurs to tamper with the articles in question."

"No, sir. The suspect has had them on since we apprehended him."

"Good. Give me twenty minutes to breakfast, then send them over."

Karl had to look away as his father, trying to appear more confident than he felt, passed his jacket, shirt, tie, trousers, socks and undershorts to the Vopo guard standing beside him, who stuffed them into a black plastic bag.

Bülow shaved in a portable basin on whose stand the words Made

115

in West Germany were plainly legible. His shirt and jacket lay beside him on the dental chair. With the lather still thick on his face he leaned over the basin to wash under his arms.

That jacket, thought Karl. He needed a way to make a trade, but how? The guard, not overbright, still had eyes...

"Major Solberg," came a voice over the intercom, "this is Deiss. We'll work from Room J, if you don't mind. Bring him down."

"At once, comrade." Solberg tossed Clay a white gown and motioned him to follow. Two guards accompanied them down the corridor.

Karl, alone in the room with Bülow and a single guard, searched his mind for an idea.

The generaloberst, who was inexplicably fond of old Marlene Dietrich tunes, burst into song:

> *Love's always been my game, play*
> *it how I may. I wasn't made that way—*
> *I can't help it.*
> *They cluster to me, like moths around*
> *a flame. And if their wings burn, I know*
> *I'm not to blame.*

Marlene, Clay thought, would have strangled him with her garter belt if she'd heard him. Lord, what a grotesque, yet never to be underestimated...

Again the speaker crackled. "Major, this is Doktor Seifert. I'm waiting..."

Karl was quickly at the switch. Bülow splashed lather and water on to the carpet as he boomed out his Dietrich repertoire. The guard, looking as though he had been bludgeoned, gazed about vacantly.

Karl bent close to the microphone. "Herr Doktor Seifert, the major is with the subject. We have the clothes ready for you. Where are you located?"

"With whom am I speaking?"

"Leutnant Karl Frassek of Generaloberst Heinrich Bülow's personal staff."

"I see... For God's sake, Frassek, what's that awful noise in the background?"

"The generaloberst, sir."

"Well, leutnant, don't bring him with you. I'm in Room L."

Karl turned toward the guard. "Wachtmeister, give me the clothes. Herr Doktor Seifert is in a hurry. Don't leave the generaloberst's side. That's an order."

The young policeman held out the bag. Karl, crisp and elegant in his uniform in spite of the hours of stress, slipped into the corridor and pulled the door shut behind him. He rounded the first corner with measured steps. Bülow's song trailed along after him down the antiseptic hall—not music, but music to his ears.

What had Solberg said about a room for special procedures? Nothing, but he had named the room . . . E, wasn't it? Yes, Karl was sure he had mentioned Room E.

Where else could Forsch's body be? Perhaps there was a room for that, too, but he doubted it. If the body had been taken to Room E it might still be there. It was only nine o'clock. Yes, Room E was his only chance. Tear off Forsch's jacket, throw Clay's over the corpse, reverse the procedure after Seifert's search.

But why would the rich American be wearing a tacky East German garment. Well, Herr Doktor Seifert, that's not the strangest part of this whole episode, I assure you. We've got a character on our hands, a real . . .

It would have to do. Time was running out and he didn't intend to hand over incriminating evidence without exhausting every possibility. The hour when odds could be calculated was long past . . .

A door opened and six guards poured into the corridor. Karl greeted them gruffly without breaking stride. Another door opened and two secretaries stepped in his path, looked up at him, startled. "Please watch where you're going," he snapped. They apologized and walked off, not seeming to be interested in the black bag he carried.

Of course they weren't, he thought. These bags must flow like mail from the interrogation room to Seifert's lab.

He marched past Room D. E should be next, but it wasn't. Where was E? Should he turn around or continue in the same direction? He must continue on, must not appear lost.

The corridor bent at right angles and descended sharply. The L on the door beside him seemed to jump into his vision. Seifert's room. He quickened his pace. A smaller hallway branched off to his left. He thought he heard a door open and sidestepped into the small hallway to regroup his nerves.

Farther down the narrow passage a dim orange light gave off an eerie glow. It was the same color as the lights outside the Friedrichstrasse station, and for a brief moment the image of the huddled visitors waiting to pass inside appeared in his mind's eye. The camps...they looked like prisoners on their way to the camps.

He hurried toward the light. Under the single bulb mounted above the stout metal door a black E shimmered. Locked? Please, no.

It was open. He slipped inside. Something moved. Then something else. "Who goes there?" echoed a sharp voice. His eyes took a few seconds to adjust to the crepuscular light. Two men in uniform were hunched over an object he could not see. He stepped closer.

"Leutnant Frassek here. From Generaloberst Bülow's personal staff."

"Whew," whistled one of the men. "Nasty job. I had a friend who once worked for Bülow. *Had* a friend." The other man laughed hoarsely.

"That will do," said Karl.

"What have you got in that bag, comrade leutnant? Must have been a small man."

"I said that will do. Where are the bodies?"

"Bodies? Why, comrade leutnant, this isn't the White Room. What's all this talk of bodies?"

"The generaloberst is in Room C. Perhaps you'd like to ask him."

"That's all right, comrade leutnant. Try the table over there. The removal crew will be along soon. How's it coming, Johann?"

The second man nodded. They stood and closed a tool chest, stepping back from the pipe they had repaired. "Good-bye, comrade leutnant. Enjoy your time with the chief."

"Go, and don't lock me in."

"Why not, comrade leutnant? You're gonna end up here anyway." Laughing, they disappeared through the door, leaving it cracked.

A narrow blade of light sliced across the concrete floor and climbed the side of a besheeted table. Forsch's body lay on top in a dark heap. Without glancing back, Karl went to it and began prying the folded arms open so that he could remove the jacket. The work was not easy: Forsch's limbs, like his spirit, seemed to have grown stronger at the end.

118

As Karl bent, twisted and pulled, his mind swarmed with ominous questions. What if the body removal crew arrived before Seifert had finished with the clothes? What if the door to Room E was locked when he returned? Should he hide his father's blazer somewhere in the corridor? If he did, how would he dispose of Forsch's jacket when the garment-search was over?

He rolled the corpse to one side, straightened an arm, pulled. The sleeve slid free. The questions began again as he worked to roll Forsch on to his other side.

He heard a voice. At first he thought it was in his mind, it was so soft. But the words soon came to full life in his ears.

"Leutnant Frassek, please turn and face me."

"Sir, I—"

"Seifert is the name."

"Herr Doktor Seifert, please allow—"

"That will do, leutnant. Where are the clothes?"

"In this bag, sir."

Seifert took Karl's arm just above the elbow and led him out. "I saw you walk past my door, leutnant. The L was quite visible, though I suppose a newcomer might manage to stumble by it. Your first visit to the facility?"

"Yes."

They walked down the narrow hallway in the spectral orange light. Seifert was old and wrinkled, looked almost consumptive. Deep shadows filled the furrows in his brow and the sagging trenches beneath his eyes. He was bent with age and walked with a limp. What was left of his white hair hung in lifeless strands over his ears. Yet his voice was rich and full, like Clay's.

"Sir, you must listen, allow me to explain—"

"Explain?"

Karl felt Seifert's hand move deftly beneath his uniform. When he looked down, the old man had already stripped him of his pistol.

"Explain if you like," said Seifert mildly.

Karl sighed. By the time they entered Room L he was so deflated he could not bring himself to speak. The doctor might be old, but clearly no fool. What was left...?

The room, like the doctor himself, was a picture of disarray. Around

119

the base of a gleaming new microscope lay napkins, coffee cups and books. Full ashtrays lined a counter with mysterious vats of chemicals, each a slightly different color. There was a word processor of the West German mark Siemens in the corner. Beside it stood an ancient black typewriter loaded with a half-typed page. Newspapers, more books, the remains of Seifert's breakfast, gloves, a hat and a black overcoat that must have been half a century old littered the bright blue Scandinavian-style sofa.

The sight gave Karl a new glimmer of hope. Maybe Seifert was living on past triumphs. Maybe he'd overlook the Hannah story sewn into Clay's blazer. Maybe he wasn't interested in, hadn't noticed, his yanking on a corpse in Room E. It was grasping-at-straws time.

Karl decided to get on a more familiar level with Seifert. "God, Solberg would shit if he saw this mess."

"He does," said Seifert, smiling and nodding. "He doesn't visit me much anymore. What that fellow needs is a good Western whore to drag him through the muck of life for a few weeks."

Karl laughed. Was there really hope? The answer crashed down on him like a blow. "The jacket, please," said Seifert. "Let's have a look at the jacket first. He was wearing a jacket, was he not?"

Karl forced himself to hand it to him. "Come," said Seifert. "Let me show you a few tricks of the trade."

Karl leaned over the old man's shoulder, feeling that the end was close. The doktor spread the jacket out on top of books and papers on the table.

"First I do a hand search. Very delicately, you see? Rodier . . . a well-constructed garment. That makes the hand search more difficult. Watch. I first eliminate the obvious places . . . inside the lining, for example. I rub the two layers of material together like this, feel for something in between. In about eighty percent of the cases, more is not needed. Your average smuggler is not very imaginative."

He fished a large magnifying glass out of the clutter. "Then I study the seams. I like to concentrate on the needle holes. Usually it is quite obvious when a seam has been opened. The holes are stretched out, misshapen, duplicated. There's some indication of tampering here, but it could also be the result of simple wear."

He looked up, smiling. "Anyway, I continue up a ladder of increasingly sophisticated procedures until I arrive at the final test. I'll move to it right now, since if this jacket contains contraband it has clearly been well prepared. This test is called a fiber analysis. I pluck my thread samples from, say, fifty spots on the seams, then compare the samples to one another under the microscope over there."

Karl interrupted, fighting to keep his voice steady. "But isn't it possible, Herr doktor, that the manufacturer might change spools at some time during the sewing? Or might he not use different threads entirely on different seams?"

"Yes, son, of course. You've got the rudiments of a good investigative mind. The situation you pose, however, is not a problem for us. We never condemn a garment on the basis of a fiber analysis alone. When a discrepancy in the thread shows up, we open the garment. Often we find nothing. In such cases, it is because the discrepancy, as you suggested, can be traced back to the manufacturer. In other cases, however, we find all sorts of interesting surprises. After all, only the most creative smugglers take us this far."

A rap at the door. Seifert straightened up as far as he could. "Would you get that, son?"

It was Solberg, who after a quick survey of the room decided he would remain in the clean corridor. "How is it progressing, Herr doktor?"

"Good, major. Care to join us?"

"No thank you, Herr doktor. It has been my experience that you prefer to work alone. Comrade Leutnant Frassek, come with me. Let Herr doktor work in peace."

"Leave the boy with me, major. He's a quick learner and he isn't disturbing. I was in the process of acquainting him with some of our newer techniques. He might find them helpful at some point in his career."

"Of course, Herr doktor. How far along are you? The orifice and x-ray searches have turned out negative. The generaloberst is growing impatient for the results of your inspection."

"So am I, major, so am I. But one mustn't let one's feelings get in the way of one's work. If he wants the job done right, he can wait. If not, he can find someone else to do it."

"I'll try to keep him diverted, Herr doktor. How does it look at this point?"

121

"Nothing yet."

"Thank you, Herr doktor." Solberg closed the door.

"And so," continued Seifert, plucking thread samples from various seams of the blazer with a special little tool which left the seams intact, "we'll just match these under the scope and see what we get."

He moved to the microscope, toyed with the focus knobs, held up a finger. "Ah-ha. Come over here, leutnant. This will interest you."

Heart stuck in his throat, Karl walked to Seifert and looked into the microscope. The patterns were so distinctly different that even his untrained eye noticed. "So...you open it up?"

"Precisely." Seifert was already slashing the stitches with quick strokes of a tiny scalpel. Soon, airy scraps of nylon floated from between layers of wool. Karl felt like Forsch, minus the final capacity for heroism. Should he kill Seifert right here, with his bare hands? Stupid...he'd be caught before he could dispose of the jacket.

He watched in horror as the canny Seifert pieced together a flock of numbered scraps. Over the old man's bony shoulder, he read:

THE EARLY DEATH OF GENERALOBERST HEINRICH BÜLOW
by Hannah Mühlendorff

Suddenly, Seifert grabbed him by the arm and pulled him close. "Go," he whispered into Karl's ear. "Lock the door. Not one sound out of you, clear?"

Karl, dizzy with confusion, did as he was told. Behind him, the doktor spoke in a normal voice for the sake of the microphones he knew were hidden in his room. "Nothing in the blazer, leutnant. Just as you thought earlier. The manufacturer must have changed threads halfway through. Now bring me the trousers..."

Seifert's hand clutched Karl's arm with surprising strength as Karl lay the trousers on the table. "Calm down, son," he whispered. "You might have to talk to them at any moment."

With those words he returned to the jacket, selecting thread that matched the thread he had cut. After he had reinserted the pieces of the final, incriminating Hannah story, he resewed the seams as effortlessly as he had slit them. In a normal voice he said, "A clean bill of health, leutnant. Nothing. I'll phone your people before I leave."

122

Then, pulling Karl close, he said in a whisper light as dust: "Go. May God be with you and Frau Mühlendorff. Heinrich Bülow deserves to die."

Clay gazed at the shadowy, defunct stations under East Berlin as the subway clattered along its familiar route. Vopo guards with automatic weapons stood in the dim light. Drab signs bearing the station names— Oranienburger Tor, Nordbahnhof, Stadion der Weltjugend—hung above the dilapidated platforms. The train crossed the invisible subterranean border to West Berlin and stopped at the Reinickendorfer Strasse station. Clay was still too dazed to notice the bright signs and cheerful crowds.

He got off mechanically at the Ernst-Reuter-Platz and climbed the station stairs, aware only of the loud ringing in his ears. The sight outside caught him off-guard. The city lay in a pristine splendor beneath the winter's first snowfall. Except for an occasional bus or plow, the roads were free of vehicles. People walked arm-in-arm down the middle of broad boulevards that normally were choked with traffic. There was laughter. Lovers wrestled in the drifts, kids out of school heaved snowballs, grandmothers strolled with their dogs.

Sheets of snow whipped down, adding rapidly to the foot already on the ground. The storm seemed to pulse through Clay, cleansing him of the venom and fear he had carried with him from his horrible night. Relief, at long last, came over him. He made a snowball and launched it toward the distant rooftops with a joyous shout. And then, turning his face skyward, he let the flakes melt on his cheeks and mingle with his tears.

PART III

CHAPTER THIRTEEN

Near the end of November the sun appeared above the gray squares and dreary buildings of the Communist capital. Soon the freeze broke. Torrents of water charged down the gutters, the Spree surged toward its high-water mark of the previous spring, cars sloshed through midtown lakes and trams spewed silver showers into the hazy blue sky.

Jürgen Adelbert loosened the long scarf around his neck and wiped the perspiration from his forehead. His days might be numbered, but he was determined to enjoy at least this fine afternoon.

He ran his knuckles over the tiny rise in his breast pocket created by the cyanide pill. He need not live in terror any longer. If he must depart, at least it would be on his terms.

As he moved across sodden Alexanderplatz he made an outrageous noise like an airplane, dipping his shoulders left and right. What a marvelous sensation of freedom. Far below he saw the ocean, choked with floating ice and ablaze in the afternoon sun. To love—and appreciate—life one must be prepared to leave it at a moment's notice.

Adelbert had just completed his long account of the Vopo, with a special section on Bülow and the White Room. He had worked and reworked the piece, a condemnation of police and state that was free of rhetoric, straight from the heart. Minutes ago he had deposited the piece with his good friend Wolfgang, a supporter of the underground.

Wolfgang had assured him that if he died, God forbid, his essay would appear from one end of the DDR to the other. The popular outrage would be great—he was, after all, one of the most beloved young artists in the country.

He pressed on toward the Cafe Warschau, boots dragging through the puddles, face turned to the sun. In front of the Rathaus a small girl in a group of visiting schoolchildren recognized him. "Adelbert," she called out. "The poet Adelbert, let's get his autograph..."

They descended on him in a big happy swarm. He looked at the children, worried they would catch cold if their feet got wet. But they all wore the same floppy rubber boots that he wore, ugly but functional.

The teacher plunged after her unruly brood. Adelbert watched her with a smile. She stopped at the edge of a gigantic puddle, pointed at her dainty fur-lined boots and shrugged apologetically.

"Ha," Adelbert said, "what do you say, children? Shall we run away?"

Laughter, rare as the November sunshine, floated over the square.

"Yes, let's run away..."

"Follow me, then." The poet as Pied Piper repeated his noisy airplane act with twenty youngsters in tow. After a few sloshing turns they made a ragged landing on the dry cobblestones beside the teacher. Adelbert introduced himself and kissed her on the cheek.

"He kissed her," giggled the children. "Did you see? Herr Adelbert kissed Fräulein Metzger." She blushed, unable to talk.

"Herr Adelbert, Herr Adelbert, give us your autograph—"

"I don't have a pen."

"Give him a pen, Fräulein Metzger, give him a pen!"

Still flustered, she dipped into her purse. A general scramble to dig notebooks out of satchels.

"I've got a better idea," said the poet, "let's all go to the cafe for a sundae."

Excited cheers and soon they were trudging across the square like an oversize family, making lengthy detours to spare Fräulein Metzger's boots.

In the cafe Adelbert ordered two dozen lavish desserts and signed his name in everyone's book. Seated beside Fräulein Metzger, he draped his scarf around her neck and pulled her close. She blushed again, but managed to look into his eyes. What warmth he saw there, the beauty ...this was life as it was meant to be. Children, sunshine, love. He actually felt a sadness for all the Bülows of the world, deprived souls who would never know such joy....

Two hours later, as he walked alone through the dying afternoon toward his apartment, the first chill of night settled in his bones. Layers of ice thin as paper had formed on the puddles. Smoke from a million coal stoves hung above the streets in stagnant layers. But the evening star still glittered clear and brittle over the stark skyline of the city.

Adelbert warmed himself with visions of the lovely young woman he had just met... He saw her in a forest near her home in Neubrandenburg. It was summer, and the sweltering heat made her fair skin flush. He sat with her on a bed of pine needles and began very slowly to undress her—

The hand on his shoulder ripped him from his fantasies. "Get in," rasped a cold voice. Spinning, Adelbert reached for the capsule in his pocket. Too late. More hands restrained him and he was lifted from his feet.

In seconds he lay bound and gagged on the floor of an unmarked gray van. He caught a glimpse of the building in which he lived as they sped south through the downtown. Then someone wrapped a black cloth around his eyes. Darkness buried him.

"Looks like cyanide," he heard the man who had torn the capsule from his fingers whisper.

Hands continued to work on him. They bound him tight to a pallet. Ropes pressed into his thighs and chest. His gag was loosened, but before he could make a sound a fat strip of tape sealed his lips.

Who were they? A terrible thought occurred... Wolfgang had betrayed him. No, not even in the bowels of Bülow's awful facility had the world seemed more cruel.

As the van swayed and bucked he felt the pallet he lay on ascend with a rubbery motion of its own. Rusty hinges squeaked. The pallet descended now, settling somewhere closer to the gritty noises of the road. Sheet metal doors clattered shut above him.

His allergies erupted, making his nose swell shut. He fought to draw air in through his mouth but the tape prevented him.

I don't care, he told himself, better to suffocate than have to face *them* . . .

His body, however, refused to cooperate. Spasms arched and twisted his slight frame. The pallet he was bound to chattered wildly against the metal bed of the van. His vocal cords shrieked in mute agony as he fought to inhale through his swollen nasal membranes. While the world blazed red and purple behind his blindfold, the van bumped to a stop in an overgrown courtyard.

"I don't think he can breathe. Give me the light." Adelbert heard the words as if they had been spoken in the foggy distance, unrelated to him.

"My God, you're right. Quick, get the tape off."

Air rushed into his lungs, but he was no longer conscious.

When Adelbert came to he was lying on a mat in a cellar. The musty smells and the damp air were reminiscent of his last subterranean visit. For a long time he lay still, not wanting to open his eyes.

Why hadn't he been able to die? Why must he face it all again? He groaned involuntarily and rolled on to his side. He heard voices, female voices among them, and a scurry of footsteps. A hand came gently to rest on his shoulder. "Herr Adelbert," whispered a woman, "Herr Adelbert, you're all right. We're sorry we hurt you. Come, try to sit up, why don't you drink a little beer?"

Beer? Limp and frightened though he was, his senses stirred. "Beer? Yes." He put a dry tongue to his parched lips, still not daring to open his eyes.

Powerful hands—the same powerful hands that had abducted him?—lifted him to a seated position. Someone wedged cushions behind him. "Drink this," said the woman, holding a glass to his lips.

He grabbed the glass from her and gulped it down. "More," he muttered, wiping the foam from his chin.

"All right, but try to drink it slowly."

130

Get the beer, get as much as they're willing to give me, pour it down. Oh, to be just a little bit tipsy before they start in on me...

His heart sank when he realized his second glass was only half full. "More," he said.

"Not yet. You'll make yourself sick." This time it was a man who spoke. "You may open your eyes, Herr Adelbert. You are among friends."

"Friends? Where am I? You're Stasi, aren't you?"

Laughter.

"We read your piece."

"How could he have done it? Why did he betray me, what did you do to him to make him talk?"

"Wolfgang would never betray you, Herr Adelbert... He's one of us, and we do not betray our friends."

Adelbert opened his eyes and stared at the half dozen men and women who stood around him. They nodded or smiled. "What? Who are you?"

"We don't have a name," said Wilhelm Jahn. "We're part of a growing underground movement in the DDR."

"You're not Stasi? Not the Vopo?"

"No," said Jahn. "And we apologize for hurting you. We should have done our research more thoroughly. We knew nothing of your allergies."

Adelbert blinked with confusion at the shabbily dressed resisters who came forward to shake his hand. "You're with the underground?"

"Yes. When Wolfgang came to us with the story he confided in us. We know you will not be in a position to give Bülow what he wants. Your piece on the Vopo need not appear posthumously. We're going to smuggle you across the border."

"What?"

"Yes, you can't stay here. We'll hide you, then you must go."

"You kidnapped me just to save my life? Why? I don't understand—"

"Nor will you for several days. Let me say, though, that our motives were not entirely altruistic. We want Bülow to believe that the Stasi is behind your disappearance."

"The Stasi? But why?"

131

"Because, Herr Adelbert, we are on the verge on the most important resistance action ever undertaken in the DDR. If we succeed in deepening the present rift between the Vopo and the Stasi, we hugely improve our odds. You see, Herr Adelbert, you are a valuable commodity.

CHAPTER FOURTEEN

Käte scarcely noticed the springlike weather. The collar on her heavy black coat was turned up as though against the cold, her gloved hands were thrust deep in her pockets. She shivered slightly as she watched the crush of employees at the main entrance of VEB Elektro-Apparate-Werke divide into four single-file lines to pass through the x-ray scan.

It was Monday morning, the second of December. She was surprised that the security precautions for Bülow's visit had begun so early; he was not due for another week. But she had prepared herself well for such problems, and was more intent than frightened.

She tossed her keys onto the conveyor belt and walked through the scan with her purse over her shoulder. The buzzer remained silent, but the man in civilian clothes supervising the operation—an outsider she didn't know—ordered her to wait. He let her stand and absorb the sting of his authority while he checked through several more employees, then held up his hand, indicating that his station was temporarily closed. He swung the same hand toward Käte and gave a snap of his fingers. "Your purse, please."

She quickly handed over the leather bag. Random searches were not uncommon when security was tight; she didn't want to draw attention to herself.

The man passed the purse to his assistant, whom Käte recognized as one of VEB-Elektro's employees. "Want me to run it through again?"

"No. Search the contents."

The assistant turned the bag in his hands like a soccer ball, then emptied it onto his table and conducted a rather cursory examination. "Nothing here, comrade," he said with a smile.

"Move it," said the security official. "Come on. Out of your seat. I'll look that stuff over myself."

He sat and began going through Käte's things. He smoothed wrinkled scraps of paper and read the notes on them, passed the currency between his fingers and fondled the coins. He screwed out the lipstick in all four tubes, held each to the light, studied the hue and shape for irregularities. He rolled a tiny plastic pet whistle between his fingers, picked up a string of painted wooden beads and dangled them from his thumb. "What are these things?"

"Worry beads." She eyed him sternly, to let him know she was someone of rank inside the firm.

"Got something to worry about?"

"No, but you will if I'm not in my office on time." She picked up her purse and tossed her things back into it. Even she couldn't tell which lipstick tubes held the 9-mm parabellum bullet casings, which compacts bore the little plastic sacks of gunpowder hidden beneath the rouge and eyeshadow...

In her office she quickly exchanged the lipstick tubes and compacts for duplicates she had stowed away in her closet. She closed her eyes, breathed a deep sigh of relief. Today was the last of three smuggling operations. The Vopo uniform Karl had brought her was stashed in a basement storeroom. She had everything she needed to rig the auditorium.

She sat at her desk and began to organize her day. Before she had made her first phone call there was a loud rap at her door. "Come in," she said.

Two men in business suits stepped toward her as though she might

134

try to get away. "Security. I'm sorry, Frau Frassek, we must take your purse—"

"You must what?"

"We will have it back soon."

"But this is outrageous. You have no right to snoop in my personal belongings. Besides, I was already searched at the entrance." She twisted in her chair and reached for her purse, which lay on a worktable behind her. One of the men beat her to it.

"We know you were already searched, Frau Frassek. That is precisely the reason we must now take the purse."

Käte picked up the receiver. "Director Scheel is not going to be happy with you," she said, dialing.

One of the men circled behind her and broke the connection. "Director Scheel has already given his permission. We will have it back in twenty minutes."

Käte followed them to the door and several yards down the corridor, protesting. But when she was again in her office, she allowed herself a smile. The security staff would be on the defensive after its futile search of her purse. It was time to go after the key she needed—the key to one of the auditorium's emergency exits.

Director Scheel had modeled his personality on the debonair stereotypes of the corporate executive he'd seen portrayed on West German television. He found himself quite charming. He was also an incomparable letch.

Two weeks earlier Käte had inveigled her way into his office to reconnoiter the famous key display on his wall, and he had arrogantly molested her. She had been forced to put up with several minutes of his panting and pawing in order to keep the door open for a return visit. She was happy to have a pretext today for behaving coldly.

She took a single key from her desk and dropped it into her sweater pocket. The key was identical in size and shape to the key she wanted. She paused briefly at the mirror on her door to straighten her hair, then walked to the elevator...

"Relax," said Scheel, when she was in his office, "as I explained I was on another line when they called. They didn't tell me it was *your*

135

purse. They said an employee in Section A, that's all. I'd no idea it was you. I trust you will accept my apology."

Scheel's dyed silver hair gleamed in the sunlight flooding his spacious office. His plastic smile flickered.

Käte stared at the key display adorning the wall behind him, trying as best she could to ignore his suffocating presence. The display was a gigantic walnut affair. The keys hung like flags of state in little individual boxes with doors of bulletproof glass. On the tiny glass doors each key's function was spelled out in silver script. Miniature combination locks jutted from the doors holding keys to high-tech and military-related areas.

Käte again located the sign that read, Right Front Emergency Exit, People's Auditorium. The glass door was low enough for her to reach if she stood on tiptoe, and it had no lock. Somehow she must get Scheel out of the room.

"Of course I accept your apology. But I would appreciate it if you would call those idiots in security and have my purse returned at once."

"Why, of course, Frau Frassek." His eyes wandered from her full breasts to her legs. She felt sick. He stabbed at the intercom. "Fräulein Lederer, call Stein in security. I want him to bring an item his men are examining to my office at once. The purse of Frau Engineer K. Frassek."

"I was hoping," said Käte, "that you would rebuke him yourself. His men treated me in a most offensive way."

"I'll talk to him when he gets here." He pressed the intercom button again. "Fräulein Lederer, make sure Herr Stein understands that he is to deliver the purse *himself.*"

"Thank you," said Käte.

"You are a model employee, Frau Frassek. Have I ever told you that before? A model employee *and*, if I may add, a charming woman."

The key hung scarcely ten feet away. She knew she could not leave without it. If only he'd go out for a moment... maybe if she asked for a drink...

"Thank you, Herr director." She moved casually over to the keys, wiping an imaginary tear from her eye. "This whole episode has been most upsetting."

"Yes, yes, I'm sure it has."

She studied the keys distractedly, as though her mind were far away. They looked almost quaint, she thought, arranged as they were in their little wood-and-glass houses.

"Do you like it?" asked Scheel.

She nodded.

"Most everyone does. A curiosity, you know. I like it too. It's a lot more interesting than, say, an aquarium."

She glanced at him, marveled at his vanity and fatuousness. The key display was not intended to be functional, but she knew it was more than just a curiosity. It was probably meant to serve as a symbol of Scheel's sovereignty over his domain.

"Yes, yes," he went on, "it's quite a nice piece. I don't use those keys, of course. The janitorial staff has its own supply. But I like knowing they're here, like knowing I don't have to depend on anyone else to go where I must."

"I see," said Käte, sighing.

Scheel pulled up behind her, his footsteps loud in spite of the pile carpeting. She could feel his breath on her neck. She knew what was coming. A pink hand landed on her breast. Another slithered beneath her dress and scampered up her leg.

She spun away and walked to the window. "No," she whispered, "not here. Get me a drink. Please. I need a drink."

The director could tell from the way she spoke that she wanted him. Of course. For the first time his new Western image was beginning to bear the promised fruits. "A marvelous idea. I usually have a *Blutige* Maria this time of day. How about yourself? A *Blutige* Maria as well?"

"A what?"

"Why, Frau Frassek, that's what our civilized friends across the Channel call a Bluedee Maahree. I always translate these English names into German. Regrettably few of our people speak English."

It took her a second to realize he was trying to say Bloody Mary. She caught a fleeting image of Clay mocking the German need to impress. Clay . . . if only she could be in his arms right now . . .

"That would be fine, director," she said, trying to sound as though she meant it.

He turned his back on her and walked to a bar on the other side of the room. She almost gasped out loud. He was not going to leave his office ... she would have to attempt the theft of the key in his presence ...

She moved back to the keys, stopping under the glass case she had to get into. He watched her while he dropped ice cubes into the glasses, smiling knowingly, as though to tell her he understood and recognized her secret passion for him. She waited. He knelt to get out a fresh bottle of vodka from beneath the counter. With a deft and silent move, she opened the glass door and slipped the key from its hook.

He stood, making what he considered a suave gesture with the bottle. She faked a shy smile and buried her hands in her sweater pockets. Her fingers found the key she had brought with her and let the stolen key fall to safety.

"Come over here," ordered Scheel. "I want to show you how to make a proper *Blutige* Maria."

Blutige Maria ... Bloody Mary ... The name had the connotation of a female drenched in blood. What a dreadful image. How idiotic of him to conjure it up in the mind of the woman he was trying to seduce. It seemed to her unfathomable that a man of Scheel's administrative talent could be such an imbecile when it came to women.

"I can make a very good Bloody Mary—"

"Yes, but there are, shall we say a few little secrets, secrets without which ..."

He dipped beneath the counter again. In a motion that seemed cued to his, Käte reached up and hung the false key. There wasn't time to close the little glass door before he stood up. He eyed her with pursed lips but said nothing.

Her heart throbbed, he must hear it ... forcing laughter she began playfully opening other doors, then glanced back at him, smiling.

Scheel still regarded her intently. "You seem nervous, Frau Frassek."

She closed the doors delicately, one at a time. "Perhaps I am."

Suddenly he broke into a broad smile, having just discerned the truth ... she was nervous about making love in the office. "Well," he said, "no need to be."

"I know ..." What else to say except this insanity?

"Now come over here and watch. There are some things you must learn." God, how he grated on her nerves. She felt no relief at having snared the auditorium key, only a sense of dread about what was coming ... where was Stein, the security chief ... ?

"What would you like to show me, Herr director?"

He hurriedly sloshed tomato juice into the glasses and cut chunks from a lemon shriveled almost beyond recognition.

"It's supposed to be a lime," he said. "Next time, lime."

"What were you going to show me, Herr director?"

"That can wait." He rounded the end of the bar, drinks in hand. She backed off. He came forward, setting the drinks on the end table. She could hear his breathing, see color rising in his face.

"Herr director, please ... I'd like to have my drink."

"No. Comes afterward. That's what my English friends tell me."

He took another step toward her. She turned to walk to the window, but he caught her from behind and pulled her down on the sofa. His wheezing sent puffs of breath across her neck. "Lie down. Hurry—"

"Herr director!"

He pushed her on to her back and got on top of her, forcing a knee between her legs. She turned her head to avoid his mouth. She had to keep her self-control. If she lost her temper, she would tear at him, ruin everything. The assassination was only a week away ... she could not afford to risk being removed from her post because she'd humiliated him.

The "safe" way was to let him go through with it, but she couldn't. At least struggle, pretend ambivalent feelings, let him sense there was hope but only later, somewhere else ...

She pushed his upper body away from her with both hands so that she could at least breathe, holding him momentarily above her. He sputtered, groaned. She tried to get his knee from between her legs, but her movements only excited him more. He lifted himself and fumbled with his fly.

When she again tried to struggle out from under him the key toppled from her pocket and landed beside her on the sofa. With a gasp she instantly let him fall back onto her and pulled his head down on her chest. She tried to move sideways but his weight would not let her budge. She felt him straining to lift his head. No, he must *not* ... he would see the key ...

She pulled his hair as though in passion to keep his head against her breasts. He strained against her, yanked himself loose. His bleary eyes stared down at her. She stared back, and calling on every ounce of control she possessed, slowly pulled up her skirt. Her eyes held his just long enough. He looked down at her bare legs and panties. The dress now covered the key, which she clutched through the material—

The intercom buzzed. She gave a lurch and rolled out from under him. "Herr director, the intercom. *Answer* it. I will *not* be compromised in this position."

He gaped at her a moment as though he might resume, then got up and dragged himself to the desk. "Director Scheel here . . . good . . . keep him with you until I call for him."

Käte slipped the key back into her pocket and hurried into the bathroom. "Herr director," she called through the cracked door, "we really should have waited."

"Yes," he said, apparently not angry. "Yes, you're right. Later . . ."

Stein entered now with the purse. Käte listened as she pulled herself together.

"Herr director," said the security chief, "a most curious thing. Take a look at this. Do you know what it is?"

"I thought I told you not to search the purse, Herr Stein."

"My men had already begun. Here. Take a look at this thing." He handed Scheel a small plastic cylinder an inch long and the diameter of a cigarette. The director examined it without particular interest.

"Well, Herr director, do you know what it is?"

Käte stepped boldly into the office. "Of course he knows what it is, Herr Stein. You give the impression that you do not. If you fellows are to do your jobs, it seems to me you should keep up with the latest gadgetry rather than wasting your time on employee harassment."

Director Scheel, who had never seen such a device in his life, did not want to show his ignorance in front of Käte, his impending conquest. "Is this true, Herr Stein?" he asked, stalling.

"Is what true, sir?"

"That you are more interested in harassment than security," said Käte.

Stein expected Scheel to reproach her, but he only gazed at her fondly.

"Is it true," repeated Scheel, "that you yourself do not know what this is?"

"That is correct, Herr director. I trust you will inform me."

"It's a pet whistle," said Käte.

Stein noted the two Bloody Marys on the table and the crushed cushions on the couch. "A whistle," he said, embarrassed. He had just realized the relationship between them and now wanted to get out of the office as quickly as possible. Just his luck to harass the director's mistress. "Sir, I must apologize," he said, shuffling from one foot to the other. "My men made a most unfortunate mistake. It was not Frau Frassek's purse we meant to search. A mistake... a most unfortunate mistake."

He put the pet whistle to his lips and forced a nervous burst of air through it. Nothing. His suspicions flared. "Whistle?" he said against his better judgment.

Käte smiled at him. "Really, Herr Stein, if you must display your ignorance, there are better places to do it than in the presence of your director."

Scheel smiled too. "I thought my security people were more knowledgeable." He turned toward Käte, because he had no more idea than Stein why the whistle had not made a sound. Except he lacked Stein's interest. Käte was too much on his mind.

"This whistle," explained Käte, "is not audible to the human ear. The frequency is too high. But a *dog* can hear it a long way off. If you have a dog, Herr Stein, you should consider acquiring one."

The security chief studied the tiny cylinder for a moment and returned it to Käte's purse. "Remarkable... I apologize again for the most unfortunate mistake." He bowed stiffly.

"I must get back to work," said Käte. She accompanied Stein to the door. The director followed close behind.

"Frau Frassek, we still have unfinished business," he said after Stein had gone down the hall.

"I must, Erhard," Käte said, her voice all warm and gracious.

"Well, good-bye for now." He gave her his knowing smile. "Next time I'll see there are *no* interruptions."

CHAPTER FIFTEEN

"So you would prefer to be with us?" Kammer said. Wisps of his thin blond hair ran straight as railroad tracks across his high forehead. His watery blue eyes remained on the pencil he twirled in his fingers.

"Yes, sir," Major Solberg said crisply. The Stasi chief's office made him feel clean and efficient. He admired the sleek tables of chrome and glass, the tan carpeting, the banks of computers along the wall. There could be no doubt about it. The Vopo was falling behind, and this was the fault of none other than its top man, Generaloberst Heinrich Bülow.

"And what, major, are your reasons? I thought you were content with your new responsibilities at the Friedrichstrasse station. Wasn't this what you told me last time we spoke?" Kammer gazed through his bulletproof window at the city. His silhouette was etched sharply against the glass—a silhouette of orderly lines and neat angles.

"Comrade, sir, I think my talents would be better appreciated here."

"Precisely what talents are you referring to, major?"

"My ability to integrate the newest technical advances into our overall system of investigation."

"You are saying that the Vopo is too old-fashioned for your taste?"

Solberg stiffened his already stiff spine. "Well, sir, not exactly. The new facility at the Friedrichstrasse station is, for example, a step in the right direction. I do not like to see it used improperly."

"Major Solberg, we at State Security make a point of getting to the point. You disagree with your boss on how the Friedrichstrasse facility is run? Is that what you came here to say?"

"Well, sir, it's really much more than a disagreement. The facility was designed for a specific type of usage. May I speak openly of Generaloberst Bülow, sir?"

"You must always speak openly in this office, major. But perhaps it would be wise for you to inquire after my own sentiments toward your boss before you begin."

"By all means, sir. Thank you, sir."

Kammer swiveled in his chair and placed his feet on a leather stool. He kept silent for several moments, peering out at the city. Solberg fidgeted.

"Generaloberst Bülow," said Kammer at last, "is a traditionalist. Some say that he is an anachronism, but I believe this is not the case. Bülow has his faults, and I certainly disagree with him on many things. As you know, we don't share the same philosophy when it comes to running a modern police and security force..."

His voice trailed off. The major strained to hear. "There has been talk that I would like his job in addition to my own. I have men who keep me informed. You have heard such talk, major?"

"Yes, sir," said Solberg cheerfully. "It would be a...relief if you succeeded—"

Kammer spun in his chair and faced his guest. His features were taut, his movements fluid, almost graceful.

"Such talk is nonsense, major. My complaint is that Bülow does not wish to work more closely with us. The Stasi and the Vopo are arms of the same organism. When you sever one arm, you cripple the whole. True, I have been frustrated in my attempts to secure his cooperation. So why do I wish to work with him? Bülow has a quality more valuable to State Security than all of our computer records and interrogation techniques. He has intuition. Perhaps you find him a bungling antique. Do not be misled by what you see on the surface. He has intuition, and we need that if we're going to find Mühlendorff before she does us more serious harm."

"But sir, if you had seen what I saw recently I think you would feel differently. This intuition of his led to a disaster...He detained an American physician at my facility for no reason at all. That man was clean. The minister of health had already vouched for him."

Kammer's interest stirred. "What happened?"

"Well, sir, the generaloberst couldn't seem to keep his mind on what he was doing. He wasted half the night on a poor old wachtmeister who was supposed to have shadowed the physician but had lost him. Then, just when the favorable hours for the interrogation arrived, he fell asleep. Right in the chair where the interrogee is supposed to sit. If I had not been convinced of the detainee's innocence I would have telephoned you to intervene. It is this type of misuse of the facility that I object to."

Kammer got up abruptly and led Solberg to the door. "We'll talk again," he said. "By the way, major, do you remember the name of the American you detained?"

"Bentley, sir. Richard Clayton Bentley."

"Does anyone know you came here today?"

"Yes, sir. My wife Lotte."

"I should like no one else to know. Consider yourself part of my organization, major. We'll discuss salary arrangements at our next meeting. For now, you will continue as though you are in the employ of the Vopo. Good day, major."

Kammer tapped intently at the keyboard. Clay's name appeared in green print on the screen in front of him.

For three hours he studied the Stasi computer records on the American, pausing briefly for toast and coffee. A single discrepancy kept his interest. Professor Hermann Kirstein, on the medical faculty of Humboldt University, had said in his transcribed interview with the Stasi two years ago: "Ah, yes, Doktor Clayton Bentley. A fine man, in my opinion. He doesn't necessarily agree with all aspects of our system in the DDR, but as I'm sure you gentlemen know, neither do I. He's no great friend of the West either. Sees faults where they exist without regard to ideology. In fact I would say that he is somewhat apolitical. He's been a great help to us in developing our new children's anesthesiology program here. He gets on well with other members of the faculty. The only time he let me down was when he did not show for his farewell party at my home. When? I'll check. Here it is—July 27, 1983. Wasn't really his fault, though. He had a bad case of the stomach flu. Said he was going to cross over to his hotel right away. The time of the call? Early evening, perhaps six."

Kammer went to work at the keyboard again. On the night of July 27, R. Clayton Bentley had arrived at the border just minutes before the midnight expiration of his visa.

Kammer called the medical faculty. Professor Kirstein had passed away the previous spring.

The Stasi chief decided that it would be useful to consult the archives in which all precomputer police records were kept.

"You *what?*" said Bülow in his customary gruff tones. He held the receiver away from his ear and stared at it, then slammed his fist on the desk.

Night had fallen. The barbed wire on the wall outside the Bouchestrasse headquarters rose in fierce loops toward the searchlights. The canvas-draped tanks slumbered beneath a pale moon. Bülow flung open the window. A breeze pushed inside, ruffling the hair on the boar's head that stared down from the wall behind him. He went back to the phone.

"You what?" he repeated.

"Comrade generaloberst," said the timid voice at the other end of the line, "you must understand that we were understaffed. We had men at his apartment, at his favorite cafes, outside the homes of most of his known friends."

"Details, Schmidt."

"Right, comrade, sir. He was at the Cafe Warschau this afternoon with a bunch of school kids. Mitzscherling had him covered every inch of the way. Adelbert caused quite a stir. He bought all the kids dessert. Then he got very friendly with the teacher—"

"Hurry up."

"Right, sir. He left the cafe alone. Mitzscherling assumed he was

146

going to one of the places we have staked out. He decided it would be best to follow the teacher. We have her here right now. She claims never to have seen Adelbert before this afternoon. Anyway, sir, Adelbert did not show up at his apartment or at any of the other one hundred fifty-seven spots we're watching—"

"*Enough*. Go back out and *find* him."

Five days until the assassination attempt. Karl had little else to do but worry. Since Clay's departure Bülow had seemed to become calm. A foreboding change that made Karl uncomfortable. Did the general-oberst know something after all? Was he just waiting for the right moment to strike against them?"

And, of course, Karl worried most about his mother. He imagined her rigging the People's Auditorium for Bülow's appearance. If only there'd been a way for him instead of her to position the blank shots that were to serve as diversions. She'd done more than her share already, and he wasn't sure how she would hold up if the prying beam of a janitor's flashlight pinned her in the act of sabotage. He wished now he hadn't told her about the long night in the Friedrichstrasse station. He'd meant to encourage her with his account of Clayton's strength and Doctor Seifert's help. But what he'd done was upset her, as he could tell from the cracks that appeared in her usual stoic facade.

As for Wilhelm Jahn, he was a great peacetime leader, no doubt about it, had held the resistance together against incalculable odds, but this was now a war. Or would be after news of Hannah Mühlendorff's attack echoed through the land.

Karl decided his job was the simplest . . . killing Bülow would be the easy part, especially given Bülow's recent calm—

The phone rang shortly.

"Get over here *now*," ordered Bülow, clearly no longer calm.

The generaloberst paced the length of his office, the stub of a cigar planted between his jaws. Karl gazed out the window at the tanks. Less than a week, he thought, and the enclosure around the Bouchestrasse station would be an empty meadow. The gates would be flung open and the steel giants would rumble onto the streets of Berlin to prowl for insurgents. Did the people really have a chance against such brute force? The episode with Doktor Seifert had renewed Karl's hope that they did...

Bülow came to an abrupt halt in front of him. He pulled the cigar stub from his mouth and examined it.

"Adelbert's disappeared, been gone a day and a half. The Stasi's got him, Frassek."

"How do you know—?"

"Listen carefully. Since I've called you in we've had several new reports. Our people have questioned everyone living within several blocks of his apartment. Three people saw someone who may have been Adelbert, saw him shoved into a gray van by a gang of civilians."

"We should have protected him as well as watched him."

"Comrade leutnant, are you interested in playing spy inside Kammer's organization?"

"Not especially, sir."

Bülow regarded him intently. "I'm glad, Frassek, that you didn't jump too quickly. You're under suspicion, you know."

"For what, sir..."

"Someone close to me is feeding that *schwein* Kammer information. How else would he have known about Adelbert?"

"I can think of several ways, comrade generaloberst. Perhaps Adelbert talked to the wrong person. The Stasi has informers all over the country—"

"Forget it, Frassek. I'll find out soon enough where the leak is. It doesn't matter at this point anyway. You see, comrade leutnant, they haven't left us any choice. If Adelbert's given them information, we must counter with the house-to-house. We'll get the underground presses that print those goddamned stories and we'll get them *fast*. If that doesn't lead us to her, she's not operating inside the DDR. I haven't wanted to do this because it blows Mühlendorff's significance way out of proportion. But I'm not going to sit on my ass while Kammer uses *my* informers to bring her in. We'll get this little matter wrapped up once and for all."

"Sounds like a difficult operation to organize—"

"Of course. But I've had the plans ready for a long time. We've got print samples from all of the underground presses. Single words, Frassek, no context. Our people don't need to be told outright what they're looking for. See here, every neighborhood Vopo will have those samples. Those fellows are moles. They'll search out every corner of the DDR, every attic and cellar, every warehouse and shed. And there's a side benefit to this approach. If it takes a while to track her down after we've got the presses, at least there won't be any stories in the interim. Think about it, Frassek. The neighborhood Vopos, the ABVs, will have their orders in the morning. We've got thirty thousand of them waiting to go, and one hundred and twenty-six thousand highly trained volunteers to help them. The neighborhood men know the buildings and the residents they'll be dealing with. We'll put our own high-level staff on the larger factories and offices—another forty thousand men. Four days are all I need, Frassek. Tomorrow's Wednesday. We'll have the presses by Sunday night at the latest."

"We need a break," Karl said. He heard his own voice echo. "This should provide it." He knew he had to get the information to his mother so that she could pass it on to Jahn. The hired driver would be arriving at the brewery with the stories any day. The brewery held the presses. Once they were discovered, the whole area would be crawling with Vopo. It would be the worst possible spot in the country for Jahn and his people to take delivery of the shipment.

Must get word, must get word, must get word . . . the thought went round and round in his head. He became a charged circuit, clearheaded, calm and energized. He watched the generaloberst stuff his briefcase full of papers. "Let's go, Frassek."

"You've already alerted your staff?"

"That's what we're going to do now. Staff meeting at my house in forty-five minutes. *Move.*" . . .

Now on the ground floor of the Bouchestrasse station they waited for the driver to bring the limousine around. Behind them was a bank of telephones. Karl looked at them and wondered if he shouldn't call Käte right away. After all, he was supposed to have a free night tonight. Why wouldn't he call his mother if he weren't able to make a scheduled engagement?

Except what could he say with the generaloberst planted like a tree alongside him? He'd end by frightening Käte without getting his message across.

He could hear the purr of the engine as the limousine approached

149

the entrance. Think of something. Once inside Bülow's home it would be too late...

"Are you treating the men to *weisswurste* tonight, sir? I noticed you've got quite a supply in the mess."

"Hungry, Frassek?"

"You did get me up from the table."

"Well, I'm not wasting my weenies on staff. They wouldn't know a good sausage from *gänseschmalz*. Go on. Grab a pair for yourself if you're that desperate. And bring along a couple for me. Hurry, Frassek."

Karl sprinted down the dingy corridor toward the kitchen. Inside, he yanked the door shut and lunged for the phone. He quickly dialed Käte's number, and after it had rung several times remembered where she was this night, and the crucial, high-risk job she had to perform...

CHAPTER SIXTEEN

The Private Incentive Program at VEB-Elektro had been initiated the previous spring without much fanfare. Now, however, it was beginning to attract the attention of industrial planners all over the DDR. During its short lifetime the program had already produced several inventions valuable to the firm, and expectations ran high that many more would follow.

The program allowed employees in research and development to stay after work and use the firm's laboratories. Materials were provided free, and there was an ample budget for technical assistance. In return the inventions generated by the program remained the property of VEB Elektro. Any invention the firm decided to manufacture afforded the inventor a modest stipend and, more importantly, honorable mention in the corporate annals.

Doktor Theo Pilka, with whom Käte shared an office and a research lab, had demonstrated the vitality of the free enterprise concept with a remarkable little device, which VEB-Elektro was now mass producing for the military regime in Poland. The device enabled the police to turn on the lights in any building in which it had been installed without entering the building. A squad car passing a shop could switch on the shop's inside lights as it drove by.

This new capability had put a virtual end to the organized system of nighttime looting that had sprung up in the wake of Poland's economic crisis—and had done so at a price even the bankrupt Warsaw regime could afford.

"Pilka's Pole Popper," as the device was known around the plant, worked on the same principle as the remote control for a television set. Pressure on the button of the portable control sent high-frequency sound waves to a tiny transonic audio receiver inserted in a light switch. The light switch was thereby activated and the lights remained on until Doktor Pilka's timer, which could be set from one to ten minutes, ticked off. Because all of the parts for the Pole Popper were already in mass production at VEB-Elektro, the new device cost only about seven marks per unit and it was easy to install, requiring in most cases less than ten minutes.

Simplicity, economy, reliability—that was how Doktor Pilka had characterized the attributes of his invention when he had presented it to Director Scheel. Those qualities were in fact responsible for its great success—and for Käte's decision to use an adapted version for her purposes in the People's Auditorium.

"Staying late tonight, Herr doktor?" asked Käte. Pilka stood at the window watching the tide of workers stream toward the S-Bahn station across the street. Though they had shared an office for five years they still used titles and addressed each other with the formal *Sie*. He gave an awkward little start as he always did when she spoke to him.

"No, no, unfortunately not, Frau engineer. It's Tuesday night, you realize." She nodded pleasantly. Doktor Pilka always tore himself away from his work on Tuesday night to be with his wife.

"The symphony again? I do envy you."

Pilka smiled shyly. His long mane of gray hair tumbled over his forehead, and he brushed it away with a nervous jerk of his hand. "Not tonight, Frau engineer."

Käte suddenly wished she had not asked. Pilka, for all his reserve and formality, liked to discuss sex as much as quantum mechanics. Not long ago he had shown her the most bizarre document she had ever laid eyes on: an intercourse record he kept with his wife. It was as explicit as a log of border crossings, complete with times of entry and exit.

"I see," she said. "Well, sometimes it's very nice to have nothing planned. One has so little time to relax these days."

"You misunderstand me, Frau engineer. We have *something* planned, just not the symphony. It appears that my performance at home has been damaged by my success with the Popper. My wife pointed this out to me last night and backed up her contentions with our intercourse record book. I could hardly take issue with her conclusions. The indisputable proof lay before me in writing. *Ja, ja,* Frau engineer, too much libido has gone into the Private Incentive Program. I must reserve a bit more of that spare commodity for my wife. The new policy begins tonight at seven-fifteen." He said it with a straight face.

Käte smiled indulgently and handed him his coat. "I'll accompany you to the gate," she said. "I'm on my way down to the lab."

"Well, God in heaven, I never thought you'd be one to participate in the Private Incentive Program."

"Inspired by your success, Herr doktor." She closed the door behind them. She was going to miss Pilka. One of a kind, and didn't realize it.

"Well, I'm sorry I can't stay with you this evening. I think I could give you some tips on how to bring Director Scheel over to your side."

Scheel . . . she hoped he'd already left for home . . . "That's very kind of you, Herr doktor. Sometime next week perhaps."

They shook hands at the intersection of two great hallways on the main floor. Pilka, eyes on his watch, continued on toward the plant exit and his duties beyond. Käte unlocked the white metal door that led to the laboratories.

Pipes hissed across the silence, rattled, fell quiet. Frick, the night security man, knocked. Käte invited him in for a short visit and locked her door when he had left.

She began at once to ready her worktable: the evening's agenda was crowded. As a diversion if someone entered, she placed a large circuit board in front of her. She switched on the soldering iron and watched it come to a glow in its holder. The big clock on the wall read seven-fifteen. With a silent good-luck wish to her colleague, Doktor Pilka, she moved into action.

Sitting on a high stool, she opened the drawer directly in front of her and pulled it back until it pressed lightly into her midriff. Positioned this way she could lean over the drawer and work on the table, and could shove whatever needed to be hidden into the drawer and close it at the first sign of danger.

Inside the drawer there appeared to be nothing of significance: perfumes, papers, brushes, a string of homemade beads, several makeup compacts, half a dozen tubes of lipstick and a picture of Karl, proud and serious in his lieutenant's uniform.

But inside the lipstick tubes, inserted in the hollowed-out lipstick itself, were 9-mm brass bullet casings. She'd hidden the casings so expertly that she had used the lipstick in front of Doktor Pilka without the slightest worry.

Inside the compacts, buried underneath the rouge and eye shadow, lay tiny bags of gunpowder—just enough to fill the six casings. And the beads were sized to fit as snugly as lead bullets in the casing mouths.

Käte spread the six casings on the table and cleaned them thoroughly with solvent. In the bottom of each she drilled a tiny hole the same diameter as the holes in the wooden beads.

Her concentration intense, she thought of nothing, heard nothing, saw only the job in front of her. Searching through a large box of spare parts that she had thrown together over the past few days, she removed six of Pilka's Pole Poppers and two 200-amp fuses. The fuses were manufactured by VEB-Elektro and used in all of the plant's main breaker boxes. She stuffed the fuses deep inside her drawer, returned the beads and bullet casings as well and soldered a few random connections on the circuit board to make it look as though she had been working on it.

Taking a deep breath, she lined up six of the poppers in front of her. The gadgets were built around tiny receivers, difficult to work on only because of their small size. Simplicity, economy, reliability, she thought, removing their plastic covers with a miniature screwdriver.

The receivers were set to function on 220-volt household current. Kate quickly altered the wiring to make it compatible with 9-volt direct current. From her supply shelf she took six 9-volt batteries, each about the size of a dime, and a roll of 22-gauge nichrome wire. She soldered the batteries into place so that each receiver had an independent source of power.

Working rapidly, she cut a length of nichrome wire and connected it to one of the receivers in such a way that, when the contacts inside the receiver closed, the wire would form an unbroken circuit between the positive and negative poles of the battery. Pausing only to wipe the fine mist of perspiration from her forehead, she removed her minuscule pet whistle from her purse and blew it lightly. As she blew, she turned the frequency adjustment screw on the receiver. Since the whistle was inaudible to the human ear she could only guess its frequency within a very broad range. She took another breath, let it wash slowly through the whistle, twisting the adjustment screw on the receiver to 30,000 cycles per second.

On her third breath, with the screw at 35,000 hz., the contact points snapped shut. In four seconds the nichrome wire was red hot—a perfect fuse. Quickly she cleared off the table and closed the drawer. A sound intruded on her awareness, a sound she did not want to hear—the sound of a key jangling in her door lock.

In the same instant she picked up the soldering iron and leaned over the circuit board, not forgetting to slip on her safety glasses. When the man entered she was peering intently at a connection she had just soldered. Wisps of blue smoke lingered in the air above her head.

"Excuse me, Frau engineer."

Käte did not look up from her work. "That you, Herr Frick?"

"No, Frau engineer. Excuse me for barging in. I knocked but you must not have heard. Herr Director Scheel wanted this to be a surprise."

"What?"

The man set a vase of Intershop roses on the table alongside the circuit board. "Director Scheel wished these to be a surprise, Frau engineer. He took your key from the display in his office and told me to come in with these if you were not here. I'm sorry again for the intrusion but I did knock. This, Frau engineer, this, on the other hand, he instructed me to leave with you only if you were in. Otherwise..."

She looked at him for the first time. He was hunched over, digging through his large briefcase. Smiling, he lifted a jar of red liquid, examined it, held it to the light. "Otherwise," continued the man, "he

155

instructed me to bring it back to his office. A very good drink, he assured me. A *Blutige* Maria, I think he called it. He said it was your favorite."

While Käte looked on, annoyed and disbelieving, the man set the jar down beside the roses and hoisted his briefcase onto the table. He pulled out a glass, a small silver bucket of ice cubes and a bright green lime and arranged them around the roses.

"What's your name? Can't you see I'm busy?"

"Wysofsky, *gnädige* Frau. But don't jump to conclusions. I'm not Polish. Polish extraction, as they say. I'll admit to that. But the name is the only remaining blemish. The Wysofskys have been good Prussians since the fourteenth century. Otherwise the director wouldn't have hired me."

He leaned toward her and whispered conspiratorily, "Do you know that we sell your colleague's device to the Polish government at *below cost?* Herr director told me so himself. He couldn't stand the thought of all that rabble emptying the stores at night. He's got a point, too, Frau engineer. If that nonsense across the border continues, who's to say *we* won't be affected ourselves one day? Who's to say, Frau engineer?"

Käte was preparing to throw him out when an idea came to her ... an idea as promising as it was offensive ... She needed an alibi for entering the People's Auditorium that night in case she were caught. So far she'd thought of at least twenty, and none of them was convincing. What if she were supposed to meet the director himself in the great hall? Hard to imagine a better cover ...

"You mean to say, Herr Wysofsky, that Erhard is still in his office?"

"He is indeed. I'm to return to him right away. I do believe he plans to visit you."

"That's wonderful, Herr Wysofsky. But he's going to have to wait until I get this circuit finished. I'll never remember where I'm going with it if I stop now ... How's his mood?"

"Good. Always is when he's drinking."

"Oh, my," said Käte. "Poor Erhard. How much has he had?"

"Well ... enough."

"That settles it. Herr Wysofsky, I hope you understand. I'm most fond of him ... I suppose the whole work force knows about us by now. But I'll not have him in here when he's drunk. I want you to give me the key. I trust you understand."

Wysofsky stood erect, a good Prussian. "I understand, of course. But I cannot do what you ask. You must also understand my position. Were I to defy the director's orders in so personal a matter it would result in my dismissal. He ordered me quite explicitly to return the key. He seems very intent on seeing you tonight."

Käte gave a nervous sigh and picked up the phone. When the director answered, his tongue was thick.

"Erhard, this is Käte Frassek. I wanted to thank you for the surprise. Herr Wysofsky is here with me now."

"Ah, thank God you're in. I must see you, I haven't been able to get you off my mind since this morning, I'll come down rightaway—"

"No, Erhard, not yet. There's a very demanding operation I must finish first."

He grumbled. She heard the ice cubes clink in his glass. "Now, now, my dear, I may be many things but I'm no fool. I know you want me as much as I want you. Do you think I was blind to how you responded to me?"

"Don't ruin things by pushing me," she whispered.

"All right, all right, but I *must* see you tonight. I don't care when or where. But it must be tonight. Käte, I don't think I've ever met a woman like you, never held a woman so beautiful. Never—"

"Erhard, there's something I've always wanted to do. Are you prepared for . . . an adventure?"

"Yes, yes, of course . . . as long as I can see you tonight."

"Good. Listen carefully. I'll be waiting for you behind the stage of the People's Auditorium at . . . let's see . . . if I speed things up here I can . . . I'll be waiting at ten-thirty. Will you meet me?"

"*Of course,* excellent *and* original thinking. Käte, you're one in a million."

Which, she thought, might be a description of the odds on her carrying this off. Well, never mind, she had an alibi for being in the auditorium at night. Elation colored the edge of fear. "One more thing," she said. "One more favor."

"What's that . . . ?" His voice sounded far away, and faintly smug.

"I want you to instruct Herr Wysofsky to leave the key to my lab

157

here with me. I don't entirely trust you after this morning, Erhard. I must be able to concentrate on what I'm doing or I won't be in the mood to see you..."

"Of course, I understand, I don't entirely trust myself... Give him to me."

She handed Wysofsky the receiver. He nodded, then hung up.

On his way out of Käte's lab Wysofsky, keyless and cheerful, encountered the security team. He wished them a happy good evening and watched as they entered the workplace of the director's mistress. He waited around a corner until they came out and fell into stride beside them.

"Pretty woman," said Frick, the night security chief. "Too bad she doesn't work more nights. I don't mind looking at that, no *sir*."

"Well," said Wysofsky, "long as you just look. She's the boss's, you know."

Frick shook his head. "What's new? The ruling class always gets the breaks. I don't care whether they call it capitalism or socialism. Same all over, Wysofsky."

Eight-thirty. Käte locked the door, went back to work. One by one she set the remaining five receivers to go off at the frequency of the pet whistle. In two of the receivers she inserted timers. She set the timers for four minutes, then lined up all six receivers and blew on the whistle. Four sets of contacts snapped shut. The two timers began ticking, ticked for four minutes and two more sets of contacts snapped shut. She reopened the contacts, set the receivers aside and turned her attention to the bullets.

Cutting six strands of nichrome wire, she passed a strand through the small hole she had drilled in each bullet casing, pushed each wire into the casing until it emerged from the hollow mouth, then caught it with a pair of needle-nose pliers, pulled it approximately halfway out and soldered it in place. When the casings had cooled she filled each one carefully with gunpowder. Finally she threaded a wooden bead on to the end of each wire and tapped it firmly into the mouth of the casing. The blanks were now ready.

She paused for some last-minute calculations. Four of the bullets were to simulate gunshots. Since the time it would take the nichrome wire to come to a glow was a function of the wire's length, she decided to trim four of the wires to 9.0, 9.1, 10.0 and 10.1 centimeters respectively. The result would be a staggered sequence of detonations, like two short bursts of fire. She trimmed the wires protruding from the four bullets to the desired lengths and connected each bullet to one of the altered Pole Poppers. The devices seemed nearly foolproof. Wherever they were hidden inside the auditorium, she would need only to blow through the whistle to set them off.

The final two blanks had a different purpose. She cut their wires to exactly the same length and attached them to the two Poppers that were fitted with the timers. From her desk she took the two large cylindrical 200-amp fuses and pried them open at the ends. Using a scrap of insulation to protect the blanks from possible heat, she inserted one unit into each fuse. Four minutes after her first breath into the whistle, the two fuses would be destroyed. She must get them into the main breaker box in the People's Auditorium so that the great hall would be plunged into darkness shortly after Bülow had been knocked to the ground by his bodyguards and given the fatal injection of curare. That was her only chance of escape...

Nine-twenty-seven. She waited for Herr Frick, who appeared with his usual precision at nine-thirty. Again, he examined the jar of Bloody Marys on the desk, the glass, the roses, the tiny ice bucket. "Looks as though there are many advantages to night work, Frau engineer."

She said nothing.

"Are you returning home now?"

"I've another two hours work stacked up in the office."

"Here, let me help you carry all that. You're taking it with you upstairs, aren't you?"

"Yes. Thank you, Herr Frick."

He carried the drinks and roses to the third floor, chatting all the while. Käte's purse, packed with explosives, dangled from her shoulder not two feet from him.

At her office desk he bade her a cordial good evening and brushed a rose petal from his sleeve. That Scheel was a lucky man, he thought, a damned lucky man.

The policy governing the use of the auditorium's folding chairs had been spelled out explicitly in Plant Directive 2754:

No employee of VEB Elektro-Apparate-Werke shall remove chairs from the People's Auditorium. If chairs are needed elsewhere in the plant, the following procedure must be followed:

1. The employee shall inform the janitorial staff (6751) how many chairs are needed, when, where and why.
2. The employee shall return the chairs to the pickup points in the hallways as soon as they are no longer needed.

It should be understood that the chairs are property of the People's Auditorium and are not intended for permanent or long-term use elsewhere. If chairs are needed in other than a temporary capacity, the employee shall turn to the Office of Supplies (5469). Violation of the above shall result in a fine of 25M per chair, to be levied against the employee at fault and deducted directly from his/her paycheck.

Hochactungsvoll,
The Direction

Käte had called the janitorial staff on Monday and asked that four chairs be brought to her office. No questions had been put to her, but she was told to have the chairs at a collection point in the hall by the end of the workday on Thursday. Because of the big event scheduled for Monday morning in the auditorium, every chair in the plant would be needed.

She carefully inspected the four chairs, removing rubber grommets from the hollow metal tubes that formed the back legs when they were opened. Three of the four grommets she had removed were already mutilated: sound waves would pass through the cracks in the rubber with ease. She slit the fourth grommet from the inside with a razor blade, tore the rubber further by hand and bit off a jagged little chunk.

Working rapidly, she cut a stiff piece of cardboard into four sheets six inches long and two inches wide. She rolled one of the sheets into a cylinder and forced it into a hollow chair-leg. From her purse she took a unit consisting of a blank, a tiny transonic receiver and nichrome wire. Bending the wire until the bullet was directly below the receiver she wedged the entire unit into the hollow chair-leg containing the cardboard cylinder. It was a tight fit, as planned.

She tapped the chair several times against the floor. The unit stayed in position an inch down into the leg. Capping the leg with a flawed rubber grommet, she moved to the next chair. At ten minutes before ten, she was finished.

The nearest pickup point was in the hallway around the corner from her office. She carried two of the chairs there and stacked them on a pile of look-alikes. Returning to her office, she glanced one last time at the wiring diagram for the People's Auditorium, then slung her purse over her shoulder, grabbed the two remaining chairs and walked toward the elevator. When she arrived at the second pickup point on her floor, which was several hundred feet from her office, she was out of breath. She unloaded the chairs but didn't pause to rest. There was a job to do, and she wanted to get it over with.

It was ten-twenty. The two altered fuses were in place in the main breaker box. The fuses Käte had removed lay in the proper slots in the spare fuse cabinet beside the main box, their innards fatally severed. Four minutes after the blanks went off, the auditorium would be plunged into darkness. It would be a darkness nearly as black as tonight's, for the colossal hall had been built without windows—a safety precaution taken by its designers in the stormy postwar era.

Käte stood at the far end of the stage. She lit a cigarette. The three-thousand-seat auditorium loomed up out of the darkness, called forth by the quivering flame of her lighter. She took a step back, as though the heavy configuration of walls and seats were tumbling toward her. The clack of her shoe reverberated through the emptiness like a spectral chorus.

She capped her lighter and stood still. In her mind's eye, in her developing fantasy, the image of the lighted hall grew brighter . . . she saw it filling with people . . . SS generals in full uniform, many of whom she recognized from her stories . . . Russian officials in dark suits, medals like brazen stars across their chests . . . Vopos of all ranks in quiet little groups, uneasy about the Stasi undercover agents who watched them with contempt . . . Workers and students pouring in, boisterous but wary, her brother Rolf among them, smiling at her as he filed toward his seat, then shouting that he was living in a police state and intended to do something about it ... Wilhelm Jahn, wire glasses askew, looking up in horror as a crush of Nazis, Russians and Vopos descended on his friend, began to dismember him, twisting joints until muscle and cartilage gave way with a sickening snap ... And Clay was there too, standing in a far corner, stunned, watching Karl enter, his machine gun in firing position, and Bülow following his bodyguard into the hall, red-faced and frowning ... *"Now,"* she heard herself call out, and saw herself throw down an armload of her stories, and repeated *"now"* ... everyone turning and looking at her ... Rolf dying, Jahn leaping to his feet and motioning to his followers, Karl turning on Bülow, pinning him against the wall with a long fusillade ... The hall erupting, fighting spilling out into the streets, breaking down doors of houses, gushing inside, spreading and rising like a tide in all directions ... The single flicker of her lighter became the flash of a million bombs, the single clack of her shoe the sound of a million troops marching from the caserns and from the Soviet Union, from everywhere ... Soon, the land lay under blood, buildings lay in ruins, people lay twisted, caked in dried blood ... she couldn't make out which were soldiers, which resisters ... The land was silent, the fighting was over, and she did not know who had won ...

Käte had doubted before, but had pushed such thoughts aside. But now, the reality so close ... Shaken, she sat on the stage and put out her cigarette. It was black and silent in the hall. And when a very drunk Director Scheel came stumbling down the main aisle toward her, she felt neither revulsion nor anger, only the sense that he was an unwitting player in what might, after all, become a nightmare ...

CHAPTER **S**EVENTEEN

The driver listened to the hum of the tires and the reassuring purr of the big Mercedes diesel. On the truck radio the West German rock group Trio sang a bizarre number:

> *Du liebst mich nicht*
> *Ich lieb' dich nicht*

He adjusted his horn-rimmed glasses, fiddled with his fake beard and joined in:

> *You love me not*
> *I love you not*

The East German border was less than twenty miles away.

Most of the snowfall from the blizzard had melted during the Indian summer, but in the Bavarian pine forests remains of drifts stretched in silver crescents among the trees. Water covered the lower-lying fields, forming vast temporary lakes that shimmered like mirrors under the cold gray sky. Fog steamed up from the saturated earth and gathered in towering banks on the horizon.

The driver was Clay, carrying the precious Hannah cargo to the East. He was glad to see the dreary German weather return. The sunshine had begun to make him nervous.

Since his release from the Friedrichstrasse station Clay's work had gone smoothly. He had found Ursula at the bank in West Berlin where she had recently been promoted to vice-president. Yes, she would have a limousine waiting all day December ninth at the Reinickendorfer Strasse station. Of course she would shop for the clothes on his list and make sure the limousine driver brought them with him. And on December ninth she would arrange for Käte, Karl and Clay to be transported to the American military airport at Tempelhof, perhaps in an armored bank truck. If so, it would be the most valuable currency that truck had ever carried, she'd told him. Of course, she knew nothing of the assassination plan, only that she was helping the trio escape from East Germany.

By late morning he was aboard the last flight to leave the divided city that snowy day.

In Frankfurt he met with his friend Jason Hobart, chief of surgery at the American Military Hospital, and asked for a large favor: could Hobart arrange to have a plane waiting at Tempelhof on December ninth?

"Bringing out that woman, Bentley?"

"Yes," said Clay. "And our son."

Hobart raised his eyebrows. "You never mentioned that part of it. Worried the Stasi will be after them in West Berlin?"

"Yes."

"Okay, friend, okay. I owe you one. We'll get you that plane. We've got a kid in the hospital now—a kidney transplant candidate waiting on a donor. So happens his father's a general. If I tell the old man the world's foremost authority on children's anesthesiology is now in Berlin and is willing to take a look at our procedures here, he'll fly the plane himself."

Before leaving Frankfurt Clay procured 200 cc. of curare and 50 cc.

164

of the antidote, neostigmine, from the hospital pharmacy. In the lab, to which Hobart admitted him, he condensed the curare into a deadly concentrate. He broke open a packet of twelve micro-syringes designed for taking blood samples from premature infants, filling eight of them with curare and two with neostigmine. When he had finished he returned the syringes to their protective plastic cylinders. The two empty syringes he put in his pocket: they would be needed when it was time to concoct some sort of holder that would fit neatly under a glove.

He traveled to Munich on the intercity express. As soon as he had found a hotel he looked up Horst von Oldenburg, the man Käte had told him to contact, and warily approached him on the subject of the DDR. It was several days before Clay felt safe revealing why he had come. When he did he could sense in Oldenburg the same determination he'd found in Käte.

Clay handed him the Hannah story, transcribed on to several sheets of hotel stationery. After he'd read it Oldenburg, immensely excited, insisted that they visit the printer that very afternoon.

Together they explained to the old man in the blue smock the unusual format they wanted for "The Early Death of Generaloberst Heinrich Bülow." Clay then pressed a bank note into the printer's hand. It was, he said, in appreciation of the printer's pledge of absolute secrecy.

Later Oldenburg scolded him. The money, he said, was not necessary. All the people they'd be working with were refugees from the East. All were devoted to the overthrow of the police state. The printer had lost his whole family in an escape attempt eight years earlier. He, as well as the others Clay would meet, understood too well the need for silence.

Sunday, December 1, was spent at the tailor's. Clay was fitted with a wardrobe of well-worn trucker's clothing. He also received a thick black beard and a pair of heavy glasses. With each glance at himself in the mirror he began to feel what he looked like, and was more impressed by the devotion and ingenuity of those he was meeting. Such people, at least to his knowledge, did not live in Boulder, Colorado.

The tailor took a look at one of the micro-syringes. "It must not show beneath a tight glove," Clay explained. "It must be held in such a way that the holder has no chance of accidentally injecting himself. And it must be in such a position that it can be injected *through* the material of the glove."

"I understand." The tailor rolled the syringe in his palm, studied the natural gulleys, smiled. "Give me your hand," he said to Clay. He placed the syringe on Clay's fingers, perpendicular to them. "Now slowly curl the fingers."

Clay watched the tiny cylinder roll into the gulley between his fingers and palm.

"We face it down," said the tailor. "If your hand is in the hand-shaking position the needle will be pointing toward the ground. Here, let me tape it."

He positioned and secured the syringe. "Can you reach the plunger with your thumb?"

"Yes," Clay said, "but it's too tight, I can't move it downward—"

"Don't worry. The holder will be made of the thinnest lambskin— like a good quality prophylactic. The material will stretch with the thumb pressure. Now, which hand, which size?"

Clay thought for a minute, conferred with Oldenburg. "One for a left hand a little larger than mine."

"You're positive he's left-handed?" the tailor asked. "The sling will not be interchangeable."

"I'm positive he's *right-handed*," said Clay. We want it on the hand he's least likely to need for something else. And I'd like you to make me a woman's too. She wears a size eight glove. Also for the left hand. Will it help you to keep the syringe?"

"Yes . . . You have extras?"

"Yes." . . .

On Monday morning, December 2, Oldenburg located the order that the Scholler Brewery in Laucha had placed with Ferkel Grains, A.G. The order had gone in at Ferkel Grains' Munich branch. It was a simple matter to fake a call from the DDR asking that the shipment be post-poned for a week. A few questions and Oldenburg had the name of the shipping company scheduled to deliver the load as well: Jobst Trans-port. He and Clay visited the Jobst office and photographed several of the company's modern grain haulers. Half a day later a used-equipment broker had located a similar truck and Clay had paid for it in cash.

Using a fictitious corporate name, Oldenburg next phoned Ferkel and placed a rush order for three thousand kilos of barley. By evening the truck was in a large modern garage with a tarp drawn tightly over its load. Body men were at work stenciling the bright blue logo of Jobst Transport on the cab and cutting a rectangular panel from the steel underbelly of the trailer.

At ten o'clock that same evening Clay and Oldenburg met with a Hans Zaisser in his plush Schwabing apartment. Zaisser was a wealthy toy manufacturer—and one of the Western world's foremost suppliers of forged documents. For a fee of eighty thousand marks he agreed to provide by noon the next day: 1.) A forged set of papers showing the truck as property of Jobst Transport, purchase date, 5/3; 2.) Full identity papers for Clay, complete with notorized employment records, in the name of Stephan Hager, citizen of the German Federal Republic; 3.) The orders, shipping papers and customs forms relating to the fictitious transactions between the Scholler Brewery in Laucha, DDR, and Ferkel Grains, A.G. in Munich.

On Tuesday morning, December 3, the cab of the truck, which had been painted in perfect replica of a Jobst Transport hauler, was lightly sandblasted to give the appearance of road use. Mud was sprayed on and washed off and a fresh repair was made on a small segment of lettering.

The stories arrived at eleven, well done. They were the size of small letters and were printed on several different shades of very light paper— so light, in fact, that a story inside an envelope would be indistinguishable from a normal letter, and a story dropped from a window would flutter like a leaflet.

The whole shipment was packed in six cardboard boxes two feet long, a foot wide and eight inches deep. The boxes were loaded into the space between the top and bottom of the hollow truck-bed. Since the hole had been cut only through the bottom panel, the barley was not disturbed.

Clay slid the slings that the tailor had made—they really did look like condoms—as well as his tiny packet of curare-filled syringes into the last box to be lifted aboard. The body men replaced the steel rectangle they had cut from the truck bed and bolted it to the mounts they had fashioned. They filled the cracks around the plate and the sunken bolt holes with a non-hardening putty, smoothed it until it was level with the surrounding metal and sprayed the bottom of the truck with several layers of undercoating and mud.

When the job was done the foreman showed Clay how to find the "door" by measuring hand lengths from an old dent on the truck bed. He got a detailed lesson on how to replace and disguise the panel when he had unloaded his cargo, then shook hands solemnly with each of the men who had helped prepare the truck. It was an odd sensation to be included in a cause that these strangers believed so passionately in. It was also a damn good sensation. He felt grateful.

The entire operation was so efficient that Clay had nothing to do his last evening in Munich. He took Oldenburg and his wife to an excellent French restaurant, then to a performance of *Carmen* at the Staatsoper. A French evening all the way around—a wise choice for a man who realized he might never again leave Germany.

That night on his hard sofa bed in the Oldenburg flat, Clay somehow managed to find sleep. He'd not have been able to if he'd known that only hours earlier Generaloberst Heinrich Bülow had ordered a building-to-building, house-to-house search of the whole DDR.

CHAPTER EIGHTEEN

The chief's men spread out over the land. In the major cities—Berlin, Dresden, Leipzig, Rostock, Schwerin, Magdeburg, Halle, Erfurt, Karl-Marx-Stadt—control centers were established. The centers monitored all operations in progress, organized incoming data and directed special units into areas of prime suspicion. In the suburbs and rural districts, local Vopos—the ABVs—worked shoulder-to-shoulder with armies of trained volunteers and, at times, with high officials from the capital.

Telephone service throughout the country was dead; the units communicated through military channels and by wireless. Interurban public transportation was also dead, and roadblocks dotted the highways. A thousand petty crimes were uncovered each hour, a thousand petty offenders hauled in with each sweep of the net.

Neues Deutschland carried no mention of the search. State television spoke only of scattered technical problems in telephone and transportation services "due to the abnormal autumn floods." But most people knew better—a nationwide police action left an unmistakable scent in the air.

"They're after Hannah," people whispered to one another in factories and schools, cafes and offices. "This time they'll find her..."

A slightly built man in a plastic raincoat and wide-brimmed hat bicycled down a country road near the village of Laucha. His wheels sloshed through deep puddles and plowed over mudbanks the rain had washed onto the pavement. He lost his balance several times, but continued to struggle ahead with surprising strength.

At the Unstrut river bridge, he stopped for a breather. Black water slapped at the bridge pilings and swirled in powerful eddies down the main channel. Steel girders screeched back and forth across their concrete supports. She won't hold forever, he thought. Too early to tell if this is to be our advantage.

He pedaled on, holding his breath. Near the center of the bridge, the slats of the road began to shake and he thought he felt the structure move. He did not panic. His nerves were good. He was accustomed to close calls.

On solid pavement again he fell into his strong pedaling rhythm. In the distance he could see his goal: the Scholler Brewery. The brewery was housed in a sixteenth-century abbey that rose from the mists of the flooded meadow like a ghost from the past. He imagined the monks of old that once lived inside. In his vision they were wearing long black robes and discussing why God had sent the flood... "The people are sinful," they agreed, "the people are sinful and must be punished.".... The people are sinful and must be punished. How little, he thought, the attitudes of the ruling caste toward the common man had changed over the centuries. How well those words summed up the way today's Party big shots felt toward the masses communism was supposed to liberate... He imagined the abbey a couple hundred years later as Napoleon's troops approached from the west, a stable then, converted by the Protestant nobility, the victors in the region of the Thirty Years' War. Stable or not, it rose from the fog to greet the French soldiers with all its original majesty. The cyclist listened in on the conversations between the French and the town notables as the invading army negotiated use of the abbey. What magnificent new ideas. Liberty, equality, fraternity! Who would have thought in those hopeful times that the twentieth-century's Buchenwald and Babi Yar, the hydrogen bomb and the police state lay in the future? He didn't know if he and people like him could change the tragic direction of history, but he was prepared to die trying...

At the spiked wrought iron gate Wilhelm Jahn got off his bicycle and buzzed—long, short, short, long. A figure in a makeshift cape appeared in the arched entry to the courtyard, then hurried out to unlock the gate and greet the resistance leader.

In the shipping and receiving room—a stark gray hall with high vaulted ceilings and uneven stone floors—the two men stomped the mud from their boots and shook out their rain-drenched coats. They opened an ancient wooden door and descended a narrow stone staircase into the cellar.

The presses loomed in the shadowy darkness like cumbersome antiques. Beside the jungle of wheels and gears on empty wooden kegs sat half a dozen men and women in worried silence. A single candle burned on top one of the kegs, and the light from its tiny flame flickered across Adelbert's face.

Jahn looked intently at each person in the cellar. He tossed his rain hat aside, then carefully peeled his black stocking cap from his bald head. "Good people," he said. "We've got damned good people." Thrusting a hand beneath his sweater, he removed a tattered envelope and tossed it to a woman sitting nearby. "Have a look, Lisa."

She pulled out the black booklet and opened it. Inside, on opposite pages, were the Stasi eagle and a picture of Jahn in a business suit. Official stamps covered the document. "All right," said Lisa, "I admit this is impressive. But what good will one set of Stasi papers do us when the whole damned Vopo descends on the brewery?"

Someone else said, "It was a mistake to kidnap Adelbert. We succeeded in making it look like a Stasi job. Great. Now the Vopo has countered with a nationwide search for the presses on which at this very second we're sitting. Wilhelm, how can you want to stay here? We've lost this round. Let's get out while we still have a chance."

"I've heard enough defeatism for one day," said Jahn. "All through my career I've found the greatest opportunities hidden in those situations that appear the most desperate. We are not facing disaster, as you seem to believe. We are on the verge of a stunning success. Go, if you want. Lisa? Manfred? I can't stop you."

"No, Wilhelm, of course we won't go," Lisa said. "I just don't see the sense in—"

"May I speak? I want you to try to envision our situation from *their* perspective. We've got one flawless Stasi ID. We've got clothes coming from Laucha that will allow all of us to dress as a high-level contingent of Stasi agents. And we've got Adelbert. He is really the key. The Vopo believes the Stasi has kidnapped Adelbert. The Vopo also believes Adelbert is in a position to deliver important information about Mühlendorff. Which means that the Vopo will hardly be surprised—angry but not surprised—to discover that their rival has beat them to the presses. A little sangfroid and we can pull it off without giving up on the shipment."

Lisa looked at the floor. The resister who had let Jahn in at the gate, a young man named Erich, sat up straight and spoke: "Don't be angry with me, Wilhelm, but there's one thing I don't understand. What do we do if our driver shows up with the stories while the Vopo searchers are here?"

"We arrest him, of course," said Jahn. A charade must be convincing.

The border! Clay first saw it off to his right, a clearing several hundred feet wide slicing through the forest, a steel and concrete watchtower jutting above the trees. He rounded a curve and slowed for the red-and-white barrier spanning the road ahead.

"Good day," snapped the East German border guard. "Passport, vehicle registration and shipping documents, *bitte*."

Clay handed him the papers.

"Park over there," ordered the guard. "I'll be with you as soon as I can. That whole caravan's ahead of you."

Clay watched the guard disappear into his dun-colored shack. There didn't seem to be anyone else on duty. He examined the crossing in all directions. The only other official he saw was high up in the watchtower, his automatic rifle propped beside him and a cigarette drooping from his lips.

Clay began casually leafing through a car magazine. The clouds swooped down and swallowed the pine-covered hills. The drizzle on his windshield became rain, morning became afternoon, the afternoon grew cold and dark. Puddles formed on the pavement and on the canvas tarp covering the barley. He started the engine and turned on the heater.

The caravan of trucks got the go-ahead at last. He watched them pull out one by one. They were loaded with chemicals and heavy machinery from the West German industrial heartland. Lumbering up the hill like an armored column, they split open the forest and pushed into the fog. Names inseparable from modern German history peered down from their cargoes—Krupp, Thyssen, I. G. Farben—names that somehow managed to survive defeat and revolution, occupation and division...

The guard banged on the window. "Hey, open up!"

"What the hell's taking so long?" Clay asked.

"Get out and help me loosen the tarp."

The guard clambered up the tailgate, extended his metal search probe full-length and began shoving it randomly through the grain. Trucks continued to enter the crossing. The guard waved them to parking spots on both sides of his hut. Passenger cars piled up in a long line behind the red-and-white barrier, their drivers grumbling impatiently. The guard continued to probe.

"Why don't they staff this place better?" Clay shouted up through the rain.

"My colleagues are on special assignment... get into the cab and mind your own business."

Clay sauntered back to the cab and turned up the radio. Fredi inundated the somber checkpoint with his groaning lyrics of love. The clumsy beat of the German rock music drew static from the speakers. But there was another sound above the static, a sound Clay had not wanted to hear, the hollow clacking of metal on metal. The guard was tapping the bottom of the truck with the small pointed hammer he carried in his belt. Suddenly the tapping rang sharp. Hollow, sharp, hollow, sharp... the beats reverberated like a death sentence. Memories of the night in the Friedrichstrasse station blazed behind his closed eyelids; his heart thumped an agitated response to the guard's tapping—stop it, get hold of yourself.

Silence. From the corner of his eye he watched the guard march to his hut and return with a large screwdriver. He kept his eyes fixed on the side-view mirror as the guard lodged the screwdriver behind a protrusion on the edge of the truck bed and pried. A round rubber plug popped loose and careened across the wet pavement.

One of the waiting truckers—a giant man with a full red beard—jumped from his cab, snatched up the errant plug and walked up to the East German. "What's wrong with you?" he said angrily.

The guard, who was running his probe into the hole he had opened, jerked his head around. "Mind your own business."

"Look, I've got a load to get to Leipzig before six tonight. Hey, don't they teach you people anything anymore? Don't you know what that hole is for?"

While Clay looked on, the trucker grabbed the probe from the guard and shoved it into the hole until it hit a frame beam. Yanking it out, he held it under the guard's nose. "Rustproofing. It's shot into the hollow areas around the wheels. Anyone with half a brain uses it these days. Now come on, let's *move* it."

Five minutes later, Clay, breathing deeply, was on his way into the DDR. Night fell. Heavy rain lashed his windshield. Patches of fog erased the road and forced him to slow to a crawl. On the radio, Munich faded. East German State Broadcasting came in loud and clear from Gera. He listened to the Dresden Philharmonic interpret Brahm's First Symphony while the road snaked toward the summit of the Thuringian Forest. Big wet snowflakes plummeted through the beam of his headlights. As he neared Gera the rain returned in torrents. By nine o'clock the highway was deserted.

A sign splattered with mud swam by on his right. WEIMAR 7KM. Below, in italics, *Buchenwald 8 km.* That said it all, he reflected. Weimar, citadel of German humanism, home of Goethe and Schiller; and scarcely a stone's throw away, that other citadel to the German past, Buchenwald, the gruesome Nazi concentration camp in which so many strands of this perplexing country's history had found concrete expression. Visitors came to Weimar in droves to bask in the glow of great cultural and architectural monuments...and then hiked over the hill to visit the barracks and ovens of Buchenwald.

The sweet notes of a Mozart piano concerto filled the cab. Clay switched off the radio in disgust. What was wrong with these people? The murderers who loaded Zyklon B into the fake showers at Buchenwald probably listened to Mozart while they worked. Germany, he couldn't understand it. He thought about the good Germans—Brahms,

174

Mozart . . . if he started there the list would go on forever . . . Karl, Käte, Oldenburg and so many others. How did this awful land, the land that historically tolerated the Bülows of this earth, manage to produce such extraordinary and extraordinarily *good* human beings? His confused thoughts led no further than they had long ago, when he'd been twenty-one and on his first visit to East Berlin. For God's sake, why worry about it any more? In five days, one way or another, he would be finished with Germany forever.

Ahead, red lights flashed across the road and the orange glow of a fire lapped at the sagging overcast. Men scurried about like ants in preparation for his arrival. A massive roadblock loomed in front of him. Again he had to fight back the panic.

Following the hand signals of a Vopo officer he maneuvered his truck onto the shoulder and inched forward until the grille was only several feet away from a line of metal drums filled with blazing coal. Makeshift tin roofs had been erected above the flames, but the rain blew back and forth in ragged sheets, hissing when it hit the sides of the drums and exploding into bursts of steam when it landed on the embers.

The officer stepped up to the driver's window while the soldiers stared on from loose groups huddled around the drums. "Passport! Transit visa! Shipping papers!" He shined a flashlight into Clay's eyes. "Vehicle registration and insurance papers!"

Soldiers scrambled up the back of the truck, tore open the tarp and began examining the load. The officer returned the papers to Clay and instructed one of his men to search the undercarriage. The tapping started, but ceased abruptly when two jeeploads of wet Vopos pulled up. There were loud greetings, handshakes and backslappings. Several of the new arrivals walked past Clay without looking up and warmed their hands at the fire. He watched their exhausted faces in the dancing light and listened best he could to their conversation.

"Sector One?"

"Nothing."

"Sector Two?"

"Nothing."

"Sector Seven?"

"Nice piece of ass on Pieckstrasse, comrade."

Laughter, more hand-warming, grumbling. The officer returned to

175

Clay's window. "Laucha, eh? You're going to Laucha tonight?"

"That's right," Clay said.

"Know anyone by the name of Robert Jenz?"

"Couldn't say till I saw him. I make a lot of deliveries."

The officer, to Clay's amazement, smiled. "Robert's a good friend of mine. We went to high school together in Laucha. I used to bump his sister."

"Yeah?"

Clay started the motor and jammed the gear shift into reverse.

"Yeah. Give her my regards if you run into her. You can't miss her. Biggest knockers this side of the Elbe. Her name's Gisela."

"I'll be watching. Who's the greeting from?"

The officer stared at Clay for a moment, trying to decide whether to give his name to a Westerner. "She'll know who it is," he said when he finally spoke. "Get going."

Several Vopos moved the roadblocks with the flashing red lights and directed the big Mercedes diesel through. Soon the lights and the orange glow were tiny images in Clay's rearview mirror. He drove through the dark sodden countryside, alone with his thoughts. Passing a final sign for Buchenwald, he turned right and did some quick calculations in his head:

Laucha was less than an hour away.

CHAPTER NINETEEN

It was, in a too-real sense, opening night at Wilhelm Jahn's "theater," and Jürgen Adelbert was not enjoying his debut as a director. The dress rehearsal he'd just run his people through had fallen flat—there was no time for another. He glanced at Erich, the young resister who'd been so kind to him after the abduction. Didn't that gray shirt look wrong on him? And what about his hair? Lisa had slicked it back, giving him the appearance of a caricature. Maybe they should—

The sound of jeep motors filled the shipping and receiving room. Adelbert sat up stiff as a rod in the high-back wooden chair to which he was handcuffed. First act. God, how unprepared they were. And the standards of tonight's audience would be high, the price of a bad performance . . . well, better not to think about that . . .

Bright headlights swung into the flooded courtyard behind the abbey. A dozen armed men and women scampered down from their jeeps and sloshed toward the entrance. There was loud knocking, shouting. Adelbert felt the cold of the stone floor beneath his feet rise into the marrow of his bones.

Erich walked briskly to the door, his eyes conscientiously narrowed to expressionless slits. He moved much better than during rehearsal, affecting a menacing front. Good. This time he'd gotten it right.

Erich opened the massive iron-and-wood door. The chill wind howled through the aperture, flinging raindrops into the room. A Vopo lieutenant mounted the stairs. Erich remained planted in the doorway. "You will wait where you are," he said.

"Nonsense," said the lieutenant. "I'm the commanding officer of this search team." His people gathered behind him. Automatic rifles, barrels glistening in the rain, rose in unison. The lieutenant nodded to his people. "Our orders come from Berlin. We are to search this brewery. Move aside." He drew his machine pistol.

Erich smiled with what he hoped was cool detachment. It was the look Adelbert had tried to draw from him earlier.

"Our orders come from Berlin as well," said Erich. "Berlin-Lichtenberg, to be exact. We are State Security, comrade leutnant. Now, if you will excuse me for a moment I will notify our officer in charge, Major Emmerich, that you are here.

The lieutenant, a local from one of the villages, was impressed with what he believed to be the secret police. He turned to his people. "Stasi..."

The search party broke up into small grumbling groups. A volunteer named Robert Jenz took the lieutenant aside. "Sir, I suggest we get the license numbers of their cars. How can we be sure they're Stasi? A quick call to Berlin and we can verify the plates."

"Good idea, Jenz." The lieutenant motioned to Jenz's sister, a slender young woman with unusually large breasts, and whispered something into her ear when she stopped alongside him. She nodded and walked over to the two black Wartburgs Jahn's men had driven from Berlin. In the yellow halo of the outdoor light they glistened black and menacing. She seemed to pause as she approached them, circled the cars warily, peered inside, crouched beside them, jotted the tag numbers on a wet pad. Two of the Vopo regulars in the search party ambled over and joined her. They inspected the cars without much interest, turning their attention almost immediately to the prodigious swells beneath her raincoat.

At the sound of footsteps Adelbert turned his head around. The leading player, Jahn, strode to the door, looking every bit a figure of rank and power. He fastened the middle button on his well-tailored black suit, set his top hat on his shining dome and went to the threshold to meet the searchers. "Who's in charge here?" he asked, his tone authoritative but not unpleasant.

The lieutenant stepped forward. "I am. Leutnant Dieter Heiz."

"Please come inside."

"Ask to see his papers," said Robert Jenz, who had run to the entrance from one of the jeeps.

The lieutenant, uncertain, cleared his throat and hesitated.

"Your man is correct, comrade leutnant," Jahn said. "You have both the right and the duty to request such information. Come inside, please."

Jahn swung the heavy door shut, leaving Jenz to stare suspiciously at them through a window. The resistance leader pulled his forged Stasi papers from his breast pocket and held them beneath the lieutenant's eyes. The effect was swift, conclusive.

"I'm sorry, sir. Of course it wasn't necessary to see your papers. Volunteer Jenz is a troublemaker."

"Come with me, Leutnant Heiz."

"Yes, sir."

Jahn turned to Erich. "Unlock the prisoner. He will accompany us to the cellar. You will remain here."

As the three men descended the ancient stone staircase, Jahn spoke to Heiz in a low voice. "Do you recognize the prisoner, leutnant?"

The lieutenant examined Adelbert like a curiosity in a zoo. The three men stopped on a landing.

"Philistine," sneered Adelbert.

"Well?" asked Jahn.

"Seems to me I've seen him on TV, sir. Is he a dancer or something?"

"Leutnant Heiz, you men in the provinces should keep better tabs on your country's cultural life. This is Jürgen Adelbert, the poet."

"Oh, yes, now I remember. I saw him win a prize on TV last month. He read a poem. Is *he* one of your men?"

"In a sense," Jahn said. "After a bit of persuasion he agreed to cooperate. Step down another level, Leutnant Heiz, and you will see the object of your search. Herr Adelbert was thoughtful enough to lead us here."

The lieutenant nearly came to attention when he saw the presses.

179

Jahn's men and women were swarming over them with pads and pencils, jotting down makes and serial numbers.

"This is Leutnant Heiz of the Volkspolizei," announced Jahn. The resisters nodded at the young lieutenant and resumed their work.

"Those are *the* presses?" exclaimed Heiz. "In *our* district?"

"Correct, comrade leutnant. And tonight we have the opportunity to carry our good fortune a step further. If all goes well we will break the back of the criminal underground in this country before dawn. It's good that you showed up when you did. You are going to participate in the making of history."

"What do you mean ... sir?"

Jahn snapped his fingers. "The documents."

Lisa clambered down from the press she was working on and rolled a file drawer on a brewery cart to Jahn's side. "Comrade major ..."

"Thank you."

Jahn pulled out the page that had been marked with a red tab and handed it to Heiz. "A shipping order, comrade leutnant. I want you to note two things—the date and the location from which the shipment will be arriving."

"Munich," mumbled Heiz. "Barley from Munich. To be transported on December the fifth. That's today, comrade major."

"Precisely. We are waiting."

"But why?"

"We have reason to believe, comrade leutnant, that the driver of this truck is the key link between our own criminal underground and its financiers across the border. We also suspect that he knows the identity and whereabouts of the underground's entire leadership—"

"Hannah Mühlendorff included?"

"I am not in the habit of being interrupted, comrade leutnant."

"Sorry, sir—"

"We are going to find out. Which brings me to a matter of crucial importance I wish to discuss with you. Comrade Leutnant, Laucha is one of the centers of the East German underground."

"Impossible, sir. We all know each other. We've all gone to school together, married each other's—"

"Irrelevant. They are among you. They are perhaps even among you *tonight*. Comrade leutnant, I am asking you and your people to join

180

with the Stasi in the most important police action in our history. This will of course delight those of you who are on the right side. But should a member of the criminal underground find himself in your ranks, you must be prepared for him. How, leutnant, would you expect such a traitor to behave?"

"Well, I don't know, sir. He might try to run. Or if he is very foolhardy, he might try to get word to his organization, warn them of what—"

"Precisely. Expect the traitor among you to show himself, comrade leutnant, and deal with him appropriately. Meanwhile, bring your people into the shipping and receiving room. Tell them about the truck and the presses. And, Heiz, keep your eyes and ears open."

"Sir," whispered Robert Jenz to Heiz, "if that truck really does show up, you can't let these people leave until we've verified their identities with Berlin. What if *they're* with the underground? Think about it for a moment. How will we look if we let them say a cordial *guten abend* and walk off?"

"Quiet," Heiz said. *"You're* under suspicion."

"For *what?*"

"For—"

The sound of an approaching diesel interrupted. Jahn entered. "Don't get up," he ordered the wet, tired Vopos who sat sipping beer with their backs propped against the wall.

The diesel engine fell to idle. Seconds later, a buzzer connected to the outside gate broke the silence.

"Men and women of the German People's Police," Jahn intoned, "I want you to stay below window level. No lights. The driver must not see you until he is in the courtyard. Only he has the information we need. Be damned certain he isn't harmed. Be on the alert for a suicide attempt. Leutnant Heiz, take one of your regulars and hide behind the cars. Grab him as soon as he steps down. *Go.*"

The two Vopos ran into the courtyard. When they were crouched behind the Wartburgs, Jahn pushed a button that unlocked the truck entrance. The thick beams of headlights entered the courtyard, followed by the enormous grain hauler. Jahn kneeled down out of sight with the others.

Clay, who had been stopped at two more roadblocks, climbed down from the truck, lifted his hands in a massive stretch, then reached back through the cab door and lightly tapped the horn. As if drawn from their lair by the beeping, Heiz and his colleague sprang from behind the parked cars and caught him by either arm. In the same instant Jahn threw a switch, bathing the courtyard in light. Clay's heart sank as more Vopos streamed toward him.

"Halt, all of you," Jahn ordered. "Heiz, instruct your men to gag the prisoner. Jenz, come here."

Both Robert and his big-breasted sister stepped forward.

"Which Jenz?" asked Robert.

"Both of you. Move."

The foursome marched out to meet the trucker. Clay watched the nightmare unfold, too exhausted to think.

"Jenz, get his papers," Jahn commanded.

This time the woman was first to move. Jenz... Jenz... Jenz. The name sounded vaguely familiar. Clay let his eyes drop to her chest as he handed her the papers. Ah, yes. Biggest this side of the Elbe. What had the officer at the roadblock said her name was? Gisela, that was it.

"Stephan Hager," said the girl, glancing at the papers.

"Good evening, Gisela..." Clay mumbled.

She looked up at him, surprised.

"Gisela," he said, "don't be angry with me. I know I told you six o'clock, but these goddamned roadblocks—"

She put her hand over her mouth and spun around.

"Gisela..." Clay pleaded.

Robert Jenz rushed forward. "Slut," he yelled "I told you, Gisela. One more time and I'd have you sewed shut. And with an enemy of the state—"

Jahn's hand fastened on Jenz's shoulder. Fists clenched, Jenz spun around, backed down in the face of the resistance leader's hard gaze and order to "get that trucker gagged *now*."

"Major Emmerich," Jenz said, "I'm sorry, but, well, the family's been having some trouble with my sister—"

"Lies, Major Emmerich," Gisela said. "I've never seen this man

182

before...Robert, you pig, there hasn't been anyone since Christmas..."

Laughter filled the abbey.

"That will be *enough*," Jahn said. "Volunteer Jenz, female, that is, give me his papers. Leutnant Heiz, put this man in handcuffs immediately."

Heiz looked at his people. "Handcuffs?" No one, it seemed, had any.

Jahn pressed a key into the lieutenant's hand. "Uncuff the poet. He'll be easier to control than the trucker."

While Heiz worked behind Adelbert's chair, Robert Jenz again turned on his sister, who let loose a stream of profanity that drowned out his words.

"I think I said that will do," Jahn intoned. Heiz sloshed back through water and handcuffed Clay, who was in the process of being roughly gagged by the others.

"The key," Jahn said. "Thank you. Kranz, Albrecht, get in the back seat of my car with him. Schneider, you will drive the truck, Kirdorf, take the poet here to Hendrich's car and tie him up. Quickly, now. Leutnant Heiz, get all of your people out here, I want one last word with them."

The search team regrouped in the courtyard while Jahn's men occupied the two cars and the truck.

"All of you," Jahn began, "this is a night you can be proud of. This is the night the forces of the law, of socialism and progress have won out over a murderous band of self-righteous criminals. With the help of these two ringleaders—Adelbert and this man from the West we've just arrested—we should break the back of the whole underground in the next several hours. The Stasi, I assure you, know how to extract information...

"The presses that were the object of your search are in the basement. Look at them all you please. They're of historical significance. But *do not* touch them. There is someone in your own rank who is under suspicion for involvement in the resistance we are shutting down. It would not be wise to leave your fingerprints...

"No one is to enter the abbey grounds without explicit permission from Berlin-Lichtenberg. No one already here is to leave. I must depend on you to watch each other. Major Kirdorf has removed your radios from your vehicles. Do not be alarmed by this. We must have the assurance of complete surprise if our raid tonight is going to succeed. There must not be a leak from here—not even to the Vopo. As you know, the Vopo is much too large an organization to be free of seditious elements. Infiltration is inevitable. Do your job, follow the orders of your commanding officer. You will have news from us as soon as our operation is completed." He gave a brisk salute and got into the passenger seat of the car that Clay was in.

The diesel erupted with a cough. The two Wartburgs turned over with soggy reluctance, then came to life. Jahn's Wartburg circled behind the Vopo search party. The diesel, driven by the resister, and the second Wartburg followed close behind. The caravan bounced and sloshed through the wrought iron gate and turned left onto the Laucha road.

It had worked so far, but, Jahn knew, it was too soon to celebrate.

CHAPTER TWENTY

Jahn manned the roadblock he had set up, stopping the few vehicles that passed and examining the papers of their occupants. When hunted, it was safest to assume the role of hunter.

Flares burned brightly above the wet pavement, casting red tongues of light to the edge of the forest. The wind groaned in the trees, and the flooded Unstrut river roared like a waterfall. Near the river Erich and his colleagues were working to open the belly of the truck and remove the stories.

Jahn slipped into the back seat of the second Wartburg, the car bearing Adelbert. "Want to leave the DDR tonight?"

"How?"

Jahn pointed toward the forest. The resisters moved like shadows between the hidden truck and the roadblock, carrying boxes of stories in one direction, tools in the other. "In the truck," he said.

"The driver is willing?"

"The driver, Jürgen, is not who we thought he was. He insists on staying with us until the operation is finished. We'll fix you up with a little grease, a beard..."

"But, Wilhelm, he's twice my size."

"I know. But you're not going to be checked by anyone. He's marked the location of every roadblock between here and the Mellrichstadt crossing. You'll take secondary roads around them."

"But the border—"

"According to our trucker friend, there's only one guard on duty. The others, no doubt, have been pulled to help with the search. When you arrive, you hand the man your papers. The instant he looks down, you hit the gas. I wouldn't be recommending this, Jürgen, if I didn't believe your chances were good..."

Adelbert rubbed a fist across his chest. The cyanide capsule the underground had returned to him sat in his pocket, just above his heart. "I think I understand... when Berlin learns what we've done tonight I'll be more hunted than Hannah Mühlendorff. You can do without that kind of a burden, can't you Wilhelm?"

"...It would be better for all concerned if you were out of the country. I don't deny it."

"All right, I'll go. But I don't want you thinking I'm running away. I'm with you, totally with you."

Jahn embraced him. "I know. Now I'd better get back to the roadblock. I'll miss you, Jürgen..."

An hour later Adelbert sat in the cab, face streaked with heavy grease. He wore the fake beard Clay had received in Munich; his blond curls were tucked beneath Jahn's stocking cap.

"Okay, baby," said the poet in English. "Wilhelm, Erich, all of you. I love you." He winked at Clay, then urged the truck slowly forward until he reached the muddy dirt road that led to the highway. The man at the roadblock flashed the all-clear signal. Adelbert flipped on his headlights and hit the throttle, launching a thick geyser of mud.

A cheer went up when he reached the pavement. The resisters allowed themselves a few moments to shake hands, then hurried toward the two waiting cars, which sped off into the night in opposite directions.

Clay, handcuffed but ungagged, sat in the back seat with an armed guard. Erich drove. Jahn, in top hat, dark suit and trench coat, occupied the passenger seat. The Stasi ID transformed the Vopo roadblocks into relatively minor impediments.

"Great," said Clay. "You pulled it off with their own divide-and-conquer technique...those Vopos are probably still at the brewery watching each other for the traitor among them. But you guys sure scared the b'Jesus out of me."

"My apologies," said Jahn. "You did great yourself. You distracted the one man among them who threatened to be trouble, that Jenz character, with your wonderful implications about his sister."

"A happy coincidence," Clay said. "So far the stars seem to be with us—"

"For the moment. In this business you never count on anything, always expect the worst."

They made another stop, dropped off another box of the stories.

"Tell me," Clay said when they were on the road again. "How do you manage to get those stories in circulation without getting caught?"

"We've had our losses," Jahn said. "But it helps that we're organized in cells. Our people don't know who their colleagues are—other than the members of their own cell. The loss of a colleague is always tragic, but it doesn't expose the organization. You cannot give up what you don't know."

"You still haven't told me how you circulate the stories."

Jahn shrugged. "Professional secret. We used a different method each time."

"And this time?"

"We've saved the most obvious ploy for the last. The mail."

"The mail?"

"Yes, we're going to use the regular mail for the bulk of our distribution. There will still be the traditional leaflet drops in the center of the big cities, but the rest will go by mail. The men we saw tonight will break the bundles down into packages of fifty to a hundred stories each. These will go to our cell leaders. From there it's a matter of putting them in separate envelopes, addressing the envelopes in a thousand different hands and getting them to the post office. We'll choose recipients at random. Once the stories are out, news of their appearance spreads like a wildfire. We get people transcribing them and circulating them who have nothing to do with the resistance. We even manage to attract a few entrepreneurial types who make copies and put them up for sale. It's a phenomenon."...

187

They entered Berlin and turned into Alexanderplatz just as the first opalescent glow of dawn appeared in the east. The rain was over now, but the sky was still overcast. The TV tower pierced the low ceiling like a sword. Clay strained to look up to the point where it disappeared into the clouds.

"Jahn," he said. "imagine the impact if someone could get up there for your midtown drop. Leaflets falling from the heavens, it would be a spectacular."

"I like the way you think," said the resistance leader. "Welcome to Berlin."

"Idiot," said Bülow into the receiver.

Lieutenant Heiz, who had previously been soaking up the head Vopo's encomiums, was jolted by the sudden outburst. "But what did you expect me to do, comrade generaloberst? An officer in the field does not have the right to question the orders of a higher officer of State Security—"

"You tell me you discovered the presses at eleven last night and waited until *now* to inform me? Heiz, you will come to Berlin at once. I want to shoot you *personally.*"

"Excuse me, comrade, sir, but—"

"Talk, Heiz. How did the Stasi find the presses?"

"They had a little fellow helping them sir. A poet. He was famous. I saw him on TV—"

"ADELBERT?"

"Yes, sir."

"Heiz, you damned fool. I'm going to make you famous too. Famous for the way you die. *They* got Adelbert to talk?"

"Evidently, sir. Major Emmerich said—"

"Major *who?*"

"Emmerich, sir. The Stasi officer in charge . . . ?"

Bülow fought to contain his rage . . . "Can you identify the people who were there? Names? License plates?"

"Yes, sir. Major Wolf Emmerich. A little bald man with expensive-looking shoes. The cars were both black Wartburgs—"

"Licenses."

"Yes, sir." Heiz tore through his pockets for the paper Gisela had given him. "Here they are, sir. C246887 and J970662."

"More, Heiz."

"Yes, sir. They caught a big fish from the West. A criminal who knows Hannah Mühlendorff. They arrested him when he showed up with a truckload of grain. When they left they took the truck with them."

"Heiz, could you identify this man if you saw him again?"

"Yes, sir."

"Give me your exact location. I'll have a helicopter pick you up in five minutes."

Adelbert watched the heavy dawn sky turn silver-gray. He ran his finger over the cyanide capsule in his breast pocket, nearly caressing it.

A wedge of geese careened southward across the desolate sky. Pines rose green and shimmering from both sides of the road. Mist lay in shreds on the soft forested hills.

I love you, earth . . . if anything happens I'm going to miss you . . . Adelbert placed the cyanide capsule on the console tray and patted the greasy shipping documents on the seat beside him. The road uncoiled in a long downward bend, then plunged into the border crossing.

He took a deep breath, held it. To his left a concrete watchtower jutted above the trees. In front of him the red-and-white barricade stretched across the pavement. He could see the border guard waiting beside his hut.

He wiped his nose with his arm, remembering how he'd wiped his nose a million times as a kid with allergies, then bit his lip and pulled Jahn's black stocking cap down over his ears.

"Shut off the engine and come inside," ordered the guard. Adelbert glanced around. Now was the moment, but inside the hut he could see a second guard who wasn't supposed to be there. A cigarette tottered between his lips, and his fingers stroked the barrel of an automatic rifle.

The capsule stared up at Adelbert in bright shades of orange and yellow. He must make a decision soon . . . he would not allow himself to be taken a prisoner.

"Deaf?" yelled the first guard. "I said, shut her down."

"Listen, I've had trouble with the truck. Look at me. Been up half the night trying to fix her. If I shut her down I'll never get her going again. Here. Take my papers."

The guard looked at him, a malignant smile spreading across his face. "Well, now, I think we'd better take a real good look at you."

Adelbert grabbed the capsule and placed it between his lips. From the corner of his eye he could see the second guard approaching. The first guard reached in through the window to shut off the ignition, turning his face sideways as he stretched.

Adelbert felt a rush of defiant strength. Now or never. With both hands he cranked up the window, catching the guard firmly by the arm. Holding the crank shut with all his strength, he ducked below the steering wheel and hit the throttle. The big diesel roared forward, accompanied by the howls of the guard. Machine-gun fire chattered in his ears. Glass shattered and fell about him in shards. Tires blew out, and the truck swerved so wildly he had to let go of the window crank and grab the wheel with both hands. How much farther to the barrier? How much . . . time stood still . . .

The driver's door flew open. The guard, who had miraculously escaped the gunfire, swung out with it, swung back, caught his balance on the running board. Adelbert saw him reach for his pistol and threw the truck into another furious swerve, flinging the guard into space. The machine-gun fire erupted again. Bullets hammered the truck and hacked up a line of trees beside the road. Adelbert lifted his head enough to catch a glimpse of the barricade in front of him. Bullets tore through the cab. Adelbert held the throttle to the floor, waited. There was a jolt, a splintering of wood and metal as the diesel burst into the West, then an ear-splitting crash.

After a moment of silence a cheer rose up from the West German customs officials, whose building Adelbert had entered through the north wall.

Across the border, sirens began to wail. Adelbert sat up with difficulty and pulled off his stocking cap and beard. He moved his arms and legs, examined his stomach. He was unhurt—in that instant he realized he still held the cyanide pill between his parched lips. He spit it out like a bean from a shooter and watched the smiling men who rushed toward him.

"God in heaven," he heard one of them shout. "It looks like we got a trophy. Adelbert, the poet. Quick. Call the TV station. This could be the story of a lifetime—"

"No, *please*," mumbled Adelbert, but no one paid any attention. They had their own priorities.

CHAPTER TWENTY—ONE

The S-Bahn deposited Karl four blocks from Bülow's home just as the first rays of the midmorning sun broke through the clouds. Black smoke rose from the skyline of the capital, where a thousand factories hummed and throbbed to the orders of the State Planning Commission. But in the suburbs the day was quiet and cool, almost lazy. A few weary Vopos were still straggling back to the caserns after their long ordeal, and some of the shops whose managers had helped with the search were opening late.

The generaloberst's house was a massive two-story gray stucco from the turn of the century. It had a red tile roof that sloped off at several bizarre angles and a front porch with thick stone columns. Abrasions in the stucco left years ago by the Battle of Berlin marred the walls, and one of the porch columns displayed a neat pattern of shrapnel wounds. The flower garden, which the state maintained and Bülow detested, stretched in gnarled autumn decrepitude to the rusted iron gate, and a lone pine with browning limbs guarded the entrance.

Karl walked quickly across the brittle vines overrunning the sidewalk, saluted the two bodyguards stationed on the porch and went inside. The generaloberst, several ranking members of the Politburo and a host of important Vopo officials were seated in the living room. Frau Leon-hardt, the housekeeper, shuffled among the intent faces with a coffeepot and a tray of rolls. Wolfie, Bülow's aging German shepherd, snored in a corner.

"Comrades," Bülow began. The room fell to a hush. "I called you here today for what was to be the first in a series of progress reports on our nationwide search for Mühlendorff's presses. I have good news. This operation has been successfully concluded ahead of everyone's expectations. The presses were discovered late last night in a brewery outside of Leipzig."

"Excellent," said one of the ministers.

"Splendid," added the assistant party secretary.

A quiet round of applause broke out.

"Thank you," said Bülow. "The credit belongs to the devoted men and women of the Deutsche Volkspolizei."

As he had done so often these past weeks, Karl willed himself to stay calm. He could feel his pulse slow. What had Bülow discovered in addition to the presses? Jahn? The stories?

"Comrades," continued Bülow, "we are rapidly closing in on that seditious voice among us. We have her presses, and we have many new leads. I want to thank you all for your support. You will be kept up-to-date. That's all for now. Good day, gentlemen."

He turned and left the room. Wolfie waddled out behind him. In five minutes the downstairs was empty except for Karl, the two body-guards on the porch and Frau Leonhardt.

Karl watched a limousine pull up outside. Major Solberg and a young lieutenant Karl did not recognize got out. The two men must have been expected because the guards on the porch ushered them right in. Solberg introduced Leutnant Heiz of Laucha and walked directly to a dust spot on a marbletop table.

"Frau Leonhardt," Solberg called, "you'd better dust today."

The old lady, who had already scampered around the living room with her rag since the officials had left, hobbled in from the dining room. "But, major, I've just dusted."

"It doesn't look like it." Solberg pointed an incriminating finger at the spot. "Do you know how many germs can live in a patch of filth that size?"

194

Frau Leonhardt had no sooner removed the dust than Bülow came down the stairs in riding dress. "Good day, Leutnant Heiz, Solberg, Frassek. I've decided to move my monthly hunt up a couple weeks. A hunt is a wonderful thing. Clears the mind. Kolski has just sent us a beauty of a fox from Warsaw. Kolski enjoys the hunt himself... an old military man like me. Leave your pistols on the table, men. I don't want you young hotheads taking potshots at my game."

The four men walked to the stables and waited in silence while the stable keeper brought the horses to the gate. The small red fox paced nervously in a wire cage beside the water trough. When everyone had mounted up, Bülow nodded at the stable keeper, who opened the cage. The fox darted into the underbrush.

Bülow drew his Luger and fired a ceremonial shot. "After him." His mare lunged forward in response to her master's expert commands. The others, good horsemen, followed at a gallop across the wet autumn countryside, a patchwork of brown-and-yellow fields bounded by fragrant pine forests. Game birds flapped up in front of them and a frightened rabbit bounded away from the pounding hooves. The fox hurtled a four-foot hedge and turned up the bank of a muddy canal.

Bülow's horse easily cleared the hedge and galloped along the narrow path in hot pursuit. "Come on, Feuerbach," Karl urged his stallion. He put a heel in its flank and the horse took off like a rocket. The fox, frantic now, jumped into the dark water and swam to the far bank; all four horses plunged in after it, splashed through the deep mud, came up on the other side and tore a semicircular swath through a field of winter wheat.

The exhausted fox turned in the wrong direction and found itself trapped on a finger of land that extended into a brown farm pond. It turned and bared its small pointed teeth. Foam oozed from its mouth; its eyes spoke the same panic Bülow was pleased to evoke in his human victims. But this was only a hunt, and Bülow the sadist of course was a lover of animals. He enjoyed the symbolic gesture of defeat from his quarries but usually let them run free in the end—

Not this time. The crack from the Luger... the fox crumpled in a heap, struck square in the head.

"Dismount," ordered the generaloberst. "Heiz, pick up the fox, throw it into the pond."

The country boy from Laucha examined the limp animal briefly and gave it a heave. Bubbles came to the surface of the pond long after the corpse had sunk.

Pistol still drawn, Bülow pulled up close to Karl. "Frassek. Solberg. Heiz. We've got a few things to settle this morning. Let's start with you, Heiz."

"Yes, sir—"

"Tell me, leutnant, just what happened last night when you and your men arrived at the brewery."

"Yes, comrade generaloberst...we were met by a Major Emmerich of the Stasi, as I explained to you on the telephone. He showed us the presses and introduced us to that Adelbert fellow who had helped State Security find them. Then he ordered us to guard them—"

"Great job, leutnant." Bülow fished a stack of photographs from his breast pocket and passed the top three to Heiz. "Well, leutnant, is this your Major Emmerich?"

Heiz laughed nervously. "Of course not. Not the remotest similarity."

"Heiz, I've had the party chairman *in person* consult the Stasi on this matter. The man in these photographs, I have been assured, is the only Emmerich with the Stasi. And the license plates of those cars you gave me do not belong to the Stasi either. Now, Heiz, who do you suppose you let get away?"

"I...sir..."

"Let me spare you overtaxing your puny brain. Your Major Emmerich was an *imposter* with the underground. And because of your idiocy, Heiz, he and his Western contact who arrived in that grain truck are now at large."

"But, sir—"

"Shut up. Can you pick out the man who drove the truck?" Bülow handed him the rest of the photographs, two dozen in all. Heiz, shaken, studied them.

"Well, sir, he had a beard and wore glasses, unlike the man in this picture...but there's a similarity, yes. I would say this is the man."

When the generaloberst saw which photograph Heiz had chosen, he turned near-purple. "*Solberg.* Recognize him?"

The major looked, was shocked, but he said..."I don't think you should come to any definite conclusions, sir, until—"

"What about *you,* Frassek?"

My God, Karl thought . . . Bentley.

"Yes, Frassek? You recognize him? Of course you do . . . Bentley. And he got away in the first place because of you, Solberg, and that goddamned bordello of yours—I'll deal with that later. Heiz, tell us again how Bentley arrived."

"In a big truck, sir."

"I have here an escape report from the Mellrichstadt crossing. At five twenty-six this morning a large grain hauler of the mark Mercedes . . . was that it, Heiz?"

"Most likely, sir."

"Well, one for us. Bentley did not go out in that truck. Our poet friend Adelbert was the only person who escaped in it. Which means that the man who is the key to this whole business is still inside the DDR. And Adelbert wasn't picked up by the Stasi, he was kidnapped by these gangsters to confuse us. Thanks to the likes of Heiz, it worked . . . but only temporarily. I repeat—we have the man who holds the key to this Mühlendorff mess trapped in the DDR. We and we alone know who he is. Therefore we, and *not* the Stasi, will find him. Am I correct in my assumption, men? *We and we alone know who this Bentley is.*"

He glared at them briefly, then went on. "At nine o'clock this morn-ing I learned that we won't be able to examine the precomputer records on this man. Why? My information chief for once had something of significance to report. We can't see Bentley's records because Kammer has already found and removed them. The time to confess has come. *Which one of you is working for Kammer?*"

"Allow me to point out," said Karl, "that—"

"Be quiet, I know it isn't you."

Karl glanced over at Solberg and did an involuntary double take. The major had turned ashen. He opened his mouth to speak. Nothing came out. He lifted his handkerchief to mop his forehead but it escaped his fingers and fell into the mud.

"Comrade generaloberst," Solberg began, "forgive me . . ." His voice broke. "I am . . . a technical man . . . a man who loves systematic pro-cedures. I felt my abilities would be of more use to our cause . . . our country if I offered them to Generaloberst Kammer. But I assure you,

I mentioned Bentley and our interview with him only in passing. All I gave Kammer was the American's name—"

"Just the name, Solberg? All you gave Kammer was the name? That man, that name—the key to our finding Mühlendorff. *And you gave it to Kammer.* Well, Solberg, I'm a generous and forgiving man. I'm going to give you a last chance to atone for your sins. Shoot Leutnant Heiz."

Bülow's gun tumbled through the air just above Karl's reach. Solberg caught it by the handle in self-defense. His eyes were glassy, his pallor gray as the clouds overhead.

"Don't do it, major," Karl said firmly, trying at least to divert Bülow's murderous rage when a blow to his solar plexis doubled him over, followed by a knee to the chin that sent him reeling backward. He regained his balance just in time to take the force of Bülow's punches, then collapsed into the pond.

"Shoot him *now*," he heard Bülow say. Before Karl could lift himself, the Luger cracked. He swallowed a mouthful of water. The point of Bülow's riding boot sank into his adam's apple. He felt his back on the bottom of the pond. Water entered his lungs. A sensation of weightlessness enveloped him as he floated to the surface, unable to move. In a voice that sounded muffled and far away he heard Bülow... "Go on, Solberg. I'm going to be generous. Shoot yourself. If I have to kill you I'll cut your nuts off a slice at a time. Go on, major..."

Karl's arms and legs came to life but he was unable to right himself before the pistol cracked again. A hand grabbed his uniform jacket and dragged him onto the mud, where he lay gasping and nauseous.

"Frassek," Bülow said when Karl was at last able to sit. "There's been a bad incident. Major Solberg shot Heiz. It seems he was outraged by the way the leutnant shamed our organization. All very understandable, but such outbursts are, of course, intolerable in an officer. In any case, Solberg would have been sentenced to death in a court-martial. Like an honorable soldier, he decided to take his own life. Get up. You'll want to make yourself presentable to deliver the sad news to the late Major Solberg's wife."

CHAPTER TWENTY—TWO

"Come in, Volunteer Jenz." Bülow gave her a complete going-over. "Sorry you had to come all the way up here from Laucha. I'm glad you did, though. I'm beginning to understand why Heiz couldn't keep his mind on his work."

Gisela bowed her head and blushed. "I don't mind coming to Berlin, comrade generaloberst. I've never been here before. This is all very exciting."

"Well, well, so it is. I'll see that you have a good time. Did my men tell you what we need you to do?"

"No, sir."

"It won't be difficult. Now you wait here with Leutnant Frassek while I get things ready."

When Bülow had left the room Gisela asked Karl, "Do you like working for him?"

"It's all right . . . tell me, were you at the abbey when all of this took place?"

"Yes, right in the middle of everything."

"You saw the prisoner?"

"Oh, yes. He was a beautiful man. It was fun having a celebrity visit us out in the country—"

"I don't mean the poet, I mean the *criminal* who arrived with the truck."

"Oh, *him*. He was terrible . . . from the moment he arrived. I'm glad the Stasi arrested him."

Bülow came back with a police artist and two technicians. The technicians quickly set up a movie projector and extended a portable screen just under the boar's head. While Karl looked on, they rolled film of Clay entering Room C at the Friedrichstrasse station. How well he had held up, thought Karl. With that story in his jacket he hadn't once lost his nerve . . .

"That's him," Gisela said without prompting. "And there's Leutnant Frassek with him."

"Lights," ordered Bülow. "Get that screen out of here. We had him once, and with your help, Volunteer Jenz, we'll shortly have him again. He's a dangerous criminal. What we need you to do is assist our artist in adding a beard to his photograph like the one he wore when you saw him."

"Yes, comrade generaloberst. He wore glasses, too. Will we draw in the glasses?"

"Yes."

Karl watched while the artist transformed his father . . . his *father*, he was still getting used to the idea . . . into a rough-looking trucker. His admiration for Clay grew . . . it would have been easy for him to hire someone to drive the truck, but he'd not been willing to take the chance on an unknown, had taken the risk on his own head . . . and what a job he'd done. The stories, and the curare, thanks to him, were now with the underground. If only Monday would hurry up . . .

The artist worked for over an hour on the sketch, seemingly undistracted by Gisela's protruding nearness—

"Stop," she said. "That's it. You've got him."

"Sure?" Bülow said.

"Believe me, comrade generaloberst. The man embarrassed me, I'll never forget his face. Could you perhaps do me a favor, sir, when you catch him? I mean, find out how he knew my name. You see, when he arrived in the truck he pretended to know me."

"I will see that he tells us . . . Care to join me for dinner tonight, Volunteer Jenz?"

"Oh..."

"Good." Bülow grabbed up his telephone and dialed. "Frau Leonhardt, is all well on the home front?... I'm glad. I'll be having a guest for dinner tonight. A very important guest. A hero of the German people. I would like you to prepare something very special... just for the two of us."

The mail arrived. Bülow leafed through the letters as he tried to make small talk with the girl. Karl saw him set aside an envelope that bore the Stasi eagle. "Volunteer Jenz, we'll be leaving soon. I'm going to take you on a limousine tour of Berlin. Please wait in the next room, first door to the left, the leutnant and I will join you shortly."

Bülow ripped open the envelope. From the corner of his eye Karl could see his chief's face reddening.

"Listen to this Frassek. 'Dear Generaloberst Bülow, sorry to learn of your early death. Take care to run your affairs more prudently on the other side. Signed, Ulrich Kammer.' This letter is a forgery, Frassek."

Karl stepped closer. Bülow turned to the next page and saw the story. He read in stunned silence for a while, then erupted. "Ha. Ever hear such rubbish? They say I'll die in the People's Auditorium of VEB Elektro this coming Monday morning. Idiots. Well, they've made their last mistake this time, Frassek. They've moved from their turf to mine. They've actually challenged Heinrich Bülow to a public showdown, on national TV. See here, Frassek, *they've* given me just the opportunity I need... I'll not only catch Hannah. I'll discredit her and her whole following."

"Sir," Karl said, "why don't you consider canceling the Monday appearance? It would make security arrangements a lot easier." He held his breath, in case Bülow should do it.

"That is *exactly* what she hopes I'll do. That's the way the officers in the stories behave. She wants us to hand her a cheap victory. Well, we're going to see what she's made of. No cheap victory this time. We'll meet her challenge head-on. I'll have every square inch of that auditorium searched. I'll have every person entering and leaving from now until I appear searched. I'll show the nation just how inept this preposterous whore really is."

*   *   *

201

Kammer sat in his office facing the large bulletproof window of tinted glass. The row of Siemens computers hummed gently to his right. He smiled at them, contrasting their neatness to the disorder of the city that sprawled before his eyes. He lit a West German cigarette, a Peter Stuyvesant, and poured himself a cup of coffee from his Krups coffeemaker. This irritation with Mühlendorff was getting a bit out of hand...

He reread the copy of "The Early Death of Generaloberst Heinrich Bülow" his aide had brought him minutes before. Of course this was a bad situation, but his genius lay in transforming liabilities into assets. And for security reasons doing it out of the public eye. Few had ever seen him, outside of his immediate staff, and no pictures were allowed.

He went to his files for the old Stasi report from 1964 on Richard Clayton Bentley, for which nineteen East Germans had been interviewed. The report had been compiled only weeks before Bentley had left Europe for the United States—never to be heard from again until he returned to the DDR in 1983 to work with the medical faculty at Humboldt University. A piece of shoddy workmanship... the agents involved had too easily been convinced that Bentley was nothing but a cocky Western kid with a peripatetic peter. But the names of the nineteen men and women interviewed had proved useful.

The Stasi chief had, in fact, spoken with four of them earlier in the week—they didn't know his identity, only that he was an important Stasi official—he had chosen the four because they were now prominent professionals. He reasoned that they would be too concerned about their careers to hedge on the truth. He was right.

It came out during his interview with a Doctor Helene Ritter Geist that Clayton Bentley had gotten involved with a young East German girl, a friend of Helene, and had tried to persuade her to leave the country. But she had remained loyal to her country and to her husband, a man of her own nationality, rejecting Bentley...

And who was this girl?

Käte Hansen, a first-year engineering student at Humboldt University.

And the East German she was married to?

Heinz-Albert Frassek.

And why hadn't all this been mentioned in the first Stasi interview two decades ago?

"You must understand," he was told, "I wanted above all to protect my friend's reputation. Perhaps I made a mistake. I am sorry if I caused any trouble..."

Kammer had promptly run a computer check on Käte. Married: Heinz-Albert Frassek, March 1964. Graduated: Electrical Engineering, June 1968. Children: son, Karl Frassek, born November 1964. Employment: VEB Elektro-Apparate-Werke, Berlin plant. Those were the details he had stored in his computerlike mind. Now, with the latest Mühlendorff story on the desk beside him, Käte Hansen Frassek's life began to take on a new significance.

Kammer called up her computer file again. Yes... as he'd remembered... she was employed at VEB Elektro, where Frau Mühlendorff now predicted Bülow's assassination...

Under "Notes of Special Interest" at the bottom of the screen, he read:

Brother, Rolf Dietrich Hansen, died April 1, 1963 while in Stasi confinement in Berlin-Lichtenberg. R. D. Hansen was guilty of the destruction of munitions shipment X-43997, proceeding by rail between Berlin and Magdeburg. Persuasion proved insufficient to extract from him the identities of his co-conspirators. Posthumous security checks of family revealed close relationship between Käte Hansen Frassek and brother, but no evidence that she cooperated with him in this or any other seditious activity. Nonetheless, she was watched until December 31, 1969, as a precautionary measure. As of that date State Security removed her from the list of potential enemies of the state...

Kammer now quickly perused the computer files of Rolf Dietrich Hansen and Heinz-Albert Frassek. Nothing of further interest. He poured himself another cup of coffee, lighted another Peter Stuyvesant and typed out the name Karl Frassek on his keyboard. Under "Present Employment" he read: "Deutsche Volkspolizei, personal staff, Generaloberst H. Bülow, bodyguard."

Kammer leaned back in his chair. Could be... Käte Frassek, Karl Frassek, Richard Clayton Bentley... sharing ties of love *and* blood ...could be, yes, indeed...

He slowly exhaled the smoke from his cigarette. And if his bold premise was correct, he had to admire what they had done for its ingenuity and daring. It almost saddened him that he would have to put an end to it.

But he would not act prematurely. If he were right...and the more he thought of it and reviewed the record the more he was convinced he was...he would let their plan unfold, let them have a go at Bülow in the People's Auditorium. If they succeeded in killing the Vopo chief, they would be doing his work. Their success would demonstrate to the party chairman what he had argued all along—that the Stasi and Vopo must be merged for maximum effectiveness—with the Stasi and himself, of course, at the helm.

After Hannah Mühlendorff had been good enough to underscore this point for him, he would take her and her collaborators into custody. Indeed, he looked forward to meeting her. And hers. Such ingenious and dedicated people. Perhaps they would be willing to provide information useful in preventing just such actions as theirs...and even more, in helping keep down the troubles among the people that would follow the assassination. Of course if they would not cooperate, he would be obliged to see that they did not survive.

He telephoned his limousine driver and dismissed him. He would be taking public transportation home tonight. And he would not be recognized; another advantage of his anonymity. He knew from early reports that the stories would be all over the city by rush hour. He wanted to ride the S-Bahn, to sit in the great squares, to sense the temper of the agitated masses. Kammer was a farsighted man...soon these masses would be his and his alone to tame and control.

CHAPTER TWENTY—THREE

Word of mouth travels like wildfire in a police state. By late Friday afternoon everyone in the DDR knew of Hannah Mühlendorff's defiant story. Crowds formed in streets and squares from one end of the country to the other. There was an exhilaration in the air, nervous and delicate as static electricity.

In East Berlin people streamed from their factories and offices into the Alexanderplatz. It was as though the city had emptied itself into a stadium for a long-awaited sports event. Vopos patrolled in pairs, pushing their way through the crowd, abruptly stopping excited conversations and laughter, but only until they had passed.

Floodlights came on to illuminate the fine old churches and glittering luxury hotels bordering the square. The cold east wind intensified as darkness fell and a misty drizzle filled the air. Still people came, by cars and trams and the S-Bahn, into the heart of the capital.

Suddenly there was a bright flash above the crowd, followed by a loud bang. Faces turned upward. And ten thousand Hannah stories fluttered from the television tower toward earth.

Was whoever had smuggled the stories into the television tower trapped? Patrolling Vopos stopped in their tracks, observed the seditious spectacle filling the heavens, and started for the tower.

From the restaurant in the bulb of the tower six hundred feet up, the diners thronged to the elevators and charged down the staircase. They had watched the young man step out on to the service balcony and throw the suitcase into the night. They had heard the bang, had listened to the young man shout out what he had done and had judged it prudent to get out of there.

The first stories fluttered into the outstretched arms of the crowd. Some were read aloud, others silently, while Vopos with lowered submachine guns shoved their way toward the base of the tower...

"Well, how do you like Berlin?" the generaloberst asked.

Gisela gaped out the window of the limousine at the TV tower, whose tip was buried in the clouds. Berndt, the driver, stared at Gisela in his rearview mirror. "Oh, I like it, sir. It's so exciting here. Is there always so much going on?"

"Yes, of course, my dear Volunteer Jenz. This is the center of a great nation—"

"Comrade generaloberst, what are those things coming down from the tower? They look like little paper airplanes. The people are all trying to grab them. What are they?"

Bülow watched the leaflets for a moment, leaning against Gisela's breasts to get a better view. "Berndt," he grumbled, "wait here." He launched himself from the limousine and plowed off through the crowd.

In five minutes he was back, shaking one of the stories in front of Gisela. "There you go, my dear," he said, handing her the tiny booklet of featherweight pages. "Why don't you keep it as as souvenir. We can laugh about it next time you come to visit me."

"But what is it?"

"A fairy tale. And one that will never come true, as these people will learn Monday night. Wait and see, my dear. Yes, that's a marvelous idea. You'll wait right here with me in Berlin and watch how the people change their tune..."

Kammer made his way through the crowd. He stopped in front of the Marienkirche, turned up the collar of his overcoat and pulled his navy blue beret further down his high forehead. He heard the bang and glanced quickly at the falling leaflets. But it was not the leaflets that interested him: he already knew their message. He tried unobtrusively to look at the citizens seated on a bench nearby.

Even though Kammer's face was not known, those who saw him felt uncomfortable under his eye. One by one the men and women on the bench stood up and ambled off into the crowd. Even before the first leaflets reached the ground, the bench was vacant.

Kammer sat down. A story fluttered toward him. Though the people were fighting each other for one of the stories not a soul came his way. Instead, the circle of bare cobblestone around him grew larger.

He tucked the story into his pocket and stood on the bench. From all directions the Vopos were approaching the exits of the TV tower. It would be interesting, he thought, to see just what the man looked like who had dared take on the national police in a battle he couldn't win, even more interesting to escort the man to the Stasi shop on Normannenstrasse. He would no doubt have some insights on how the underground was organized...

As Kammer prepared to make his way to the tower, a spontaneous event took place that took him by surprise. The crowd closed ranks in front of the Vopos and refused to let them pass. Here and there an officer readied his machine gun, but each time this happened a thicket of civilian arms grasped the barrel and wrenched it skyward.

The people who had been in the tower reached the exit and melted into the growing crowd. And Erich, dressed in the same suit he had worn at the abbey, slipped unobtrusively to the edge of the square, watched the final leaflets skip over distant rooftops and take off toward alleys and side streets, then entered the Alexanderplatz station and boarded the S-Bahn for home.

Not far from Alexanderplatz an old woman was walking her dachshund. She wore an olive-green pointed hat and a thick coat of the same color, tattered from decades of use. On her arm hung a shopping net with a loaf of dark break and a kilo of butter. She stopped to rest in front of the National Gallery, reaching down to rub her dog behind the ears.

"Smell that, Fritzchen?" she murmured.

The little dog lifted its nose, snuffled, whined.

"You smell it, too, don't you?" She warmed her hands and let herself down on a bench. High above the city she watched the lights of the television tower come on.

"That's Berlin for you, Fritzchen. There's trouble brewing again. Now listen here, I don't want you conking out on me just because there's trouble. If you're going to live here you've got to accept it. That's what I tell them when they come complaining to me . . . It smelled like this way back before the Kaiser ran off to Holland. The next day he was gone and the mobs were in the streets. Oh, some time that was. They dumped Rosa Luxemburg in the river right over there. I knew her, Fritzchen. She was a fine woman, a sight better than what's coming along today."

Her eyes began to water from the cold wind. She looked down at her dog, who was shivering and apparently anxious to continue its walk.

"Listen, Fritzchen, you'd better get used to the cold. When the big trouble comes they'll shut off the oil and stop the coal deliveries. You'd better get used to it if you want to stay in Berlin . . . It didn't get much better here after we got over the killing. We had a government, sort of, but we had a spell when you'd have to take a wheelbarrow full of money to the baker to get a loaf of bread. Little dogs like you were running round loose all over town because people couldn't afford to feed them. Oh, things did improve for a little while. I married, you see. There was more to eat. And Berlin was lots of fun for a few years there. My husband and I used to go to the cabaret up on Schönwalder Strasse nearly every Saturday night . . . But then the Nazis came along and spoiled it all. You should have seen those boneheads, marching and singing like idiots. Pretty soon old President Hindenburg died and the Führer was at the top, leading us to slaughter like cattle. By the time his war was over all of this you're looking at now was rubble— all of it, Fritzchen, as far as you can see."

Pedestrians hurried by in the direction of the Alex, paying no mind to the old woman who sat blathering to herself. The dog shivered violently as the wind sliced through its fur.

"Hush, Fritzchen. Stop all that complaining. I told you, if you're going to live here you've got to accept the hard times. It's going to get bad again, little one. I hope not as bad as it was then. After Hitler's armies collapsed, the Russians headed toward the capital—millions of them. We were living like moles in the subways. The bombs came down day and night. We watched our friends and families die all around us. And those of us who still had addresses got those little telegrams from the War Ministry. Our sons, our husbands—until there were no men left to love and protect us. That's when the Russians came in. Animals... no offense, Fritzchen. And those first winters after the war—nothing to eat, nothing to burn. We froze and we starved here in the ruins. And the Russians never left. But *we* started to leave, to go West. So they built the Wall to keep us in... Well, it looks better here now, doesn't it, darling? We've got the ruins cleaned up and we've got heat and food. But underneath things haven't changed that much. I tell you, Fritzchen, Berlin was not meant to be a happy place."

A gust rattled a street sign beside her and sent a flock of pigeons on a noisy flight. An old man from her neighborhood recognized her and walked up to the bench. *"Guten abend,* Frau Wollweber."

"Guten abend, Herr Sachsel. Will you sit and join us?"

"Ach, thank you, Frau Wollweber. But they say there's a celebration in the Alex. I'm on my way over there to see what it's about. Why don't you accompany me?"

"No thank you, Herr Sachsel. The news will reach me soon enough."

Her words were prophetic. As the old man hobbled away, one of the stories rose on a gust, cartwheeled over the Friedrich Bridge and landed at her feet.

"Well, well," she clucked, "don't just sit there shivering, Fritzchen. Fetch it."

The dachshund lifted the Hannah story to her, wagging his tail. Frau Wollweber settled back on the stone bench and read in the weak light of a streetlamp:

The Early Death of Generaloberst Heinrich Bülow

On a blustery December 9 of the year 198–, Anna von Ettinger rose at dawn. She dressed in a heavy wool skirt and sweater and pulled on her fur-lined boots. She wanted to walk the entire distance to VEB-Elektro, where Generaloberst Heinrich Bülow, chief of the People's Police, was to give a speech.

"Won't you consider taking a taxi," asked her mother. "You'll be frozen to the bone by the time you arrive."

"The cold doesn't bother me," Anna said. "And there will be many people who want to speak to me on the way to the factory."

"Can't you wait until afterward for that? Undercover agents will be waiting for you everywhere. Anna, why are you inviting disaster?"

"There's nothing to fear, mother. The people are with me, they'll protect me."

She walked briskly through the old town. The sun rose and touched her youthful face with its morning freshness. Chimes struck the hour, filling the frosty air with clear, hopeful music. Anna stopped at her favorite bakery for a hot roll.

"Morning, Fräulein von Ettinger," the baker said. "I've got a fresh batch of Berliner pastries in the oven now. Care to wait?"

"Certainly, Herr Bolz." She placed her purse on the counter. The baker stared at her in shock.

"Anna, my dear . . . you must be . . . more careful. I can see the outline of your pistol. Put it away. Quickly! Here comes Major Eberle."

"Don't trouble yourself, Herr Bolz. You can see it. He cannot."

The baker, perplexed, moved to his oven. The major pulled up to the counter beside Anna. "Morning," he said. "And a pretty morning it is."

"Indeed," said Anna. "Herr Bolz, come here with those."

The baker changed course with his steaming tray. Anna and the major each plucked a pastry from it and ate. Her purse remained on the counter only an arm's length from the major's eyes. He paid and went out, his mood still buoyant.

"Anna, don't scare me like that," the baker said.

She smiled. "Herr Bolz, we have feared them long enough. Don't you think it's time we stopped?"

He watched her, shaking his head, as she resumed her walk.

Along the way to the factory, she stopped and spoke with several people.

"Anna, careful," whispered the people.

At the main entrance to VEB-Elektro Anna submitted calmly to a search by two female Vopos. Quickly, she passed into the plant. The crowd streamed toward the People's Auditorium. She followed, nodding pleasantly to those around her as they showered her with good wishes . . .

Generaloberst Heinrich Bülow sat on the stage, listening to an insincere introduction. He gazed contentedly out at the sea of people watching him and directed a glance at the TV cameras. He was watching for Anna, of course. His death had already been predicted in a million leaflets. Still, he was surprised when he caught sight of her approaching the stage through the crowd. He stood and pointed.

"Men, stop her! MOVE!"

The plainclothes Vopos occupying the first four rows turned in unison, watched Anna as she strode confidently down the aisle, but did nothing to stop her. She smiled at them. The hall became silent.

The generaloberst turned on her. "You are undermining our new order. I'll have you, and your kind, eliminated once and for all—"

"You haven't the power," said Anna, climbing onto the stage.

"Arrest her," Bülow ordered.

She smiled. "You cannot arrest Hannah Mühlendorff. Hannah Mühlendorff is a spirit that defies physical laws. You can put bars around her but they will do no good. You can snuff out her physical manifestation in this person or that—in a hundred thousand or a million people—but she will only grow stronger. Hannah Mühlendorff is the part of the human soul that demands to be free. You are helpless against her."

"We'll see about that." Bülow began to move toward her, but the spectacle taking place in front of him made him freeze. All those he had murdered during a lifetime of cruelty surged onto the stage from the wings, gathering into a quiet army of men and women as unflinching as Anna... His tone began to change... "Listen, all of you, I'm not the guilty one, there are others, the party leaders, the Stasi. They've forced me to do what I did..."

Anna drew her pistol. "I'm sorry, generaloberst. You don't convince. *You* are guilty of the most terrible crimes, as the men and women here with me will attest. You must pay—"

"But Anna," an old man said who had stepped forward from the audience. "Must we not show compassion even to this monster? Aren't we adopting his own hideous standards by taking his life?"

"I've struggled with the same question, as have all of the von Ettingers. And I've decided, at last, that men like the one standing before us don't understand compassion. Our humanity is wasted on them. It only encourages them in their belief that they can behave as they do without retribution. No, the cycle must be broken. We must vanquish them at their own game, even though we would wish not to play it. *We have no choice.*"

She snapped off the safety on her pistol.

The generaloberst had apparently recovered some of his malign bravado. "Go ahead, kill me, do you think it will do any good? There are thousands waiting to take my place. They despise you and your underhanded colleagues even more than I do. And after they see what you've done they'll treat you a thousand times more harshly than you ever dreamed possible."

211

"I think you're wrong," Anna said. "And if not—if things do not improve for our people when you are gone—we will continue our work. This has been a bleak century for us Germans because of people like you. Well, the darkness is over...good Germans have decided to stand up, to speak out. And from now on they will be speaking a language even you understand."

She aimed her pistol at his forehead. The audience clambered to its feet. The television cameras zoomed in. Bülow began to tremble. He leaned forward as though to attack Anna physically. But in the end his fear got the best of him. His heart burst, and he tumbled forward on to his chest.

"Let this be a message to others," Anna said, turning to the crowd. "You are in the end, alone. You too are moving to your own self-destruction. If you are still capable of it, look within yourselves. You have time to change. But time is running out."...

Anna returned to the streets and began her long walk home. All along the way people greeted her and offered her congratulations. The news of what had happened was already known.

"I'm afraid this is only the beginning," she told them. "The road will be long, and painful. Are you prepared for it?"

"Yes," people answered her. "We must. We have no other choice."

The old lady tossed the story into the air, watched as it skittered off to the west toward the Friedrichstrasse station. Her dog leaped off after it, yanking the leash from her grasp.

"Fritzchen, come back here. Let it go. Now it's for someone else to read."

The dog returned, wagging his tail. She stood with difficulty and pointed her hunched and brittle frame into the wind. As she struggled ahead, she resumed her monologue.

"Well, Fritzchen, I do hope she succeeds. There's still some fight left in me. They've all tried to beat it out of me. The Kaiser, the Führer, the Party and, now, time. But when I go, I'll go kicking."

A band of frightened youths rushed past her, followed by a phalanx of antiriot police. She watched the policemen's granitelike faces as they stormed ahead.

"But there is one thing that bothers me, Fritzchen. That girl in the story...Anna was her name...she's young. She doesn't realize that Bülow is telling the truth when he says there are a thousand like him waiting to take his place. I don't know why this is so, Fritzchen, but

212

it's the truth. There are so many out there who *want* to treat others cruelly. You don't live for eighty years in Berlin and believe otherwise."

When they reached the Alexanderplatz the people had been dispersed. Vopos in high riding boots crisscrossed the great square in groups of three and four. The wind kicked up a few stories and swirled them about. A Vopo caught one of the errant brochures and shoved it into his pocket.

The old woman slipped under a thick rope and walked diagonally across the cold cobblestone expanse, the shortest route to her flat. Fritzchen followed several steps behind. The hair on his back stood on end and his belly drooped until it almost brushed the ground. Three Vopos stopped the old woman and her dog near the television tower. They stared at her.

"What's wrong with you?" one of them asked.

"Can't you see that the Alex is cordoned off?" said another.

"We'll have to take her in," said the third.

"I told you, Fritzchen," mumbled the old woman. "There's trouble coming to Berlin."

CHAPTER TWENTY—FOUR

There was great excitement at the VEB-Elektro plant. Hannah Mühl-endorff's story had, of course, done that. Her colleague, Doctor Pilka, was astonishingly indiscreet in his confidences to Käte, which momentarily startled her as she stood at their office window watching the Vopo search teams, complete with dogs and electronic sensing devices, enter the main building.

"Take my word for it, Frau Frassek," he was saying, "Hannah Mühl-endorff knows what she's doing, she's timed her strike to coincide with a low point in the Soviets' ability to interfere. They're bogged down at home and abroad. We've only our own to worry about..."

She devoutly wished she could share his certainty. "Herr doktor, you must excuse me. And I should caution you to be less outspoken. You never can tell who...well, never mind," and she turned away from him to go back to the plans for an electrical generating station Scheel had asked her to review. At first she could scarcely keep her mind on what she was doing, but when she at last settled down she happened on to a glaring error. It was a fortuitous discovery, allowing her to become absorbed in the complicated equations required to correct

215

the mistake. When she looked up again, the half-day Saturday shift was over.

She arranged her soft blond hair in the mirror on her door, pulled on her heavy black coat and walked into the corridor, where she was engulfed by crowds of employees anxious to get home, sweeping her along toward the exit. Trapped in the maelstrom of moving bodies, Käte suddenly felt faint. She dug into her purse for a handkerchief and stopped beside the wall. What's wrong with me, she thought, watching the last of the departing workers disappear around the corner.

Alone in the hallway, she closed her eyes, and her horrible image returned . . . a field of mutilated corpses stretching to the horizon, resisters, soldiers, victims—it was impossible to tell one from the other in their naked, dismembered state . . .

God, was this what she was laying the foundation for? An uprising fated from the start to disintegrate into carnage? She must get *hold* of herself. Jahn was right, she must not think of such things. Single-mindedness was imperative right now. Besides, she told herself, she wasn't inviting mass slaughter. She was only setting the stage for a gradual liberation . . .

She took a deep breath, forced herself to open her eyes. And in that moment saw that she had not been alone. Several feet from her, leaning casually against the wall, stood a trim, middle-aged man in a Western pinstripe suit. He was looking at her with emotionless, pale-blue eyes. His blond hair was combed straight across his high forehead, and his slender white hands were folded in front of him, as though he were praying. Momentarily his eyes held her in a look that, like him, was at once neutral and yet remarkably powerful. She felt as though she was being penetrated. The feeling was fascinating and terrifying at the same time. The corners of his mouth bent into a beginning smile as Käte finally broke the connection, but that smile followed her out of the plant and across town to the birdhouses. It was a smile she hoped never to see again.

"Don't you people eat anything but these damned weenies?" Clay said.

"They might be the last food you get until you're out," Jahn told him. "I'd eat them if I were you."

216

"When's she coming?"

"Soon. Congratulations, you've become a national celebrity," Jahn handed Clay the mug shots that had just been circulated to all Vopos in the DDR.

"Great. How do you like me? With or without the beard?"

"Alive. We're going to move you as soon as it's dark."

"I'm not going anywhere until I've seen her—"

"I understand, but you're aware that she doesn't know you're here . . . it will be quite a shock for her."

"Could you do me a favor and give her a little advance warning?" Clay asked.

"Certainly."

"Thanks. Whose place is this anyway?"

"It belongs to an old misanthrope named Sacher. Must be ninety. He lives here off and on throughout the year. When he's away, he's with his son in Dresden. That's where he is now. He has no friends, and the neighbors pay him no mind. My men will come for you at seven this evening with the ambulance. You'll be taken out on a stretcher. If anyone sees us, they'll simply assume the old man has died. There's no problem where you're going. Our people occupy all six of the apartments in the building. It took us over a decade to maneuver ourselves into that position."

"I'll be fine right here, I don't see why I have to move again—"

"You must. And it must be tonight."

"I don't want to sit around for two days with a bunch of nervous assassins."

"Don't worry. You'll be alone most of the time. You're going to stay in the tunnel."

"So you've decided to tunnel us out after all. Well, I like that notion better than the subway."

"Sorry, you'll still be leaving on the subway. The tunnel only goes as far as the last subway station in the East."

Clay took a nervous bite of his *bockwurst*.

"Electronic sounding under the Wall has become too sophisticated," Jahn went on. "This tunnel is safe. It runs from the basement of our apartment house to within several feet of the underground wall of the Stadion der Weltjugend station."

217

"So we're in the tunnel," said Clay. "We dig the last feet of earth away from the wall. Then what?"

"Let us worry about that..."

"Jahn, I think I've a right to know."

Jahn nodded. "I guess you do... The entire operation must be done in such a way that the electronic sensors in the station detect no abnormalities. Otherwise the power to the trains is automatically turned off and you find yourself trapped under East Berlin."

"You mean we have to get on a *moving* train?"

"Exactly. Several of the U-Bahn motormen in the West are ours— refugees from the East who used to work with us. Over the years we've developed a simple code for communicating with them. The trains passing through the Stadion der Weltjugend station on Monday morning at 11:34 and 11:54 will open their doors. They will hold their usual speed of twenty-two miles an hour through the abandoned facility. What we must do is neutralize the Vopo guards on the platform."

"What about closed-circuit television?"

"It's only at the Friedrichstrasse station."

"So we go from the tunnel to the platform, get rid of the guards and jump aboard the train?"

"Either that or you stay here with me and help build a revolution."

"I'll jump," said Clay.

"You must think to give the door a good lead. Let one or two cars go by. Get a feeling for how much in advance of the door you must jump. It might help to throw an object such as a coin through one of the passing doors to get a sense of the time-space relationship involved—"

"Jesus. What about Käte?"

"Don't worry about her. We've spent a morning practicing with a car and a pillow. She's quite athletic." Jahn glanced at his watch. "I've got to go. She's probably waiting now. Until Monday morning."

Clay shook his hand. "If you ever get out of here I hope you'll settle in the States. I'd like to help set you up there—"

"Thank you, Clayton, but this place is my home. No matter what, I won't leave." The resistance leader buttoned his synthetic leather jacket, pulled his new black stocking cap over his bald head and went out into the gray December afternoon.

Clay settled into a dilapidated wicker chair beside the back room window. Through a crack in the drawn curtains he peered at the vines and trees and thickets surrounding the cottage. It had begun to rain, that fine cold winter rain the heavens spill with such sombrous monotony on the plains of northern Europe. Crystal beads of moisture appeared on the brown ivy and lent a frosty sheen to the pines. The great barren oaks bent and shuddered in the breeze, and a leafless vine rasped against the window pane.

It was after four o'clock when he finally saw her emerge from a wet tangle of vines near the back door. She had closed her umbrella to slip through the undergrowth, and her hair was soaked. She looked pale, disoriented, as though she had just wandered away from a bad accident. He hurried to the door and motioned her inside.

She collapsed in his arms. "I'm not going to cry, Clayton," she whispered. "I've promised myself."

"I had to come, I couldn't bring myself to stick anyone else with the job—"

"You're out of your mind."

"Sure. Sane people don't get involved with women like you."

She managed a smile. "Wilhelm says he'll take us out together. He didn't seem to mind. I just spoke with him."

"I hope he told you I was here."

"Yes, that's why I'm late. I had to sit in the rain for a long time before I could come. Clayton, the last thing I wanted was to expose you to more danger—"

He squeezed her to him. "Shhh. Everyone who's behind you is there because he or she wants to be. Let's just make sure we don't slip up in the home stretch. Is Karl all right?"

"I haven't spoken with him since the story came out. Too risky. I hope no one has noticed his mother works at VEB-Elektro."

"And if they have? I've got the curare and the hand slings for the syringes. I'll show you how to use them later. When will you get them to him?"

"I'll put it in the drop tonight—Clayton! I can't believe you're really here."

He took her hand and led her into the bedroom, where he helped her out of her coat. She sat on the edge of the bed and unzipped her boots. "Wet all the way through," she said.

"So I see. I was depending on you to warm me up."

Her smile vanished as quickly as it had come. "Clayton ... I've got a bad feeling ... I saw a man in the corridor when I was leaving work today. I had the awful feeling he was a Stasi agent ... and my feelings in this department are pretty reliable. I also had the impression he knew something ... maybe everything ..."

"Last minute jitters, darling. I've been having them too. Everything's right on target, you've done a tremendous job ... the others have too ..."

She sighed, willing, wanting to accept his reassurance ... because if the man was Stasi ... but she wouldn't let herself think any more about that. She couldn't afford it.

He was kissing her neck now and pulling her wool sweater up over her head. No time or inclination for bad thoughts ... Clayton, only him ... She raised her arms, let them fall back on to the bed. He took off her shirt and bra, stockings and panties and tucked her under Sacher's thick down quilt. As he undressed she watched him and shook her head, a smile on her lips.

"My God, you're cold," he said, sliding under the quilt. He rubbed her hands in his, rubbed her shoulders and back, held her freezing feet between his legs. When he pulled her to him, her nipples felt like tiny spots of ice against his skin.

"Clayton ... I don't know if I can. Damn it ... that man ..."

"Come, come, darling. Like this ..." He entered her very gently and rubbed her buttocks and legs to bring some warmth to her skin. "Do you remember the first time? I was such a kid. It was a dream, Käte. Do you remember?"

"Yes, oh yes, I remember." She hugged him with more strength. "It was hot—hot and windy. It wasn't far from here. We've never gone back to that place. Maybe we should have."

"I wish we could. Listen, Käte ..."

She was moaning softly, clutching at his back with her nails.

"... there's a high meadow not far from what's to be your new home. You can look out past the city and see the farmland stretching to the horizon. And if you roll over, you'll see the mountains. They're mag-

220

nificent. The wind is hot there in the summer too. We'll go next August. You'll see." He kissed her for a long time. The heat rose to her skin. She wrapped her legs around him.

"Clayton, I love you. Don't let me become sad when we're over there. I don't know why, but I feel as if I will. Don't let me, please."

"You won't be sad. I personally guarantee it. You'll be very happy, and you'll make me very happy . . . I've lived for this, Käte. Thank God you're finally coming with me . . ."

They made love as the afternoon darkened into night. The rain beat in raucous waves against the window. Perspiration glistened on her forehead and neck. She held him still more tightly . . . "I won't scream, I won't—"

He held his hand over her mouth and felt her teeth sink into his flesh. Pleasure exploded from his loins. She grasped him by the shoulders, rolled on top of him, sank down on him. For an enchanted moment, while their cries of love filled the room, they forgot the coming ordeal.

CHAPTER TWENTY—FIVE

Rostock is a port city in the north of the DDR situated on the estuary of the Warnow river. From the town center it is but a short bus ride to the sandy shores of the Baltic. It was to these shores that Käte headed on Sunday morning. There was something about the sea that calmed her and gave her new strength.

The express train from Berlin bumped and swayed through the sparsely settled lake country of Mecklenburg. Käte gazed out the window, sticking to her pledge not to think about tomorrow. She poured herself a cup of strong black coffee from her thermos and spread butter on one of the hard rolls she had brought along for the trip. Suddenly the brakes came on with a screech, sloshing coffee from her cup and raining luggage down from the overhead racks. The train shuddered violently, coming to a clangorous halt in a grove of pines. There was no station in sight.

Whispering filled the coach. "I knew it," said the woman seated behind Käte. "I told you we should have stayed home today. They'll be searching every person out on the streets until this thing is settled."

"Shhh," said the man traveling with her. "What difference does it make? You're not Hannah Mühlendorff."

"Listen, father," said a young boy. "What's that noise?"

The earth beneath the train began to quiver. A deep rumble rose from the forest. A Soviet tank burst from the pines, stopped for an instant with its cannon pointed at the train, then turned onto the dirt road running parallel to the tracks. Another tank appeared, then another. The rumbling in the forest grew still louder. In quick succession now dozens of tanks streamed from the woods and headed north, crossing the tracks just beyond the waiting locomotive. They were followed by armored personnel carriers, mobile missile launchers, truckloads of soldiers and occasional jeeps bearing bemedaled, fat-jowled officers.

Käte studied the faces of the passing soldiers. Most were Karl's age. They smiled and laughed like young men anywhere, apparently undisturbed by prognostications of trouble in the land they occupied. One of them, a blond youth with Nordic features, pointed at Käte. Several other soldiers looked her way and waved. She lifted her hand in wistful reply, and the whole truckload of Russians began to wave and throw her kisses. Just boys, she thought, full of energy and innocent mischief. What do they care who governs Germany?

The train continued at last, arriving half an hour behind schedule. Käte took the bus out to Graal-Müritz, where she had often brought Karl when he was a child. During the ride she thought about the wild lavenders of the heather, the pristine white of the sand, the aquamarine of the ocean. But when she stepped from the bus everything—heather and sand, water and sky—was gray. The dunes were higher than she remembered, windswept and capped with hardy tufts of grass.

She walked slowly along the deserted beach. The sea was calm. Great crescents of glassy water stretched to the horizon, where a freighter etched a smoky course westward. Gulls cawed and swooped in the stagnant sky.

Käte indulged herself with long-denied tears. She thought of Karl as a boy playing among the dunes. And she saw herself when she was younger—calm and determined, her head lifted into the breeze. Then, peering through tears into the gray distance, she saw the face of the blond stranger from VEB-Elektro smiling at her from the surface of the sea. Clayton was wrong...somehow she would meet him again. But she was no longer frightened. She was ready.

                                    *   *   *

Wilhelm Jahn lived for the movement. He did not torment himself
with unanswerable questions. Was it not clear that the present system
was evil and existed only because people allowed it to exist? Was not
freedom something worth fighting and even dying for? If you believed
these things, further philosophizing led only to flabbiness that inhibited
action.

How could one translate the anger of the steelworkers over the new
five-year plan into general anger toward the Party? How could one get
word of the shootings in Schwerin to the electrical workers in Zwickau?
How, most immediately, to get a police car inside the grounds of VEB-
Elektro on Monday, December 9?

Jahn believed firmly that Generaloberst Bülow's death at the hands
of a legendary resistance writer would set in motion the uprising of the
East German people, and he hoped to preside over that process, guide
it into a full-blown people's revolution.

On Sunday, December 8, he sat alone in the nearly empty Cafe
Warschau, Adelbert's old purlieu. There wasn't much time for a respite,
he had a lot to do in the coming hours. But he wanted to write his
mother in case anything should go wrong. He wrote her now in Czech—
the Jahns were Germans from the Sudetenland—periodically glancing
around the cafe to make sure he was not being watched.

Dearest Mama,
    I hope all is well with you. I can't tell you how much I regret the
infrequency of our get-togethers.
    Mama, I haven't time for a long letter now. I've never told you this
before, and I know the news will upset you. But you must know. If
anything should happen to me in the weeks ahead I don't want you for
a moment listening to what the authorities will tell you about me.
    I work with the underground in our country, and have for many
years. I needn't tell you what we are trying to do, nor why. You, if
anyone, will understand what motivates me.
    As you've no doubt heard, an important event is about to take place
in Berlin. I am part of this operation and of others scheduled for the
future. That's why I have no wife and little ones—an answer at last to
your question.

                                     225

Don't worry about me, mama. The people are increasingly behind us. And if I should die it will be knowing I have at least lived for a good cause. You should not regret my passing too much. I won't have suffered.

More likely, though, I am going to live and succeed. In the not so distant future we'll be setting up a provisional government in Berlin. I promise you this, mama . . . when the capital is safe for decent people I'm going to bring you here to live with me.

Now I've got to go. I see my friend coming. Please don't try to write me for a while. I'll be in touch with you as soon as things settle down.

He signed the letter "Your devoted son" and put it in an envelope he marked "L." At no point did his name or that of his mother appear. The letter would go through the underground post on Tuesday, but he did not know when it would reach her.

Erich came to his table and sat down. "Come on," he said quietly but tensely, "they're cordoning off the plant. If we want to get our car in with the others we'll have to do it now."

"I'm ready," Jahn said. They hurried across the Alex toward the S-Bahn station and took the train to their garage in Weissensee.

An hour later Jahn and Erich approached the giant factory in the Vopo squad car the underground had stolen eighteen months earlier. The car identification and license number had been altered. The two wore Vopo uniforms and were armed with the correct papers, but they had been unable to get information on the exact police procedures being employed at the plant. Wilhelm Jahn seemed unworried.

"We drive to the center of the action," he told Erich. "There will be search teams moving in and out, a lot of checking and questioning. We'll set up our own little operation in the most obvious spot. We will stop all entering Vopos, check papers, ask about assignments."

Erich blanched and took his foot from the gas pedal. "Not again," he protested.

"It's our best bet. You know how we Germans are. Someone asks us for our papers and the fight goes out of us. Anyway, I'd rather be doing the asking than the answering. Calm down, if we try to make ourselves inconspicuous we won't make it till morning."

"All right, all right, where do you want me to turn in?"

"The main entrance. Where else?"

Erich stopped at the gate before reaching the first Vopo cordon. Jahn jumped out in time to flag down a column of arriving police cars. In the background paramilitary bomb-search crews were preparing to enter the factory and scour the People's Auditorium for the sixth time. The activity at the gate attracted no special attention.

"Papers," Jahn demanded.

"Papers, major?" The man in the back seat of the first car was clearly annoyed. "Don't you know who I am?"

"I don't care who you are. No exceptions. Orders from the top."

Jahn examined the documents, pleased that his first contact was not with a flunky but with the notorious Generalleutnant Spitzer, district chief of the Mecklenburg Vopo. "Very well, comrade generalluntnant. Everything in order." He spoke courteously but with no hint of servility. "Have a productive stay in Berlin."

After watching Spitzer explode at the next ID check, Jahn returned to his work. One by one he stopped the arriving vehicles, asked about specific assignments, examined IDs, stared long and hard at faces suddenly grown uneasy. When night fell he and Erich found themselves not only inside the gates of the plant but in virtual command of a sector that ran from the main entrance down to the river.

Steam from the plant's huge exhaust pipes hissed out over the cold water of the Spree. The moon flickered briefly through a seam in the overcast. A train whistle tugged plaintively at the silent edge of the night. Twelve hours, thought Jahn. Twelve hours until their judgment day.

"Okay, okay. If it was a hamburger I'd be less generous. Go on. Take it." Clay tossed a scrap of pumpernickel and his last bite of *bockwurst* down the black tunnel. There was silence, then a soft scamper of tiny feet. The rats moved away from him. He lit a match. A couple of stragglers near his leg stared at him with red beady eyes. "Get!" he shouted. He picked up a clod of earth and threw it at them, putting out his match in the process. The scamper of tiny feet resumed. He felt a light drumming on his abdomen. "Goddamn it," he shouted,

227

striking another match. He looked at his watch. Noon. He'd always hated Sundays, but this was unbearable. Twelve hours till midnight, another eleven till Käte showed up...

He opened the bottle of Sliwovitz he'd sworn to save for the last night in the DDR and took a long swallow. "Paris," he whispered to himself. "Ah, Paris. That's where we'll go first. Fly into Frankfurt and right out again. How about it, Hobart, old buddy? You know how it is when you've had it with a place. East Germany, West Germany... I've had it. Just stick us on a military transport to Paris and have the pilot tell us when we cross the Rhine. We'll wait till then to celebrate."

A light appeared at the head of the tunnel. Clay watched two men with sawed-off shovels slide through the tiny entrance from the basement of the apartment complex. They approached on hands and knees, the tunnel at this point being less than three feet high.

"Bentley? You down there?"

"Nope. Already left for the West."

"Let's go. We've got another six feet to dig before morning. That's a lot of dirt to haul."

"Jahn said we were only a couple feet from the subway wall."

"Jahn's an optimist. Let's go."

"You fellows want a drink?"

The men took a quick swig from the bottle, then continued on all fours down the narrow passage far below the streets of East Berlin.

"Let me eat my sundae first." Adelbert was almost pleading. "I can't talk all the time."

"But this is going to be a live broadcast," the television journalist said. Crews swarmed everywhere, setting up lights and cameras. "The whole world wants to hear about your escape."

Hundreds of fat and jovial Munichers pressed in on the flustered poet, slapping him on the back and thrusting papers in front of him for his autograph.

Adelbert pushed his sundae aside. He was no longer hungry. Since his arrival in the West they had pursued him like a hunted animal— journalists, TV people, publishers, West German police and immigration officials, advertisers, university spokesmen... he couldn't keep track any more. "I thought Sunday was a day of rest in the Christian world."

The West German television announcer repeated his words into the microphone. "With these words DDR poet Jürgen Adelbert began his interview at the famed Schwabing Cafe. We go now to my colleague, Hans-Christian von Schleier. Herr von Schleier, how would you..."

Adelbert twisted his hand around in time to see an English and a French reporter pushing at each other. How was he going to get out of here? As far as he could see in any direction his path was blocked by people, wires, cameras, microphones.

An American TV journalist began his report. "As you can see, East German wunderkind Jürgen Adelbert, who has just made one of the most daring escapes in recent memory from the armed camp that was his homeland, is eating a sundae. A fitting symbol of his new life." The reporter shoved his way to the table. "How's the sundae?... how's it to be here?... what's it like to be free after all those years of slavery in the East...?"

The German crowd became silent. English was being spoken, and it was a national pastime in West Germany to measure your erudition by the amount of English you understood. Perhaps there would be a chance to utter a few words of the language into the reporter's microphone.

"Well, Mister Adelbert, won't you say a word to our American audience of twenty-eight million?"

"My English is not very good," Adelbert said in very good English.

"Tell our viewers what it's like to be free. What's it like to sit down and eat a sundae without worrying about the police?"

They were reducing what had happened to a sundae? What Jahn and the others were risking to a sundae?

Adelbert put his hands to his temples. The questions rained down like artillery shells. The crowd pressed in closer. The camera lights grew hot, the air stale. Adelbert's claustrophobia attacked with a vengeance. He wrapped his head in his arms. He had made a mistake. These people meant well, but they didn't understand. How could they? He didn't belong here. He had to go back. At once...

On his way to Bülow's house for his Sunday afternoon shift Karl stopped at the Pankow drop, where his mother had said she would leave the curare. And it was there, in a small glass bottle hidden in the hollow limb of an old linden tree. He would pick it up when he returned...

Ten minutes later he stood on the generaloberst's porch chatting with his bodyguard-colleague, Klaustermeier.

"You on duty tomorrow?" Klaustermeier asked.

"Yeah," Karl said. "I think we all are. Worried?"

"Sort of. I'm with the boss in thinking it's a hoax. But what if the people in the audience decide to make the prediction come true? That's what happened with the von Ettingers at the end. Remember?"

"But those were just stories. That's not how the real world works."

"Well, you and the chief see eye to eye on that point. He doesn't seem to be nervous. He's spent the whole day with that girl from Laucha."

"Du lieber Gott. Is she still here?"

"As sure as you're standing talking to me. Frau Leonhardt is pretty upset about it. The big boys have been in and out all day—the assistant party chairman, the generalleutnant in charge of security at VEB Elektro, some district heads. She spilled coffee on someone and overcooked the sausages too."

"What's he doing to the girl?"

"I don't know. There's not a peep from her when he's in the parlor with his people. But when he goes back into the bedroom the howling starts. What do you think? Does being the top man at the Vopo give you the right to treat a girl that way?"

"Rights, rights... Klaustermeier, if you stop and think about it you'll see that rights go only as far as one's power. If she hasn't got the power to stop him I guess he's got the right to do whatever he's doing—"

The howling started again inside the house. Karl put his finger to his lips. Her words were faintly audible. "No, generaloberst. No. Please. My family's waiting for me, I've got to go back home."

Guttural laughter. "Home, eh? We know what you do back home. I just called down there for a reading of your security report. You spread your thighs for all those bumpkins. Be glad you've moved up in the world."

"Please, please let me go—"

"Want me to tape your mouth shut again?"

She sobbed loudly. "Please, generaloberst, let me go home—"

"I thought I instructed you to call me Heinrich. What kind of whore are you? You're to do exactly as I say. Now lie down."

"You're hurting me."

"Shut your mouth. I'm going to teach you what a real man is. When I'm through with you, you'll have no more kind words for little faggots like that Adelbert. You're going to say, 'I once knew a real man named Heinrich who did it to me right.' Here, put your mouth right here—"

The screaming started again, followed by slapping sounds. "Goddamn it, I told you to shut up. But since you insist on defying my orders we'll do things differently."

"Let me *go* . . ."

"You'll go when I'm so sick of you I can't look at you anymore. Just now, you're getting pretty interesting. I like the nasty ones, especially when they're tied up. Give me that blanket. Turn over. I'm going to show you something you'll never forget."

"My God," Klaustermeier said.

Karl felt sick to his stomach.

"I hope something happens to him tomorrow," Klaustermeier blurted out. Karl gave him a long hard stare. To his surprise, Klaustermeier did not retract his words.

Beyond the dead garden a group of army officers marched by. "Maybe it would be best," Karl said, gazing blankly at the soldiers. "But our job is to protect him under all circumstances."

"Unfortunately," said Klaustermeier.

Karl was impressed, and for the moment, encouraged.

Kammer spread the plans to the VEB-Elektro plant over his desk for a fourth and final review. With a red pencil he circled the four emergency exits from the People's Auditorium. He poured himself a fresh cup of coffee from the Krups coffeemaker and lighted a Peter Stuyvesant. With his feet propped on a leather stool he listened to the soft, reassuring hum of his Siemens computers. Beyond the smoked-glass window of his Lichtenberg office the last lights of the city began to flicker off.

That's it, then, he thought. All of the emergency exits from the

People's Auditorium lead into the basement. The flight of his fugitives would begin there. But where would it end? If they stayed below ground in the labyrinthine tangle of tubes and boilers their only chance of escape would be the plant's giant exhaust pipes that hung out over the Spree. He would have a boat in the river somewhere nearby just in case. But it was much more likely that they would make use of police disguises and try to blend into the hubbub following the assassination. From the basement they would take one of the many staircases to the main corridor, from which they would make their way to the principle exit. A good plan, the one he would have adopted had he been in their shoes. But it was not good enough.

He glanced at his digital watch: 00:01 DEC 9. Some history would be made this day. More importantly, though, he, Kammer, would lay the foundation for a more rational system of rule in the DDR. And ideally he would do so with the help of those who had put an end to the Bülow era.

If he was right in his educated surmise that the voice of Hannah Mühlendorff was one Käte Frassek, scientist of note, administrator of talent, he was also right in believing that she had been seduced by extremist politics, mostly because of her brother's death. Well, that was understandable. He himself had once flirted with the dissident doctrines while a student. She was a modern, rational type—he had studied her face at the plant before she had become upset. With enlightened guidance—his—she would discover her error. She would understand that her emotions had clouded reason. He would make her see that the future belonged not to those who served causes, ideologies and religions—but to those who helped create and accept the triumph of logic, of the computer, and wisely chose to ride the crest of the future.

Justice today, as he intended to demonstrate, was synonymous with predictable order. The old struggle between the nebulous abstracts of Good and Evil had been supplanted by the more meaningful struggle between the Rational and the Irrational. He would give Hannah Mühlendorff and her co-conspirators a chance to redeem themselves. If he was to build a more rational and efficient society, he would need the cooperation of the best minds hitherto monopolized by the resistance.

He placed the plans in his briefcase and buzzed for his driver, satisfied with the results of his eighteen-hour day. Inside the limousine he switched on the interior lights and studied the photographs of Karl and Käte that he had assembled. Intelligent, wholesome-looking people, he thought. Not wild-eyed romantics stupid enough to die for an emotional cause. Yes, he believed they would work with him. They might even learn to enjoy it. Especially Käte. A damn interesting woman.

PART IV

CHAPTER TWENTY—SIX

On the morning of December 9, Bülow rose before dawn. He telephoned the night staff at the Bouchestrasse station and made arrangements for Gisela to be picked up. She was, he told his officer in charge, to be placed in solitary confinement. The evidence pointed to high treason, and the generaloberst intended to pursue the case personally when his schedule permitted.

His first business of the day taken care of, he climbed under the shower and abandoned himself to song. The racket traveled down the hallway to his bedroom, where Gisela, still bound, heard it and commenced alternately crying and shrieking. When the cacophony reached Wolfie in the maid's quarters the old dog briefly pricked up her ears, then lodged her tail firmly between her legs and squeezed under Frau Leonhardt's bed.

Frau Leonhardt, who had not slept a wink all night, got up and pulled on her housecoat. She fled to the kitchen, where she rattled pots and pans as she worked. At least the sounds made her feel better— good healthy household sounds unlike the lubricious notes of Bülow's all-night labors.

It must be a bad dream, she told herself. She peeled several pounds of new potatoes, sliced them and dropped a thick glob of goose fat into the iron skillet. A bad dream, indeed! Generaloberst Bülow, the highest police official in the land, the guardian of law and order, could not possibly be such a man. Yet she knew he was, and she was not sure how she would be able to face him when he appeared for breakfast.

She took four enormous *weisswurste* from the refrigerator and placed them into a pot of boiling water. After washing her arthritic hands, she dumped the potatoes into the hot goose fat and covered the spitting skillet with a lid. Then she ducked into the pantry to fetch a rye bread and some marmalade. The door swung shut behind her, leaving her stranded in the dark. Turning too quickly in search of the light switch, she struck her head on the corner of a shelf. She reached into her housecoat pocket for a handkerchief to swab her cut, found instead the crumbled sheets of feather-light paper one of the visiting officials had left on a marbletop table in the hallway.

She continued groping for the light switch while she dabbed at her wound with the papers. When she at last found the light and flicked it on, she saw she had bled rather profusely. The large splotch on the first sheet of paper was still moist and expanding. She watched the movement of her own blood with fascination, then saw the words beneath the stain: "The Early Death of Generaloberst Heinrich Bülow." Befuddled, she continued to read. Soon, her heart was beating wildly and she was gasping for breath. These resisters were, of course, awful. And yet . . . the very thought caused such guilt to rise in her that she felt as though she were being strangled—might it not be a blessing in disguise if Bülow were . . . removed?

She shoved the story into her pocket, wishing she had never seen it. Gathering up the bread and jam with motions made jerky by fear, she hobbled back into the kitchen. When she looked up she was staring at the generaloberst's medal-bedecked chest.

The sight caused her to gasp. The loaf and jar leaped from her hands and took off across the floor. She fell to her knees, trying to intercept them. Her abrupt movement creased her housecoat beneath the pocket and sent a blood-stained page of the story tumbling to the floor. Bülow pushed her away with his boot and picked it up. "Hurry with breakfast," he said gruffly. "I've had a long night."

In his chair he emitted a few more stanzas from his shower medley and turned his attention to the page. He read several lines, held it up to the light, scraped the dried blood away from his name with a thumbnail. His face darkened.

"Frau Leonhardt, where did you get this? Why is there blood on it? What were you doing in the pantry? Come here. *Answer* me."

The old housekeeper scurried up to the table with coffee, sausages and potatoes.

"TALK!"

"I will explain . . . everything, sir . . . Now, eat, you see I've made you your favorite breakfast. It will get cold—"

"Know something, Frau Leonhardt? You remind me of that goddamned Polish housekeeper we had when I was a kid. The witch would have poisoned my father quicker than you could pull a trigger. That's why he made her taste every bite of food she prepared for him. Tell me, Frau Leonhardt, you weren't planning to poison me, were you? To give me a little something that would make me drop during my speech today?"

She looked at him as though he had struck her. "I . . . sir, Herr generaloberst, I have always been so loyal—"

"Loyal, Frau Leonhardt? Do you take me for an idiot? Running around my own house with my death warrant signed in blood. How did they sneak you in here? Let's get a few matters cleared up. The story . . . we'll start with the story. Who gave it to you? *Who?*"

"Sir, I swear, I just found it this morning, lying on the table in the hallway—"

"Ox shit. I want the truth."

"That is the truth, sir." Frau Leonhardt put her hands over her tear-streaked face and let herself down in a chair.

"What about the poison? Who put you up to it?"

"Poison, sir? There is no poison. I fixed you your favorite breakfast because—"

Bülow was on his feet. "We'll see about that. *Eat.* You heard me. *Eat.*"

He stood behind her with clenched fists, his short stout neck throbbing. She lifted a forkful of potatoes to her mouth. He knocked the fork across the room.

"The *sausage*, eat the *sausage*." He reached over her shoulder and cut off a large slice, speared it with a fork and pushed it against her lips. She took it into her mouth, chewed. But in her agitated state she could not swallow. While Bülow cursed and threatened, she broke into violent sobs. The lacerated morsel shot from her mouth and splattered on to the tabletop.

"Not poisoned?" Bülow said triumphantly. He stared at her for a moment in disgust, then kicked the chair from under her. The brittle bones of her hip splintered with a crack as she hit the floor. He sank his boot into her ribs, bent over her and folded his thick fingers around her neck. "TALK. WHO PUT YOU UP TO THIS? WHAT ARE THEIR PLANS FOR TODAY?"

She said nothing. He shook her so violently that the table and chairs rattled like rail cargo.

It took him several minutes to realize that she was dead.

He got to his feet, clearing the table with a ferocious sweep of his arm. So one of his men was involved? So much, at least, was clear. How else could Frau Leonhardt have gotten the story? Frau Leonhardt, who never left the house. Maybe it wasn't *one* of his men. Maybe it was one hundred. No matter. He would find and eradicate every last one of them.

He had been careless. He had taken the most drastic measures to assure that no one would enter VEB Elektro with a weapon. And yet he had almost allowed over a hundred armed Vopos into the very hall where his assassination was to take place. He'd better get moving. There were going to be a lot of men to search and disarm before his speech got under way.

He went out of the kitchen amid the potatoes, sausages and broken plates. Shedding his boots, he padded silently through the dining room and into the parlor. The two night guards were standing on the porch, backs to the window, automatic rifles propped against the rail. They were silhouetted against a dirty gray pink dawn. The smoke of their cigarettes rose in blue wisps above the steam of their breaths. He studied them. They were clearly engaged in casual conversation, their gestures revealed no hint of any nervousness. Those two were reliable, Bülow decided. Besides, neither of them had enough initiative to work for the underground. That would require someone more like Schmidt . . . or

240

Frassek. These two would have to do. He opened the front door. "Morning, men."

"Morning, comrade generaloberst. A pleasant night?"

"Thank you, yes. Now listen carefully. There's been a change in our security arrangements at the plant. The three of us are going there right now. We're going to set up an additional search facility inside for our own people. The Vopos entering the auditorium today will carry no weapons. The policy begins now. Give me your pistols. I'll take your rifles, too."

He locked the weapons in his vestibule closet, then pulled on his boots and went to his study. He put his speech into his briefcase, as well as the list of all Vopos scheduled to work inside the People's Auditorium that day.

He began to feel better once in the car. He had turned the tables on his unknown adversaries at the eleventh hour. There would be only one weapon inside the auditorium—his. Their poisoned food had not worked. This would make for a confrontation to his liking. Today was going to be his triumph...over the Mühlendorff nuisance *and* over Kammer. His practices as head of the Vopo would be vindicated. A sweet personal victory.

He briskly saluted the small officer with the wire-rimmed glasses and the intense face who greeted him at the main gate of VEB-Elektro. "Everything in order, comrade major?"

"Yes, sir."

"What's that ambulance doing inside the compound? You fellows expect me to be needing it?"

The intense man smiled. "Hardly, sir. But someone else might."

"They're not worth saving, major."

Jahn saluted and waved the limousine forward.

Karl closed his fingers lightly around the tiny syringe and lifted his fist to the thumbs-up position. The needle, held by the tight lambskin sling in the trough between his palm and fingers, pointed toward the ground. He moved his thumb. Perfect. He would be able to push the plunger down without difficulty, thrusting the needle through its rubber sheath, through his glove and into whatever part of Bülow he could hit most easily. He put on his gloves. Thus positioned, the syringe hardly interfered with the normal movement of his hand and fingers. Nothing short of an exhaustive body search was going to expose his weapon...

The van from headquarters arrived at twenty minutes to eight. Six Vopos scrambled into the back. Karl climbed in beside the driver. "Go."

The private took off with a lurch. "Gonna be inside today, leutnant?"

"Yes," said Karl coldly.

"What d'you make of the whole thing, leutnant? Gonna be trouble?"

"Just drive, wachtmeister. It's not our job to speculate."

"Yes, sir." The chastened private cleared his throat and hummed quietly as he negotiated the streets of the capital.

Though it was rush hour, Berlin seemed subdued. Crowds had gathered in the usual places—in the central squares and around the S-Bahn stations. But they were docile crowds, the composite of many individuals lost in their own thoughts. And indeed, Karl thought, there was much to think about today. If Hannah Mühlendorff's predicted assassination succeeded, a polarization within the DDR would be inevitable. The future would not remain free of confrontation and bloodshed.

For some this was not a disquieting prospect. But for the old and cautious it was. How indelible were the memories of nights spent beneath the earth while bombs exploded overhead and rubble-strewn streets glowed like blast furnaces. How fresh the memories of sons and lovers, whose charred and tangled corpses were all that survived of their exuberant idealism. How fresh the memories of Russian troops venting their hate-stoked lust in mass rapes of German women.

Freedom, you say? Ah, yes, but what is the price? How much do you expect us to pay? We have already paid dearly just to stay alive. Would the people stay passive in the face of tyranny even if his mother succeeded? Would they erupt in a suicidal uprising led by unorganized hotheads? Or would they see the message Käte had tried to convey in twenty years of stories... that there *was* a third course of action, a gradual, sure building of opposition fueled by decisive, meaningful acts such as Bülow's assassination? Would they join the gathering force of Jahn's movement, willing to risk and sacrifice but sustained by a realistic hope for a better future? The people would have to decide. His role was to help them have their chance.

242

"So this is you?" the surly Vopo captain at the plant entrance said. "Frassek, Karl, leutnant?"

"Correct, sir."

"Hmm. Seems to me I had another Frassek come through earlier. Two Frasseks on duty today?"

"Excuse me?"

"I said, two Frasseks on duty today?"

"Not to my knowledge."

"Name looks mighty familiar."

Karl was forced to make a split-second decision about what he should reveal to keep the greater secret intact. "You're probably talking about my mother," he said.

"Don't get wise with me, leutnant."

"No. I'm serious. She works here."

"Works *where?*"

"At VEB-Elektro. Look on your other list, the one for the firm's employees. You probably remember her name from there."

The captain leafed through the computerized lists. "Well, so she does." He brought his red pencil to rest beneath the name Käte Hansen Frassek. "Your mother, you say?"

"That is correct."

"Bet they gave the two of you a going over, what with all the threats on the big kahuna's life."

"Routine."

"Routine? Does Bülow know?"

"Yes. I'm on his personal staff."

"Well, well... you fellows expecting action today?"

"We're prepared."

"Think so? You must not have heard the latest."

"No..." Karl said. He was unpleasantly aware of the light pressure the syringe exerted on his palm. Was he holding his left hand naturally? He felt self-consciousness creep into his gestures.

"Come on, captain," yelled a Vopo waiting in line. "This isn't the railway."

The captain smiled at the crowd, enjoying his hour in the spotlight. Slowly, he returned his gaze to Karl. "Well, listen to this, leutnant. Bülow's disarming his own people. Right in there behind those curtains. Don't you think that's a little strange?"

"The generaloberst," said Karl, "usually has good reasons for what he's doing. I don't make a habit of trying to second-guess him. Now, if you don't mind, I'm due at my post."

The captain scratched his head beneath his cap. "One more thing, Frassek, you say your boss knows you've a relative on the work force here? It doesn't seem to me he'd allow that type of situation, with all those stories about family cells—"

"Captain, if you want to question his judgment, that's your business."

"Yeah, leutnant, maybe I do. Maybe we're not talking about judgment either. Maybe he doesn't know. Move on."

Karl parted the heavy brown curtains, frustrated by the bad luck that had met him at the plant entrance. He felt his composure unraveling, took a deep breath. Behind him the captain glowered at the impatient crowd, then jotted Käte's name on a scrap of paper and motioned a colleague to his side.

Enter One At a Time read the makeshift sign on the door Karl opened. He passed into a brightly lit room that was empty of furnishings except for a large metal desk in its center. A television camera whirred from a high corner, a green light blinking from its nose. Affixed to the tabletop was a long yellow sheet of paper, on which was typed:

MEN AND WOMEN OF THE GERMAN PEOPLE'S POLICE:

We will carry no weapons today during the award presentation ceremony in the People's Auditorium of VEB-Elektro. I have ordered this procedure to demonstrate to the East German people the farcical nature of the threats on our organization and its chief.

Place your rifles and pistols on the table. Any ammunition remaining on your person should be placed on the table as well. When you have finished proceed through the door marked "A" to the bottom of the stairs. You will be met there by Leutnant R. Clausen, who will issue you a receipt for your weapons and ammunition and further direct you.

Before leaving this room, stand in front of the camera and state clearly your name, rank and serial number.

Generaloberst Heinrich Bülow

Beneath the note was Bülow's signature, overlaid by the official stamp of the *Deutsche Volkspolizei.*

Karl quickly shed his rifle and pistol, worried that the needle was distorting his motions. At the bottom of the staircase he picked up his receipt from Lieutenant Clausen, who told him to proceed to Room B at the end of the corridor.

Karl passed through a series of x-ray scans, walking briskly but not rapidly. What would he say if the captain upstairs had passed word of his mother's presence to Bülow? How would he explain his failure to mention that fact to Bülow? He was worrying this one when the generaloberst's voice exploded through a loudspeaker in the hallway.

"Move to the white line, stop and identify yourself."

Karl stopped. There was a camera nearby, he assumed, but he didn't try to locate it. "Karl Frassek, leutnant, personal staff, Generaloberst Bülow."

245

"Come forward, Frassek. Enter through the door marked B. Hurry, we're behind schedule."

Karl walked thirty feet to the door, opened it, entered an area black as night. The door swung shut behind him, he heard the lock close.

"Identify yourself," the voice ordered again. This time the loudspeaker sounded as though it were above him and to the right.

"Leutnant Karl Frassek," he said in a strong steady voice. "I believe you are acquainted with the relevant details."

Blinding lights came on, a favorite Bülow technique. Karl fought not to flinch . . . this was hardly the time to show nerves. He glanced at his surroundings—a janitor's lunchroom hastily converted into an interrogation facility. The wires to the speaker climbed the cinder-block wall like vines; the burlap front of the speaker looked soggy with age. Just below the speaker was a door with a single window. The window was covered by a square of one-way glass held in place by thick duct tape. Fifteen feet to Karl's left, stiff as a statue among buckets, mops and brooms, stood Leutnant Bloch, the newest of Bülow's bodyguards.

"Well, well, Frassek, I've been waiting for you," came the voice through the speaker. "I have a note here from the people at the entrance. The note, signed by Captain Helmstedt, says that you have a relative on the work force at VEB-Elektro. Is this correct?"

"Yes, sir, what of it?"

"Your mother has worked here for years. You did not inform me."

"Why should I have? When I started work for you less than a year ago, a full security check was run on my family. I assumed you had checked on and knew about the status of my mother. It's in your files."

"Why did you not inform me?"

"I told you, sir. I thought it would have been superfluous."

Karl could hear him pick up a telephone. "Captain, Bülow here. A question on the Frassek matter. Has the other person by that name passed through our stations yet?" Silence while Bülow listened to the answer. "Good," the generaloberst continued into the telephone. Then, into the speaker: "Leutnant, the full name of your mother."

"Käte Frassek, *geboren* Hansen." Better keep that needle in striking position. I might have to kill him ahead of schedule . . .

"Käte Frassek, *geboren* Hansen," said Bulow into the phone. "I want her followed to her seat by two of your people. They will remain with

246

her until the ceremony is over, at which time they will bring her to me at the Bouchestrasse station."

"Well, Frassek," said Bülow after a pause, "how do you think she'll like our facility? Frassek, what's the matter? You look nervous. Is that true, comrade leutnant. Are you nervous? ANSWER ME."

"Comrade generaloberst, I must protest any harassment of my mother. If there is a problem, settle it with me—"

"Well, well, Frassek. Large talk from a leutnant. Take off your clothes. Everything. Don't stand there gaping. Move."

Karl fought down panic. "...nor, sir, do I appreciate being singled out for—"

Bülow cut him off. "Feel singled out, do you, Frassek? Open the closet, Leutnant Bloch. Singled out, eh? Well, Frassek, if you look in there, you'll seen an entire rack of new parade uniforms. You're not the only one who's changing clothes for the event. It's a big event, Frassek. A big day for the Vopo. No reason my own bodyguards shouldn't look their best. Bloch, throw him the sizes he wants. Everything, socks, shoes, gloves, underwear. Leave what you're wearing now on the floor. You heard me, Frassek. Undress. I'm anxious to see how you, the big talker, is hung."

Karl went numb. *"Faster.* We don't want to keep our television audience waiting. Come on, does it take you this long to undress when you're bumping one of your floozies?"

Karl placed his socks in his boots, then stepped out of his trousers and folded them neatly. He was about to shed his undershorts when Bülow ordered, "The gloves, damn it, get the gloves off."

He pulled his right glove off and laid it on his trousers, caught his left glove by the fingers and slid it off as well. He began unbuttoning his uniform jacket. The sling was skin-colored and tight-fitting. Seen from the back of his hand, it was nearly invisible. Bülow, however, left him no time to hope.

"Frassek. Hands toward me. *Now.*"

Praying for the miracle he knew would not happen, Karl held both palms toward the square of one-way glass. There was a long silence. When Bülow spoke at last, he seemed genuinely shocked. "Is that a *needle*, Frassek? A medical needle?"

"Yes, sir. A micro-syringe."

"What's in it?"

"Insulin, sir. I'm a diabetic. I didn't want anyone to know. I was afraid for my job and my athletic career—"

"*Ox shit*. Take the needle out of that rubber thing and place it on the table. Shove it gently toward Bloch."

Karl slid the syringe from its holder. It was still a potential weapon, and he clung to it a second too long.

"*Now*. Send it down to Bloch."

Should he make a move? Disarm Bloch and lunge through the door Bülow was standing behind. A quick glance at the door convinced him he should not . . . it was fitted with two heavy dead bolts, both clearly locked.

"Now, Frassek, or I'll have to have Bloch shoot you."

Karl gave the syringe a light push. It spun like a miniature hockey puck down the long table toward the man who still held an automatic rifle trained on his throat. Bülow came in now, face calm and businesslike. He drew his Luger and pointed it at Karl's head, careful, though, to keep a safe distance from him.

"Leutnant Bloch, pick up the needle. Frassek, don't move or I'll be obliged to put a bullet through your skull."

The young lieutenant examined the syringe, keeping one hand on the trigger of his rifle. Bülow stepped back toward the door. "Insulin is in there, Frassek?"

"Yes."

"What would insulin do to me?"

"Nothing."

"To Major Bloch."

"Nothing."

"To you?"

"Prevent an attack."

"Want to take it?"

"At eleven o'clock."

"Why not now?"

"I don't need it."

"And it definitely won't hurt Leutnant Bloch?"

Karl didn't answer. It was clear no one would leave the room until

248

Bülow had decided on a guinea pig and tested the contents of the syringe. If he didn't tell the truth Bloch would die from the injection and he would be in no better position than if he'd confessed.

"Well, Frassek, let's hear it once more. Will this stuff harm Leutnant Bloch?"

"It will kill him."

Bülow laughed. "And it was intended for me. What's in it?"

"Curare."

"I've read about that somewhere. An old Indian poison, they used it on the tips of their spears. *Right*, Frassek?"

"Yes."

"Well, well, my trusted bodyguard. A man I took a special interest in, furthered his career in every possible way. And what does he do? He tries to poison me. What do you think of that, Leutnant Bloch?"

"Very bad, sir."

"Yes, Frassek, very bad. Now tell me more about this curare. Could it be it has some medical, some scientific use these days?"

"I don't know—"

"The hell you don't . . . It has a medical use and you got it from that goddamned American doctor. I'll tell you something, Frassek. I don't know what he is to you but I'm going to hunt him down. If he somehow gets out of the DDR I'll find him in America. You heard him invite me to visit him, well, believe me, I will. Now, Frassek, how does this curare work? No more lies."

"Inject me," Karl said.

Bülow smiled. "Not so fast, too easy for you. Besides, I can't spare you, leutnant, until you've led me to the others. Bloch!"

The lieutenant stiffened.

"Yes, sir."

"Inject yourself."

"What, sir?"

"I said, inject yourself!"

"Don't do it," Karl told him quickly, taking half a step forward until Bülow turned on him with the Luger.

"Stay where you are," Bülow ordered.

"Bloch," Karl said, "you see what he is, why we have to kill him—"

249

"One more word, Frassek and I'll be forced to shoot you ... Bloch, put the syringe on the table."

"Yes, sir," the young Vopo said, breathing with relief.

"Now put your rifle inside my door. We don't want Frassek getting any more ideas for sacrificing himself before I'm ready."

Bloch did as he was told, then returned to his post among the mops and brooms.

"Now, Bloch, take the needle in your right hand, and stand at attention like a *soldier*. Good, good."

Bülow, his eye still on Karl, trained the Luger at Bloch's head. "And now, Leutnant Bloch, inject yourself. *That is an order.*"

Prussian-stiff, in a sudden, frantic gesture Bloch buried the needle in his forearm. In the same instant he fainted, collapsing on the linoleum floor. A broom with a metal handle tumbled onto his back. Seconds later he opened his eyes. "What happened?" He groaned. "Where am I ... ?"

"Get up," Bülow ordered. "You will stand at attention until I dismiss you."

Bloch, standing straight as a rod again, could not suppress his joy at having escaped certain death. After a full two minutes of silence he allowed himself, "What strange stuff, comes on with a bang but I feel fine now."

"Too small a dosage," Karl told him, to give the man a few more seconds of illusion. "You're going to be—"

Karl stopped in mid-sentence. Even Bülow looked on in shock. Abruptly the lieutenant's face broke into bright red hives. His eyelids drooped eerily, as though pulled by some great invisible weight. He tried to speak but all he could produce were a few strangled vowels.

Karl, hoping the lieutenant's falling body would distract Bülow for the necessary split second, dove beneath the table and threw himself forward. But where Bülow's boots had stood was now Bloch's corpse, the bright red splotches on his face darkening to the purple of varicose veins. Karl got to his feet, spun around, cornered ... But Bülow was no longer in the room. What was—?

"Get dressed, Frassek," boomed the voice through the loudspeaker. "You are really too obvious. Get dressed, new clothes from the closet.

250

Hurry. You, my trusted lieutenant, are going to sit up there with me on the stage. I want all your friends to see you there squirming. Yes, indeed, Frassek, I'm going to enjoy this little ceremony. Hurry. After all, your good mother will worry if you're not with the others."

CHAPTER TWENTY—EIGHT

A black Wartburg sedan came to a stop at the corner of Pushkin Allee and Eisenstrasse. Kammer, alone in the back seat, lifted his field glasses to survey the enclosure around VEB-Elektro. He counted fifty-four Vopo squad cars and one ambulance.

There were, he estimated, two hundred paramilitary Vopos within the compound. Should things get out of hand the tanks from the Bouchestrasse station were less than four blocks away. Yes, Bülow had arranged this part of his operation well. Any more police presence would have made him seem too concerned, any less would have been careless.

A driver stopped behind the Stasi car, which was blocking the right-turn lane, and flashed his lights. "Enno," said Kammer politely, "pull up on the shoulder."

Major Enno Obermeyer, a twenty-year veteran of State Security, glanced at his boss in the rearview mirror. "Sir, that would mean driving on the grass—"

"Of course, Enno. And that is forbidden. We will reprimand ourselves properly at a later time."

The Wartburg climbed the high curb, tipped steeply and stopped on the brown grass between the pavement and sidewalk. Several of the curious motorists who had been circling the plant followed Kammer's example. In minutes, two dozen cars were parked on the grass across from the factory.

"Our countrymen are losing respect for the law," Major Hans-Jürgen Kiefer remarked from the front passenger seat. "Deplorable."

Kammer lighted a Peter Stuyvesant and poured himself a cup of fresh black coffee from his back seat bar. He swung the tiny color television set around on its adjustable arm and wiped the dust from the screen with his handkerchief. "Perhaps, Hans-Jürgen, you should welcome the phenomenon we have just observed. True, they disobeyed a traffic law. But they did so because *we* did it first. They are followers. Be grateful for that. When they cease to be followers, we shall cease to be leaders."

Hans-Jürgen, seven years Enno's junior and, like his colleague, an awesome specimen of physical fitness, twisted uncomfortably in his seat. "What I don't understand, sir, is why the three of us are here alone. If it's so important to capture this Hannah Mühlendorff, why are we taking such chances?"

"Major, we are here on, shall we say, a hunch of mine," Kammer told him. "If I brought out the entire Stasi each time I had a hunch, however educated it might be, we would be foolish indeed. Further, Generaloberst Bülow has made it clear that he wishes to face and defeat this particular threat on his own. A matter of honor, I suppose. He has been adamant in his refusal to accept my assistance." Kammer could hardly explain to them that he wanted the resisters to dispose of Bülow for him.

"Suppose, however, that your hunch is correct, sir," Enno said. "In which case you might indeed capture the assassin ... but only after she has succeeded in her plan against Generaloberst Bülow. Would it be correct to assume that this would place you and the Stasi in a most favorable position, leaving you, sir, in control of the whole police apparatus of this nation?"

"That, Enno, would be a reasonable assumption." He would have to watch Major Enno Obermeyer more closely in the future. He adjusted the volume on his miniature TV set. "It seems, gentlemen, that they are switching to live coverage inside the plant."

254

The search procedures at the entrances to the People's Auditorium were exhaustive. Käte passed through two x-ray scans, gave her purse over to three separate examinations and underwent an uncomfortably thorough hand search of her clothes and body. She was relieved to see that the Vopos were not armed, and she entered the hall anxious but confident.

When she took her seat, it was nearly ten o'clock. The crowd inside was as subdued as it had been at the plant entrance, its silent gaze directed at the activity on the stage. Television cameras glided overhead on mobile platforms. Technicians swarmed among the tangle of thick black wires crisscrossing the floor. Official photographers scampered about behind a fat yellow cordon, snapping pictures of the company and Party officials who had already begun to take their seats.

A soft ripple of applause greeted Director Scheel as he came from the wings and crossed the stage. Next came the generaloberst's bodyguards in their parade dress. Käte squirmed in her chair, caught a glimpse of Karl behind a knot of his colleagues. Could it be possible ... they were only a single step from realizing a twenty-year goal ... ?

A coterie of somber Party officials emerged, followed by the plant's top administrators. Then, after a short pause, the generaloberst himself burst into the stage lights. Squat as a petroleum drum, he surged forward with powerful steps, his bemedaled chest leading the way. He was smiling.

Scheel clapped and moved to a podium draped in the flags of Berlin, the DDR and the Soviet Union. The TV cameras whirred; the announcers in mobile glass booths became silent, and Scheel launched into a long-winded introduction of the guest speaker.

After about ten minutes Bülow coughed and tapped at his watch. Scheel glanced at him, nodded. Käte twisted in her assigned seat to consult the clock on the wall; saw instead two uniformed Vopos in the seats directly behind her. One of the Vopos was a much-decorated male officer in his forties. He smiled pleasantly. The other was an enormous woman of lower rank whose stare was distinctly unpleasant.

Käte returned her attention to her purse, fidgeting nervously with the zipper. A hot breath passed along the right side of her neck, the side on which the Vopo woman, Unterleutnant Holz, was seated. Käte froze. Clearly she was being watched.

Director Scheel's words... "And now, *meine damen und herren,* I present to you our distinguished guest, interior minister and chief of the German People's Police, generaloberst..."

Now. It must be *now.* She felt those malevolent eyes on her and slid forward in her chair. The hot breath on her neck followed.

"... Heinrich Bülow, who has done so much to create a stable, peaceful social order conducive to productivity in our great land..."

Her fingers plunged into her purse, found the cigarette package, groped for the cigarette that was hard in the center, found it, closed around it. The breath was very near, seeping intimately through her hair. She hunched over, putting the cigarette between her lips as she moved. A thick arm came down on her shoulder, wrenched her upright, pinned her against the chair. Another hand tore the cigarette from her lips. Too late—Käte had already exhaled through the hidden pet whistle.

The first two shots cracked near the center of the auditorium just as Bülow got to his feet. Screams, shouts from the audience. Two more shots cracked near the stage. Three of the generaloberst's bodyguards hurled themselves at their boss, three more stayed back, keeping a tight circle around Karl.

Bülow spun out of their protective grasp. Nobody was hurt, nobody hit... "Blanks, get back, false alarm." The three lieutenants, looking a bit stunned, did as they were told. The generaloberst stepped boldly to the edge of the stage, raising his arms like a misshapen de Gaulle.

"Meine damen und herren," he announced in a voice that did not require amplification, "so much for the resistance. Those, as you have seen, were blanks. Big noise, no substance. Like the whole so-called resistance movement." He marched to the podium, where Scheel was still lifting himself cautiously from the floor.

The fat Vopo woman behind Käte was saying, "Look at this... a device of some sort in her cigarette. *She* set off those blanks."

Käte could not even react. She had watched the three bodyguards form a ring around her son. The existence of the two Vopos behind her was no coincidence—Hannah Mühlendorff had been discovered. She pictured herself and Karl being dragged in front of television cameras a few minutes from now, exposed and humiliated. There was only a single remaining hope, slender as thread. When the timers had ticked through their cycles, the two charges in the main breaker box would go off...

Bülow, full of himself, slammed his fist into the podium near the microphone. *"Meine damen und herren,* today I was threatened by this seditious criminal who calls herself Hannah Mühlendorff. To show you how seriously I took her threat, I ordered the men and women of the German People's Police to accompany me to your fine plant without their arms. I thank them for their devotion and courage.

"Meine damen und herren, today you have witnessed a triumph, not mine but yours. We in the Party have dedicated our lives to bringing the people of the DDR the type of country *you* want, a democratic society in which we all can prosper and be free. We are not fully at our goal yet, but we have made great strides. With your continued support, we shall stay the course."

The Party dignitaries and company brass seated on the stage applauded, feeling greatly relieved after the shots were proved to be blanks. Old Heinrich had pulled it off. He'd even somehow found the good sense to sound relatively civilized...

"The German Democratic Republic, unlike its neighbor to the west, has broken the stranglehold of the Nazi past. We have built a system in which the horrible practices of that day are only a tragic memory..." Something in the crowd distracted him and he squinted out over the sea of heads.

Near the back of the auditorium an old man had gotten to his feet, was waving his arms in the air. When Bülow paused, the old man called out in a surprisingly strong voice... "We don't want to listen to your lies, generaloberst. We've heard them too long—"

"Leutnant Klaustermeier," Bülow ordered, "usher the gentleman from the auditorium. He is obviously out of his mind, a sick man. He needs help..."

Klaustermeier hopped down from the stage, but before he could reach the old man the voice rang out again... "Do you fear *me*, generaloberst? Or do you fear my words? The truth?"

The audience stirred. Klaustermeier took the old man gently by the arm, removed his cane and began to lead him toward the aisle.

"Generaloberst, you said this is a free country. Haven't I the right to speak? Or is it only free for you and those who agree with you?"

Purple rose in Bülow's cheeks. Who was this old fool? Bülow's bodyguards moved to the edge of the stage. Men planted in the audience stood and moved toward the aisles. Bülow would not allow a confrontation. His men were unarmed. There could be no worse embarrassment than to have to call in forces from the outside.

"Back, members of the German People's Police," Bülow called out. "There's no need."

The Vopos stopped in their tracks.

"You, too, you men in the audience. Return to your seats. This troublemaker can have his say. He is proof of what I have been saying. Now, old man, what is your name?"

"Is your memory failing you, generaloberst? Seifert. Doktor Max Seifert. I work for you at the Friedrichstrasse station."

Bülow's painfully self-enforced calm slipped away. Seifert! The criminologist who had given the clean verdict on Bentley's clothing. "All right, that's enough ... take him out of here."

"You will not leave this auditorium alive," Seifert said as two Vopos took him by the arms and began to lead him away ...

Käte looked on in a state of near-shock. She forgot about the two Vopos behind her, even about the blanks in the main breaker box about to go of ...

Seifert wrenched one arm loose and pointed his cane at Bülow. "Hannah Mühlendorff has taught us how we must deal with you. And we *will*..."

Bülow snapped. He drew his Luger, ordered that Seifert be brought to the platform. And in the same instant, as if in accompaniment, two shots went off in the wings, and a blackness darker than night engulfed the auditorium.

CHAPTER TWENTY—NINE

Karl moved through the darkness, agile as a cat. Near the podium he fell to his hands and knees and slid to a point on the stage he had fixed in his mind's eye. He had been studying an eight-foot length of electrical cord before the lights went out. It took him only seconds to find it, unplug it at both ends and tie it into a stout noose.

Bülow's voice rose above the commotion. "Get those goddamned lights on . . ."

The words served as a beacon of orientation. Karl shed his boots, lifted the cord so that it would not rustle across the floor and padded cautiously in the direction the voice had come from.

"Someone at least light a match," the generaloberst called out. On stage, not one match flickered, not one flashlight shone. The police and Party officials, relieved that their televised fiasco had been hidden by darkness, moved quietly toward the wings.

Karl continued forward, veering slightly to his left. One more word . . . one more word and I should have him . . .

But that word remained unspoken. The generaloberst had suddenly remembered Karl's presence on stage. He turned, furious. Karl, not five feet away, could sense the animal energy of his movements. The breeze generated by Bülow's sudden bodily shift brushed across him.

Karl had seen Bülow draw the Luger just before the lights went out. He knew that he risked being shot the instant he made contact. But if he was going to use the noose he must get closer. He took a silent step, another, until he could hear the man's breathing. Slowly he raised the noose. He knew he was vulnerable in that position but he had no choice—

Bülow again spun, brushing Karl's stomach with his Luger. Karl darted backward and to the side. In the same instant he let the noose fall over Bülow's head. The generaloberst felt the cord land on his shoulders, ducked instinctively. But Karl's reflexes were too fast for him . . . the noose closed around his neck with a sharp jerk.

Now Karl knew he must keep moving—quickly, unpredictably. And at the same time he must keep tension on the cord. If Bülow got loose . . . He launched himself at Bülow's legs. Bülow, upended, fell like a boulder. As he struck the stage Karl bounded to his feet and hauled back on the cord with a savage yank. The darkness erupted with a strangled gurgling.

Karl lunged again. A shot exploded in his ears, and the flash of the Luger illuminated Bülow's face in a freeze-frame. The chief was far from dead. He was on his back, left hand clutched to the thick black knot on his Adam's apple, right hand clutching the pistol. Karl fell on Bülow's right forearm, grasping it with both hands as he drove his knee into the iron muscles between the wrist and elbow. The gun refused to clatter to the floor. He pounded his knee into the arm, sure he had broken bones, sure those bones were being pulverized. Still Bülow held on, and as he did his desperate clawing to free his neck from the stranglehold was transmitted to Karl along the bizarre communication line between them. Karl tried to draw the cord tighter but couldn't without letting go of Bülow's right arm. Bülow began to breathe in great rasping gulps. The stranglehold was broken, he must go for the gun—

Bülow's knee hit Karl in the small of his back with sledgehammer force. Karl skittered forward on his stomach while the black world of his vision burst into a pyrotechnic of red and orange. At the same moment he felt a sharp pain as the cord cut into his fingers. At least he still had him. A shot went off as he flung himself sideways, the bullet entering the floor so close to his hands he could feel its impact on the wood. He got to his feet, still reeling. Bülow fired two more shots, wild. Karl yanked the cord with all his strength, and the terrible gurgling sound recommenced.

Fast . . . it must happen fast. The darkness wouldn't last forever. Die. In the name of God, *die*. He lurched this way and that, trying to make himself an elusive target. Briefly, he let the cord fall slack, then gave it a short, fierce jerk. The Luger finally tumbled from Bülow's grasp, hitting the floor with a clatter, to Karl as sweet as any sound on earth.

Karl dragged his burden out of reach of the gun. He jerked, let the cord fall slack, jerked again. Bülow's thick neck refused to snap. Karl stepped closer, winding the cord around his fists and lifting with all his strength. Revulsion filled him so that he thought he would be sick. Die, in the name of God, die . . . How long could they stay locked in this obscene struggle?

The gurgling abated. An unsteady hand clawed at Karl's pantleg. The weight of the huge mass on the end of the line became so heavy Karl let it fall to the floor. Then, in frustration, he yanked the cord.

The noise, delicate as a dried twig under foot, caught him by surprise. He let his arms drop; the generaloberst's head hit the stage beside his feet.

Move. Don't let up. He stooped down and removed the noose while death spasms took hold of Bülow. He forced himself to go through a quick mental checklist while he untied the hangman's knot. His boots . . . he couldn't leave the auditorium without them . . . Bülow's assassination was only the beginning. Now he needed to escape. Outside the plant he mustn't come under suspicion—

Noises in the wings. Think. He stretched the eight-foot cord to rid it of the worst kinks, then swung it in a low circle while he moved slowly sideways. The end of the cord struck an object. He went to the spot, gathered his boots in one arm and, orienting himself by the slender grooves in the floor, made his way to the edge of the stage. A little over a minute after the main breaker box had blown, he entered the tumultuous crowd.

Someone slammed into the oversized torso of Unterleutnant Holz and tried to squeeze past her. As she momentarily took her hands from Käte's shoulders and latched on to the offender, Käte plunged into the crowd, moving ahead until she tripped over an outstretched ankle. Staying on all fours, she tried to crawl. A thicket of legs blocked her path. A heel landed on her hand, making her bite her lip to keep from crying out.

"She's *gone*," Holz called out. Her voice seemed to come from directly above. Käte pushed herself flat against the floor and squirmed beneath a heap of collapsible chairs thrown topsy-turvy by the fracas. The crowd, elated but panicky, surged toward the exits.

"Police, here," yelled Holz. "We need light. Give me some matches."

Nobody was listening. And the people had but one thought—get out of the auditorium.

"Police," repeated Holz. "I order you to give me your matches—"

"Unterleutnant Holz," her colleague Oberst Röhm said, "kindly remove your hands from me. And calm down. No one can get out. The doors are locked. When the lights come on we'll find her." . . .

Käte stood and pushed to her right with all her strength. But the crowd had become a powerful current, and the current ran in the opposite direction, sweeping her away from the emergency exit, whose key she carried.

As the charging bodies buffeted her, Käte lifted a hand and brushed it over the top of passing heads. Soon, she had plucked a pointed felt hat from a woman who had all but crushed her. She set it firmly on top of her blond head. It might only gain her seconds, but seconds might make the difference.

People who had been seated on the periphery of the auditorium were quick to find the exits. The Vopos entrusted with preventing any movement into or out of the hall stood guard at the locked doors, but the people organized themselves into groups and set about rhythmically pummeling the stout metal doors.

Whispers darted through the night. "He's dead," said one to another. "He's dead . . . I'm sure . . . Hannah has succeeded . . ."

"Hannah, Hannah, Hannah." A chant rose at one of the exits. The words seemed to add fresh vigor to the demolition crew. There was a screech as the hinges failed, the door broke open with a crash. People streamed into the deserted corridors of the plant; light streamed into the auditorium.

Four Vopos pushed a plant technician to the main breaker box. The technician was pleased to discover and announce that the spare fuses had been gutted. The Vopos grabbed him by the arms, ordered him to find a solution or be shot.

The auditorium lights came on in a brilliant burst of white. It was as though the police had caught the audience in a collective criminal act. But the lights did nothing to slow the tide. At the three other main exits keys were torn from the pockets of resisting Vopo guards. The doors flew open and the crowd stampeded into the corridors.

"Stay where you are," a Party official ordered into the microphone. But Karl's use of the amplifier cord had cut the power supply to the podium. The official's voice fell like a sparrow's chirp on the roar of the stampede.

Käte steered a determined course toward the emergency exit, sometimes pitting herself against the current. She was making good progress when a man twice her size slammed into her and knocked her hat from her head. She glanced to the floor, hoping to retrieve it, and saw only pounding feet. She resumed her upstream journey, cleaving the current of anonymous flesh until she reached a point where the crowd had thinned. She rushed forward, feeling exposed. The east wall of the auditorium was less than one hundred feet away—

The shouts of Unterleutnant Holz rained down on her . . . "There, there she is, let me *down*."

Caught in the beam of approaching lights, Käte froze, then saw the enormous woman standing on a chair far in the crowd, buttressed by two uniformed arms behind her buttocks. The arms stiffened in a vain effort to keep Holz's body aloft, then folded like overtaxed beams, and Holz fell backward, disappearing into the sea of people.

Käte joined a group charging up the main aisle along the east wall. She had less than forty feet to cover now to reach the emergency exit, but it was forty feet in the wrong direction. As the crowd rushed toward the exits at the back of the auditorium, she inched ahead step by step, bracing herself against the wall.

Each time she paused for breath, the crowd carried her backward. She felt herself beginning to lose strength. Her bracelet caught in someone's sweater, she was spun around, stumbled. The crowd seemed to respond with renewed fury, carrying her back to the same place where she'd entered the current. She looked up at the ceiling lights, and ahead caught a glimpse of Holz bearing down on her, swinging arms like Westphalian hams as she knocked men and women out of her way.

"Stop her," Käte called out. "She's trying to kill me, stop her..."

Someone heard, a thud reverberated near where Holz had stood, followed by a yelp of pain. Exhausted, Käte squeezed her way out of the aisle, stumbling down a row strewn with capsized chairs.

The auditorium was half-empty now. She made rapid progress in the direction of the stage, holding her skirt above her knees and stepping over the rows. She continued past the emergency exit, then reentered the aisle and let the human current sweep her along. Gradually, she made her way toward the wall.

Her shoulder brushed the concrete. Ten feet ahead, the emergency exit sign glowed above the crowd. She dug into her sweater pocket for her keys, closed her fist tight around them, threw back her head and went forward...

In front of the door, sweat splattered across her low forehead like raindrops, stood Unterleutnant Holz, arms folded across her chest, eyes dancing with a *schadenfreude* of repellent intensity. Planted like a tree beside her stood Oberst Röhm, a glittering display of medals on his uniform jacket.

Käte willed herself to run, but her legs cramped. A burning spread through her lungs, her arms trembled with exhaustion. She turned to the people streaming by. "Help me, please..." But her voice was too weak to be heard.

"*Guten tag*," Oberst Röhm said. "I didn't have the chance to introduce myself earlier. Götz Röhm. No relation, of course—"

Käte saw Holz's mouth fall open, and in the same instant Röhm dropped to the floor like a sack of potatoes.

"Hurry," Karl said. "Open the door, don't just stand there, mother."

Käte fumbled to find the right key while her son's voice floated in her ears like music. Holz, mouth agape, inched sideways. As she put out an arm to block Käte from using the key, the point of Karl's boot caught her on the wrist. She drew back her hand in pain.

Käte managed to get the key into the lock and turn it. "Go in," Karl told her.

As Käte stepped over the threshold Röhm's unconscious body skidded past her on the floor, propelled by Karl's push. Holz followed, helped along by the first right hook Karl had ever unloaded on a woman. She stumbled several steps, tripped over her prostrate colleague and went down with a crash. Quickly, Käte relocked the door.

"Karl, thank God, are you all right?"

"Yes, sure..." He bound Röhm's legs together with the oberst's own belt. "You?"

"So far. Do they know our identity outside the plant?"

"I don't know. Where's your uniform?"

"Here. First door."

"Get dressed. I'll drag these two somewhere I can tie them up better." Holz stirred. Karl checked her eyes. "I might have to hit her again."

"Karl—"

"Mother, hurry. We're at least thirty seconds behind. If we miss that subway—"

"Karl, is Bülow..."

He smiled. "Yes, Hannah, he's dead."

They rushed down a labyrinth of basement passageways, joining the crowd in the main corridor just before the plant exit. The people poured out the great arched entryway, sweeping Karl and Käte into the cold gray morning.

Vopo squad cars blocked the gate to the city beyond. Submachine guns bristled from tight knots of troops. The corpse of a man who had tried to scale the wrought iron fence around the enclosure hung impaled on a spike fifteen feet above the crowd, blood still oozing from the bullet holes in his back.

Karl scanned the enclosure for the ambulance. A sound he knew too well distracted him. Air and earth commenced to vibrate in unison as the tanks from the Bouchestrasse station rumbled up from the east. The first tank to reach the factory paused at the corner of Eisenstrasse and Pushkin Allee, as though observing the battalion of cars parked illegally on the shoulder, then swiveled on its heavy steel treads and trained its cannon on the crowd. A column of tanks appeared behind the leader, splitting in two at the corner. Half of the tanks went down the Eisenstrasse to the river, plowed over a barbed wire fence and bumped up a service road ringing the factory. The rest bent into Pushkin Allee, meeting the first column on a narrow side street along the plant's western boundary. Helmeted gunners appeared behind machine guns mounted on top of the tanks while cannons maneuvered nervously. An eerie silence fell over the prisoners in the plant complex.

Spotting the ambulance near the center of the crowd, Karl told Käte to follow and started forward. Vopos from the auditorium began arriving at the plant entrance in large numbers. A disheveled officer directed them to a basement room where their weapons had been stored.

"Leutnant Frassek," one of the bodyguards who had been in the auditorium called out. "Leutnant Frassek, what happened?"

Karl faced him down. "I don't know, get out of the way. He might still be alive."

Karl turned and walked off. The bodyguard followed him. Käte took the young man by the arm.

"Please do something helpful," she said. "This has been a bad day for all of us."

"What can I do?"

"Start clearing a path between the exit and the ambulance. We'll need to move it back to the steps. Hurry. I understand the generaloberst might still have a chance..."

"All right." The bewildered soldier flagged down a colleague and went to work.

"Have you alerted the hospital?" Karl barked at the ambulance driver.

"Yes, sir. Hospital Friedrichshain. Ten minutes with a good escort."

"Good. Back the ambulance to the entrance. I'll organize your escort."

"That's already been done, sir."

"By whom?"

"A major who's been running the show out here all morning. A little guy. I forgot his name but that's his car over there."

"Very well. Warm up your engine. If the generaloberst dies on the way you were driving too slow."

"You, you and you," Wilhelm Jahn shouted. "Get in your cars and pull up to the gate. I want to be at the hospital eight minutes after we hit the street. Move."

After giving his orders to the sluggish group of officers he turned to Karl and Käte. "You and you. Into my car. You, take them."

Erich saluted and ushered mother and son into the back seat of Jahn's stolen Vopo squad car. He slammed the door, circled the car, jumped into the front seat and without looking at his passengers started the engine.

The ambulance backed to the plant entrance. A muffled cheer came from the people as a stretcher appeared. Bülow was underneath a white sheet, bouncing with each step of his bearers. His huge chest towered above his head and legs, giving him the appearance of awesome physical vitality even in death. Karl looked away.

Jahn got into the passenger seat. "Drive."

Erich engaged the clutch and crept cautiously ahead.

"Faster," Jahn ordered. "Use your horn."

Erich nodded and cut a blaring path through the throng. After a moment's hesitation the others followed—six cars and an ambulance, a procession of howling sirens and flashing lights. The gate had been opened, but a line of Vopos with submachine guns stood blocking the exit. One last check.

"*Go,*" Jahn ordered. "Foot to the floor."

The squad car lurched ahead; the guards dove for cover. By the time they'd struggled back to their feet the whole motorcade had roared through the gate, squealed left on Eisenstrasse and headed for the Spree river bridge.

The bridge was only several hundred feet from the plant. Two tanks had stopped just in front of it, closing it to all automobile traffic. Erich screeched to a halt underneath the cannon of the first tank and laid on the horn. The motorcade pulled up tight behind him. Several officers jumped out. The commander of the tank opened the hatch and looked down.

"Get these things out of the way," Jahn shouted. "Bülow's been hurt, we're trying to get him to Friedrichshain."

The commander yelled something back about orders, and a jurisdictional dispute ensued. "I'll have to radio for permission," the commander finally said.

Käte, trying to keep calm, looked abstractedly at the line of cars parked on the grass shoulder to their right. Her eyes seemed drawn to the window of a black Wartburg. The face she had seen in the corridor of the plant, the face that had stared up at her from the iridescent surface of the Baltic, now looked back at her—tranquil, almost friendly. She clutched at Karl's arm.

"What's wrong?" he said, his attention focused on the tanks.

"That man . . ."

Karl looked at her. "What is it?"

"That man . . . I saw him in the plant on Saturday. That's him. Don't let him see you're looking. Over there in that black Wartburg." She glanced at him again, hoping her mind had been playing tricks on her. The man smiled pleasantly, as though she were an old friend.

"Erich," Karl said, recognizing now that it was Kammer, whom he'd met once with Bülow. "Kammer's here. To your right in the Wartburg."

"What?" Erich looked in his mirror. "*That's* Kammer?"

"Yes."

Jahn got back inside the car.

"Frassek says that's Kammer over there," Erich told him.

Jahn did not look around. "Some luck."

"What are we going to do?"

"Back up," Jahn told him. "The tanks are coming forward to let us on to the bridge."

"But, Wilhelm—"

"Just *drive*. This is not time to panic."

Erich nodded, stuck his head out the window and signaled the other cars. The motorcade pulled back twenty feet and stopped. The tanks pivoted directly in front of Jahn's car and rumbled away from the bridge. Erich pressed the gas pedal to the floor. Karl and Käte watched through the back window as Kammer's turbocharged car slipped effortlessly into the speeding procession.

Beside them an S-Bahn train clattered over the river, rolling in the opposite direction, slowing for the Treptower Park station. It was the Number Five, the train Käte had taken every day from Pankow to VEB-Elektro.

She took Karl's hand in hers and squeezed it, looking at him as was her way—directly but tenderly. "I'm sorry, darling. I should never have let you get involved. I'm afraid this is the end, we're going to—"

"Quiet," Jahn said. "You're not going to anything. Not now... Faster, Erich. Damn it, *faster*..."

CHAPTER THIRTY

Near the Stadium of World Youth is a subway station of the same name. Like the other stations along the eastern leg of the Number Six it has been closed for many years. The Stadium of World Youth station is less than four hundred yards from the Wall and West Berlin.

On the morning of December 9 a lone Vopo guard walked the platform of the defunct station, glancing impatiently at the faded dial of the big railway clock. It was almost eleven. Soon his colleague would arrive. He did not particularly care for Hugo, but it got damned lonely down in that damp, deserted cavern. Lonely enough to make him long for company—even Hugo's.

Five years, and he'd yet to witness an escape attempt. He wondered why the Vopo wasted its manpower on the post. There was no possible escape to the West anyway, with or without guards. It took two keys just to get inside. And if somebody managed to get inside, so what? There were too many high-tension wires for anybody to run down the subway tunnel, even if he was a tightrope walker. And nobody could get out by train. The trains didn't stop, and if the fool tried to cling to the outside of one of the coaches the concrete scrapers on the tunnel walls would make quick work of him. And if a train did stop? Well, in that case the sensors in the track would make sure it didn't roll another foot. Even he, a guard on the border of the police state, couldn't get to the West from here...

A train roared through the station, wheels screeching, couplings clanking. For a moment the Vopo guard imagined he heard something behind him...a tapping that seemed to come from deep inside the concrete station wall...He hurried to the spot, put an ear to the concrete. Nothing. God in heaven, was he starting to hear things? That's what happened to old Fritz. He started hearing things—little noises at first, then bigger and bigger ones until he couldn't take it any longer. He'd jumped down onto the tracks and ended up crisp as bacon...

Another train rumbled by. Again the guard heard the tapping. *Verdammt*. He was going to have to speak with the boss right away. He'd request a job with a little more activity, maybe even a little more danger. Anything to keep from going out of his mind...

Clay and two of Jahn's men worked inside the narrow tunnel, chiseling holes into the station wall for half a dozen charges. The work was tedious: they could only chisel when a train was passing. Worse, they were forced to work in total darkness. Light might find its way through the cracks and pores in the concrete, alerting the guard in the station. Käte and Karl were due any minute. Clay tried not to think about his options if they should fail to show.

In the park bordering the entrance to the station, Andreas Dengler lit a cigarette, pulled up the collar of his overcoat against the cold and took out the previous day's *Neues Deutschland*. He continued to watch the street over the top of his newspaper.

For two weeks Andreas had observed the comings and goings of the Vopo guards who worked in the station. He knew that a second wachtmeister would soon arrive to join the man already underneath the street. Overlapping shifts. Probably helped keep them sane, he thought.

At five after eleven the wachtmeister appeared on the corner. As he turned to descend the stairs leading to the locked station doors Andreas overtook him.

"Officer, come quickly, a horrible thing has happened. There's been a murder in that building across the street."

"What?"

"A murder. *Come*. They sent me to find a policeman."

Andreas ran across the street. The wachtmeister followed, if a bit reluctantly. "Quickly," Jahn's man said at the entrance to the apartment building. "It just happened a few minutes ago."

Andreas opened the cellar door and led the Vopo down a staircase covered with coal dust. "Here, to your left."

As the wachtmeister saw nothing and turned to protest, Andreas plunged a butcher knife that he'd hidden beneath his coat into the man's solar plexus and guided it upward toward his heart...Five minutes later he emerged from the alley exit of the building in full Vopo dress. The keys to the station were in his pocket, and he was armed with the standard automatic rifle. He circled back through the park, unobtrusively descended the station steps and unlocked both sets of sturdy metal doors.

Inside the dank, dimly lit passageway he paused to catch his breath. Rust-colored water stains drooped down the tile walls. Cigarette butts and newspapers yellow with time littered the floor. He followed the passageway to its intersection with the platform. The station clock pointed to 11:19. Better get this matter handled before the guard reports his colleague's tardiness. He strode on to the platform. The guard did not notice him, crouched as he was beside the station wall in a dark corner, his ear pressed attentively to the concrete. Andreas smiled. He liked easy jobs. He continued forward, the rifle slung casually over his shoulder. Get close. Make clean work of it.

A train arrived with a clattering roar and tumble of lights. To Andreas's surprise the guard remained in his crouched position with his ear to the wall. As the last coach of the train disappeared down the dark tunnel, the guard stood, scratching his head.

Andreas raised his rifle and directed a short burst of fire. The guard slammed into the wall, slumped to the floor, never having seen his killer.

Knocking his rifle butt near the spot on the wall that had attracted the guard's attention, Andreas alerted the others that the way was clear.

273

Three dull thuds came back in response. Then the chisel returned to work with a staccato of sharp blows.

Andreas dragged the body to the stationmaster's booth and stuffed it inside. He stepped to the edge of the platform and walked its full length, keeping an eye on the spot where the other resisters would break through the wall. It was hidden from the passing trains by two thick pillars and the dark shadows they cast. Even in the event of bad timing it should do...

When the next train roared by Andreas was standing in the shadows himself, a cigarette hanging from his lips in characteristic Vopo fashion, a foot propped nonchalantly on a bench.

Clay's back ached and his hands throbbed from a grueling night of physical labor, but he felt strong. A lantern made his work progress more rapidly. Not long after Andreas had given the "all clear" signal he put down the hammer and chisel and smiled at his two companions. "Well, gents, there it is, the work of a craftsman. Now see if they'll fit."

The men inserted small cylinders of explosives in the holes he had fashioned and began attaching detonation wires. The sound of heavy breathing in the tunnel made them stop and look around.

A wiry young man emerged from the blackness, crawling swiftly on his hands and knees. When he reached the widening in the tunnel he stopped and sat with his back against the earth, sputtering. "They *did* it! And on national TV..."

Clay and the others embraced, backslapping. "Are they all right?" asked Clay, who had crawled near enough to grab the messenger by the arm.

"So far. We've had two sightings from our people. They're at the head of the motorcade escorting Bülow's ambulance—"

"He's not dead?" one of the men asked.

"Of course he's dead," Clay said. "I told you about the injection. When do they get here?"

"There are complications... Kammer's car seems to be in the procession with them."

"Who the hell is Kammer?" Clay asked.

274

"Who is Kammer? You're making a revolution and you don't know who Kammer is?"

Clay's digging companion said, "He's an American, a friend of Mühlendorff. He brought the last batch of stories in from the West. Clay, Kammer is the head of the Stasi."

"God...you mean to tell me the head of the Stasi is after them?"

"Possibly."

"What the hell are we going to do?"

"We can't do anything, it's in Jahn's hands."

Clay leaned back against the dirt wall and closed his eyes. Fear for Käte and Karl took hold of his gut. He could face anything except the notion that the lifelong dream of bringing her out was slipping away.

Led by Erich, the motorcade careered down the drab boulevards of the capital, a fury of lights and sirens, revving engines and screeching tires. Erich spent as much time watching the rearview mirror as the road, fantasizing that something would go wrong with Kammer's turbocharged Wartburg and wanting to make his move as soon as it did.

Karl and Käte sat in silence in the back seat knowing that Kammer knew, that the Stasi was waiting for them somewhere.

"Fake engine trouble at Leninplatz," Jahn ordered. "Pull over, I'll get out and raise the hood while you signal the others past."

Erich lifted his foot from the accelerator, then hammered it up and down. The car jerked spasmodically. The squad car directly behind almost plowed into them. Brakes squealed, horns blared and headlights flashed as the chain reaction rippled toward the rear of the motorcade.

Erich signaled the angry driver behind him to go on as he brought his own car to a stop at curbside. Jahn rushed out to the hood, flung it open and buried his head in the engine compartment. The ambulance passed with a swish of air, followed by Kammer's black Wartburg. They held their breath to see if it would slow down. It did not! Käte squeezed Karl's hand, almost risked a smile.

Jahn got back into the car. "Left on Lenin Allee, full throttle."

They squealed around the square and headed west. Karl and Käte twisted to peer out the rear window. It actually seemed as though their ploy had worked...But the black Wartburg soon returned to where

275

they'd stopped, slowed, then came on after them once again. Its acceleration was phenomenal. In a matter of seconds it was in its previous holding pattern a mere hundred yards back.

Jahn turned to Käte, leaning over the front seat to get closer. He looked very serious. "Käte, we mustn't give up. You're going to need all your wits about you to jump on to that subway. But...we must also be prepared. Should something go wrong...if, for example, you should be trapped in the station—"

"Yes, I understand. What do you suggest?"

Karl began to protest, then turned away. Without further words Jahn opened his ammunition clip and handed Käte two of the tiny plastic cylinders containing the syringes. "The one with the white cap is the antidote—"

"I'll take that one," Karl said.

Käte stuffed the syringe in her pocket. "All right, enough talk about getting caught," she said. "What now?"

Jahn had no time to answer. "He's pulling closer," Erich shouted. "Shall we fire at him?"

"No," Jahn told him. "You can be sure the car is bulletproof. Go north on Brunnenstrasse. Just past the Hungarian restaurant is an alley. Turn in. Karl, Käte...as soon as we're out of sight the three of us will get down low. If Kammer thinks we've left the car he'll stop. Maybe we'll be able to lose him then. If not, Erich, take us home. We'll jump out at the courtyard. If he's followed you once after our heads have disappeared he'll follow you again."

"Which will leave him chasing *me*."

"I have faith in you, Erich. Hang on. Two hundred yards to the alley."

The car lurched wildly in the turn. "Now," shouted Jahn. "Get *down*." Karl, Käte and the resistance leader crouched low while the car skidded down the alley, sideswiping a row of garbage cans. The car bounced over the potholes and burst onto a main street. As Erich turned he caught a glimpse in his mirror of the Stasi Wartburg nosing into the alley. A series of loud crashes followed as it slammed into the rolling garbage cans.

"Good work, stay down," Jahn said.

"*Verdammt, verdammt,*" Erich was muttering. He had covered two hundred yards without encountering an intersection, when Kammer's car careened out of the alley and roared after them.

"He's still there, like glue."

"Never mind," Jahn said. "Everyone up."

They got upright as Erich heaved the car into a sharp turn. The smell of burning rubber struck in their nostrils.

"Erich," Jahn said, "better take us direct. If we blow a tire..."

"Right, hang on, a couple more turns and we're there."

"Listen carefully," Jahn said. "We three will be exiting to our right. When Erich says go, jump out. You'll be less than twenty feet from the apartment door."

Käte nodded, took hold of her son's hand and squeezed it as though she would never let go.

"He's gone crazy," Major Enno Obermeyer said to Kammer. The sleek Wartburg skidded through a right-angle turn, knocking over a pushcart and breaking up a small curbside gathering of citizens who had come out to talk about the assassination.

"Easy," Kammer told him. "The distance is not important so long as you don't lose them. Is the gas ready?"

"Yes, sir." Major Hans-Jürgen Kiefer patted the launcher lying on his lap, then slipped one of the green metal canisters into position.

"How many canisters do we have?"

"Four."

"That should be more than adequate," the Stasi chief said.

The car again lurched as Obermeyer fought to keep up with the resistance driver ahead. "Crazy," he mumbled.

"Relax, Enno, they're not going anywhere," Kammer told him.

"What if they don't go inside a building?" asked Kiefer. "What if they get out and run?"

"They won't. They're not fools. Just foolish, and misguided."

Obermeyer whipped through a sharp turn just in time to see Erich's car slide broadside into another alley.

"Go," yelled Erich. Karl hit the ground on his stomach. Käte landed on top of him. The gravel thrown up by the wheels as Erich sped away fell on them like hailstones. Just ahead a colleague stood holding the

door open. The Frasseks scrambled to their feet, reaching the apartment house at the same moment as Jahn. The heavy door slammed shut. Jahn remained at the peephole. The black Wartburg nosed into the courtyard, an ominous intruder, slowed as though about to stop, then sped on after Erich.

"Into the tunnel," ordered Jahn. "MOVE. I caught a glimpse of the launcher. He's got gas."

The word spread among them...*gas.* They knew about the stuff Kammer's people used...instant temporary paralysis. When you recovered you were in the hands of a Stasi "persuasion" team. Death, certainly, was preferable. A ten-man stampede toward the tunnel, until Jahn, standing at the basement entrance, converted it into a more orderly flight...

"Turn around," ordered Kammer. "He dumped them."

"How do you know, sir?"

"Rear springs. Hurry."

Two minutes later they glided into the courtyard again. Kiefer rolled down his window just enough to stick out the launcher.

"Shoot," Kammer ordered.

The first bomb smashed through a ground-floor window.

"Now the fourth story," Kammer ordered.

Keifer jumped out of the car, wary of gunfire, took cover behind a fender and fired. Pieces of glass fell on to the stones below, tinkling like chimes.

"Second story."

"Right, sir."

"Enno," Kammer said, "get the masks ready. I want this business concluded quickly. We'll get Mühlendorff out first, then bring a truck from Lichtenberg for the others. It's getting on to lunchtime."

"A celebration lunch, sir."

"Third story..."

"Yes, sir," Kiefer called from outside.

"...And you're right, Enno. It will be a good lunch. There's said to be a fine country tavern outside Dresden. We'll make a little trip down there in the company jet."

"With Mühlendorff, sir?"

"Yes. It will be better to get her out of Berlin."

Kiefer jumped into the car with the launcher. "All floors purified, sir."

"Good, Hans-Jürgen. Thank you. Shall we have a look around?"

When the first gas bomb crashed through the kitchen window of Apartment 2, Jahn was the only one still in the building. He heard the glass break, heard the hiss. He quickly went into the tunnel entrance and crawled as fast as he could. He knew it would only be a matter of seconds until the gas seeped into the tunnel and rendered them all helpless. He was glad he'd planted five hundred pounds of explosives in the earth above...

He counted under his breath as he crawled. Thousand-two, thousand-three, thousand-four. The phosphorescent handle of the detonator glowed in front of him in the darkness. Now he yanked it from its mount on the earthen wall and pulled out the safety with his teeth. Thousand-six, thousand-seven. He must reach the first bend in the tunnel if he was to avoid a living burial. As he plunged ahead his knee landed on the wire trailing from the detonator—the wire that ran to the massive charges above. The faint snap told him he had broken a connection. Thousand-nine, thousand-ten. Stay calm. Light a match. Find the severed connection. Thousand-eleven, thousand-twelve, thousand-thirteen. You've got to hold it with both hands. Ten feet to the bend. Too far. Better stay put. If the gas gets in everybody is lost. Thousand-sixteen, thousand-seventeen. No more time. Bring down the earth. Maybe you can make it...

He held the wire and match in one hand, the detonator in the other. Touching the wire to the severed connection he pressed the "Fire" button with his chin. A violent explosion smashed him into the mud. An enormous mass of earth landed in front of him. Behind him, the entire ceiling came down with a deep, ominous thud. He lunged ahead, squeezing between the tunnel wall and the fallen mass while the ceiling delivered a burst of stone and dirt. Another explosion erupted, closer than the first. He heaved himself forward toward the bend. Too late. His head collided with a slab of ceiling on its way down. A ton of earth fell on his legs, pinning him.

He was able to light a match, ignoring the fissure in the sagging roof six inches above his skull. 11:39. They had missed the first train, but should be on the platform for the second. Jump straight, Käte. See that you jump straight, my brave Hannah...

Clay held her tightly in his arms. The charges closing the tunnel had just gone off, sending tremors through the earth and a blast of air into the widening beside the subway wall.

"My God, was he through yet?"

"I'll go check," Karl told her.

"No," the messenger told him. "If you miss your train, there won't be another. Not ever."

A man arrived at the widening, his face twisted with grief. "Come on. Jahn's buried."

Ten men crawled off in silence while Karl and Clay tried to keep Käte calm. The day was beginning to take its toll.

Kammer ripped off his gas mask as soon as they were back inside the car. "Enno," he said, "please drive to the Friedrichstrasse station."

"What sir?"

"Bahnhof Friedrichstrasse, please."

Obermeyer drove the car into a driveway and turned around. "I don't—"

"How long a journey?" interrupted Kammer.

"Ten minutes."

"You've got five. You saw that tunnel entrance. She's down in the Stadium of World Youth station. I don't believe she plans to stay."

"But, sir," Obermeyer said, "can't you just phone ahead and have the stationmaster shut down the net?"

"Certainly I can, Enno. But you forget our dilemma. If others learn we are on her trail so soon after the assassination they will make certain unfortunate assumptions..."

"Such as, sir?" Kiefer asked as they sped down a broad boulevard.

Obermeyer was smiling as he passed a truck at ninety miles an hour. "They will assume, comrade major, such things as that our chief knew who Hannah Mühlendorff was long before the assassination, that he allowed her to strike in order to get rid of Generaloberst Bülow."

Kiefer nodded. "Even our party chairman might assume such things, which could be damned unfortunate..."

Kammer merely said, "Gentlemen, it's true, people can be cruel in their suspicions...so I trust you both understand how important it is to keep such notions to yourselves. We'll get her today, no question. The essential thing is that only the three of us know about her capture. Then in a few weeks we'll arrange for one of our less gifted agents to make a sensational arrest. Meanwhile, she will come to understand that her future is with us at State Security. We must restore order in this country, and our task will be less difficult with the aid of Mühlendorff. And so my insistence, gentlemen, that we not only take her secretly— but take her unharmed...

"And, Enno, Hans-Jürgen, I wish to make clear that if a word of this *ever* gets out, I shall be obliged to kill you. This would, of course, be distasteful to me, but I would have no sensible alternative."

"Don't worry, sir," said Obermeyer, who was already warming to the prospect of a foray into West Berlin. "It would clearly not be sensible for us to talk."

"I'm glad you understand," said Kammer. "Do you both have your Western papers?"

"Yes, sir," said Kiefer happily. "We never doubted we would be using them."

It was 11:44 when the Stasi trio reached the Friedrichstrasse station. They inserted their cards and typed in their personal codes at the special Stasi entrance, bypassing the Vopo checkpoint and arriving on the platform anonymously. The Number Six arrived at 11:49. Kammer had already studied the subway schedule in the car. He knew that this train would be the first to pass through the Stadium of World Youth station since the resisters had climbed into the tunnel. So one thing was certain: he would get to West Berlin ahead of her. Or at least at the same time.

CHAPTER THIRTY—ONE

Karl and Käte changed into the civilian clothes the resisters had brought them. Karl handed his revolver to the messenger. "I shouldn't be needing this," he said. "Put it to good use." He took his mother's arm, turned her away from her silent vigil, gazing down the tunnel. But no Wilhelm Jahn appeared. Miracles were in short supply.

The messenger called out for everyone to stand back, that it was time to blow the wall.

The explosives shook the earth and filled the tunnel with acrid smoke. Käte opened her eyes on a gaping hole in the station wall. A "Vopo" stuck his head into their lair. Käte put her hand over her mouth and started backward, reacting instinctively.

Andreas in the Vopo uniform shook hands all around, looked at Käte with admiration, told her there was no time, she'd better get going. She nodded, accepting finally that Jahn was not coming, and climbed quickly down, helped by Andreas.

"You'd better get in position by the tracks," Andreas told her. "Stand about fifty feet from the front of the station. I'll put the other two behind you at forty-foot intervals. The trains are still running and they're on time. You have about two minutes."

She walked across the cracked and littered concrete. Behind her the resisters who'd gone to look for Jahn scurried out of the hole and hid themselves in the long corridor. They would wait inside the station until Käte, Karl and Clay had been aboard the train long enough to cross the border, then they would rush out on to the street, where two dozen resisters waited to help in their getaway...

A faint rumbling became audible on the platform. Clay glanced at Käte. She was alarmingly pale, but after all she'd been through, he had to believe she'd hold up. No matter what, she had a way of pulling herself together when she had to. "Don't forget to lead the door," he called to her.

The rumble grew rapidly, swelling to a roar that echoed in their ears and shook the concrete beneath their feet. The train's headlight exploded in the dark stretch of tunnel leading into the station. Fat sheaths of wiring writhed in the dancing light. The old rails lit up with silver gleam, signaling the train's approach. And then it was on them—a thousand tons of metal that mocked their soft flesh and fragile bones.

The first two cars were already past...Käte seemed frozen as she watched the passing patterns of glass and metal—window, window, door, window, window, door, window, window, door...She could see people in the coaches waving their arms at her, make out the word "jump" on their lips. Window, window, door, window, window, door, window, window...In her peripheral vision she saw the empty station unfolding behind the train. The last car was approaching. Panic hit her at last, a panic she had to fight down to time her leap. She broke into a run alongside the train. Window....window...door...window... NOW. She lunged, half-expecting to slam into the side of the coach. But she flew through space, landing with a jolt on her hip and shoulder and sliding across an aisle. Applause, nearby passengers helping her to her feet...everyone talking at once, asking her if she was all right...

"The others?" she managed to gasp out. "Did the others make it?"

People pressed in close, trying to hear what she was saying. Through the cluster of heads she saw activity near the front of the coach. "Anyone jump into this car?" she heard someone yell in an officious voice. "We got two of 'em up front."

The red-faced official now came into view, a subway employee who had unlocked the door joining Käte's coach to the one ahead of it. She saw people pointing in her direction, smiled.

Clayton and Karl were safely aboard.

But her joy was short-lived. Behind the subway official three men in trench coats were pushing their way toward her, explaining something about West German immigration procedures for escapees from the DDR. The eyes of the man in charge of the group settled on her. The same man. The one she now knew was Kammer. And he was smiling at her—that same terrible, knowing smile.

She shoved her way toward the rear of the coach, put her hands into her pockets. Yes, she had remembered to transfer the syringe . . . Her left thumbnail sought the cap on the hard plastic container. Whispers, murmurs followed her journey down the aisle. The passengers who moments before had applauded her escape now seemed to want nothing to do with her . . . Why was she running from the West German authorities, was she crazy . . . ?

The cap at last popped free. She bit her lower lip and gradually worked the syringe out of its container, removed the rubber sheath from the needle and, with her hand still in her pocket, rolled the syringe to the edge of her palm. She made a loose fist around it. The plunger was within easy reach of her thumb, the needle protruded just beyond the base of her little finger . . .

The train was very crowded. If she could somehow reach the last set of doors before Kammer and his men caught up with her, she wouldn't need to use the lethal device, if not . . . The brakes came on suddenly, causing her to bump into several people preparing to get off. She muttered apologies, shoving her way ahead. The doors opened on a world of polished tiles and brightly colored advertisements. The *West*. She tried to move faster, but the wall of passengers in front of her was impenetrable, and a fat woman with active elbows was trying to board before everyone had gotten off. Seconds ticked by with agonizing slowness. Between two tall heads blocking her path she could see Karl and Clayton running through the crush looking for her. She was moving forward again, but so slowly . . . A few more steps and she would be out, yet she knew even before it happened that she would not make it.

Powerful hands caught her from behind. More hands searched her for a gun. A white handkerchief found its way into her mouth and prevented her from uttering a sound. An efficient, silent force pulled her unobtrusively backward through the flow of descending passengers. She got one last glance of Clay and Karl. They had spotted her, she'd seen raw horror wipe out their smiles of a moment before.

Kammer's men pushed her into her seat so smoothly that no one seemed to notice, and those who did merely assumed Immigration was doing its job, if a bit overzealously. There was a sickening hiss. The doors slammed shut, and the train sped out of the station.

Karl and Clay passed a moment of stunned silence on the platform, as though mesmerized by the red taillights of the train retreating into the black tunnel. Then they gathered themselves and broke into a run toward the station exit.

"Is someone waiting?" Karl shouted.

"They'd better be."

Father and son burst out into the hubbub of the busy metropolis. The black Mercedes limousine was across the street. Clay pointed. Karl led the way into the dense traffic, waving angry motorists to a halt.

"Wedding Bahnhof," Clay said as they jumped into the back seat. "Step on it . . . those track repairs still going on between here and there?"

"Far as I know, Herr doktor."

"We've got to intercept the train we just got off."

The driver merged into the flow of cars and buses, accelerated a bit, weaving expertly in and out of the traffic. "Big risks involved, Herr doktor. Insurance, speeding tickets, chauffeur's license. I'll have to add five hundred—"

"Five thousand if we beat the train."

"Well, Herr doktor, in that case . . ." The big engine came to full life.

"Have you got the packages from Ursula Landau?"

"Of course, Herr doktor. Frau vize-präsidentin made sure of it."

"All right, good. Now listen, keep the engine running when we get out at the station . . ."

Kammer sat directly across from Käte. She was slumped slightly forward, kneading her loose left fist with the fingers of her right hand,

286

a distraught woman wringing her hands, praying, imploring God. She appeared too devastated to speak or even to look into Kammer's penetrating gaze. Standing beside them were Kiefer and Obermeyer.

"Allow me to congratulate you," said the Stasi chief in his quiet, silky voice. He shuffled through a stack of newspapers he had lifted from the vacant seats beside him. "I admire your professionalism, however misdirected. I assume you know who I am..."

She did not speak, did not look at him. He went on. "Now, Frau Frassek, we haven't much time. I want to make you an offer. I very much hope you will accept, because otherwise I will be forced to kill you between here and the next stop. This does not serve our purpose as well as I would like. And it certainly does not serve yours."

She lifted her eyes to his, as though she were mildly interested.

"I have been studying you for some time," he said. "What I have learned, Frau Frassek, is much to my liking. You are a woman of science, a modern, rational woman..."

Käte felt the train slow, knew it was too soon for the station. From the corner of her eye she could see laborers at work on the tracks. The blue flame of a welding torch flickered eerily on the dark tunnel walls.

"Now, Frau Frassek, the four of us are going to get off the subway at the next station. We shall be taken back to East Berlin by my men here in the West. You have nothing to fear. This is the Stasi, I am not like Bülow. We could, of course, stage a showcase trial. We could force you to make a public apology before sentencing you to death. But these things are of little lasting value. Frau Frassek, I want you to join my organization. I am going to give you the opportunity to atone in the best possible way... You will work with me for five years or until the back of the disruptive underground in our country is broken—whichever comes first. Then you will be quite free to go to the West. And we need never reveal to the East German people that Hannah Mühlendorff has been caught."

The subway stopped deep inside the tunnel. A train moving in the opposite direction swayed by close enough to touch. A bright collage of faces tumbled past, people secure and confident, knowing where they were headed.

"I understand it will distasteful for you to work against your friends. But surely it will not be as distasteful as your alternatives. Rational people like you and me, Frau Frassek, do not, in the end, die for causes. And we do not sentimentally sacrifice ourselves for personal attachments. That would be destructive self-indulgence. You will be comfortable with us, and your work will be intellectually challenging."

The train crept forward, shuddering over a stretch of temporary track. She looked at him directly now. His everlasting smile made her want to scream.

Now he was saying, "I'm afraid our time is up. I must ask you for your decision."

Käte extended her right hand. He took it in his—a soft hand almost feminine in its delicacy. In a quick and precise motion she slammed her left fist down on his thigh. He jerked his leg back and twisted, but there was little room for movement in the cramped seat. By the time he was able to tear her hand loose, the syringe was empty. It remained stuck in his thigh like the stinger of an insect, spent and quivering. Obermeyer and Kiefer quickly took hold of her, unsure what to do.

"You'd better let *me* talk now," she said, surprised by the strength in her voice. "Herr Kammer, if *you* wish to live, you will tell your men to take their hands from me. I can save *your* life, but it will require the cooperation of all three of you."

"Enno, Hans-Jürgen, we shall listen briefly." The smile began to fade, and Käte could discern the first traces of fear beneath the slick cadence of his words.

"You have been injected with a lethal dose of curare," she told him. "I'm sure you know what curare is. The antidote is with my son and his father, the two men you no doubt saw jump onto the train ahead of me. They know what happened to me. They were near the subway door when you stopped me. I expect them to arrive at the next station by the time we get there—"

"She's bluffing," Obermeyer said.

"No." Kammer, sniffing the syringe that he had gingerly lifted from his thigh, added, "No, I don't believe she is." He turned in his seat, abruptly pulled a pistol from his breast pocket and draped one of the papers on his lap over it. "Enno, Hans-Jürgen . . . your revolvers . . . put them down here beside me. Quickly."

"But, sir—"

"Now."

288

They did as they were told. Kammer covered their weapons with a second newspaper.

"Sir, I don't understand. Why—"

"Because, Enno, it would, as Frau Frassek has no doubt realized, make sense for you two to let me die. You could then take Mühlendorff back yourselves and collect the rewards. Gentlemen, move to the front exit of the coach. It seems the time has come for us to go our separate ways. I'm sorry—"

"Sir," Kiefer said, backing into the aisle, "you must save yourself. And we'll go to our people in West Berlin. That way . . . all our interests can be served."

Käte listened uneasily. There was nothing she could do to prevent Kammer's two subordinates from activating the notorious Stasi operation in West Berlin. For now, Kammer himself must be her only concern. As long as he held his gun, her own life was still in danger.

"Your pistol remains a problem, Herr Kammer," she said when the others were twenty feet down the aisle.

"And so it will until I have the antidote, Frau Frassek. Don't make the mistake of assuming our little chess game is over. And one more detail . . . if I feel myself beginning to fall under the effects of the drug *before* you have filled your part of the bargain, I shall be obliged to pull the trigger."

"Stand up," she said. "Walk to the rear exit and prepare to get off. Your time is running out—"

"Our time, Frau Frassek." He put his gun in his trench coat pocket but kept it pointed at her through the material.

The train swung into the bright station and stopped. The doors hissed open. Kammer pushed Käte ahead of him down the steps, holding her firmly by the shoulder . . . She spotted Karl and Clay running down the station stairs and called out. Clay waved back as he and Karl disappeared into the crowd.

Kammer guided her toward a fat steel pillar, turned around and leaned against it. He tightened his grip on her shoulder, shoved the barrel of the gun into her spine. Karl and Clay were running toward her, until Kammer's words stopped them. "Another step and I will kill her."

"Does he have a gun?"

"Yes, Karl...I injected him in the thigh with curare almost two minutes ago. Show him the antidote."

Karl rummaged through his pockets and produced the plastic container. Clay snatched it from his fingers, took out the syringe and removed the rubber sheath. "Neostigmine," he said. "You drool a lot, but it works."

Kammer nodded. "You will inject me immediately, Herr Doktor Bentley."

"I will when we've worked out an exchange. Right now you could shoot all three of us after I've given you the antidote."

"You think I want to spend the rest of my life in a Western jail for killing you? Inject me. *Now...*"

Clay toyed with the syringe. "You still have time, you're not showing the symptoms yet."

"The instant I feel anything I shoot."

Clay ignored him. "Käte, Karl, what this man knows and you maybe don't is that he's immune to justice in the West as well as the East. There's nothing Western intelligence would like more than to have this man on their side. He can shoot us with impunity, go down in history as the man who finally solved the Mühlendorff riddle—and go to work tomorrow morning for the Federal Republic. Better computers, bigger villas, BMW's instead of Wartburgs, a higher salary—"

Kammer took a step forward, pushing Käte in front of him. "Enough of your nonsense..." His eyelids drooped eerily as the curare began to take effect. Bright red hives appeared on his face. "You've ten seconds before I shoot..."

Clay put the syringe back in its container and pitched it into the crowd. "And you have roughly the same amount of time to save yourself."

Kammer looked at him in disbelief. For an instant he hesitated, watching the cylinder roll beneath an army of feet. Then he abruptly let Käte go and rushed ahead. A teenage girl picked up the bizarre object, examined it. "Give that to me," Kammer shouted at her. "Give ...tha—"

The girl gaped, bewildered, as the Stasi chief strangled on his words and collapsed at her feet, his hives going from red to purple.

She began to scream for help, and the crowd closed around the stricken man. The Frasseks and Clay circled behind the tumult. Clay helped Käte climb the long staircase and led her into the waiting limousine.

Käte fought to catch her breath. "Clayton, the other two ... they'll alert the Stasi undercover people here ..."

Clay busied himself giving the chauffeur orders to take side streets to Ursula's bank, pretended not to hear her.

"Clayton, do you think we'll ever get out of West Berlin ...?"

He still didn't answer.

"Don't worry," said Hegel, director of Stasi undercover activities in West Berlin, into his telephone. "No, no, Major Obermeyer, it will be all right. You say you got the license number of the limousine. Very good. And even if you hadn't we would still have solved the problem. Yes, well, thank you, a fine job. Good-bye for now ..."

And on the other end of the line Obermeyer hung up the pay phone receiver, checked the change slot for a possible overflow of Western wealth and winked at his colleague. "He congratulated me. And we're in luck, Hans-Jürgen. They're obviously not going to take a train or car out. That would mean reentering the DDR. Which leaves the airways. Tegel Airport will be covered in five minutes. We're to head for the American military airport at Tempelhof. Hegel told me he's coming with a large contingent of men. That, obviously, is where he expects her to show up."

CHAPTER THIRTY—TWO

"How do I get privacy?" Clay said to the driver. Käte and Karl were sitting opposite him on the car's velour bench.

"On your right, Herr Doktor, you will find a little black door. Open it. The first button deactivates the microphone contact between us. The second, third and fourth will give you visual privacy."

Clay pressed all the buttons. Louvered blinds on the side and rear windows rotated shut with a small motor-induced hum. Ceiling lights came on. A gray curtain separating them from the driver descended electronically as they moved through the busy city.

Karl lifted the edge of a blind to peek out. He saw an old tower whose gold-armed clock pointed to 12:20. How was it possible? Less than thirty minutes had passed since they had jumped onto the train. That dark and cracked platform beneath the Stadium of World Youth seemed a lifetime away.

Clay looked into one of the boxes stored beneath his seat and handed it to Käte. "Do you mind changing? For lunch?"

She reached over and dug her nails into his wrist. "Clayton, have you lost your head? By now all of Kammer's West Berlin undercover people are looking for us, and you talk about clothes...I thought you said there would be a plane waiting for us at the American airport."

"There is, Käte, but I'm worried the airport is surrounded by Stasi. We need some time to think things through. And the fancy duds are at least a sort of disguise. Make us look less like who we are and where we've been. Okay?"

Karl had already spread his new clothes out on the seat. "Clayton's right, mother." He held up a navy-blue Rodier blazer.

Käte shook her head, shrugged. "New clothes...? Okay, okay," and she allowed a smile as she unwrapped a white silk blouse and spread out a tweed suit on her lap.

Once they'd changed, Karl saw his mother as he'd almost forgotten she could be, and Clay could only stare and shake his head in admiration.

The driver tapped on the curtained window as he stopped. He came around to curbside and opened their doors. They hurried into the bank. The driver watched them, amazed...three very strange, very well-dressed people with dirty hands, going into a bank. He climbed back behind the wheel, figuring he'd seen it all.

"Ursula," Käte was saying, "you never told me you were a vice-president." Tears were still in her eyes from their reunion that she'd never allowed herself to think would actually happen.

"I was afraid you'd think I was bragging...oh God, Käte, you've been through so much—"

"More than you realize," Clay said, "and Karl too. Karl, tell her about it—" Käte shook her head emphatically. "No. Not yet. We've a long way to go still..."

And the memory of Jahn was too fresh. Of course Ursula knew nothing about her real work, what she had done or why this was the moment she'd been asked to help them escape to America.

"I've arranged for us to use the executive dining room," Ursula was saying.

"That was thoughtful of you," said Clay, "but we'd better stay here in your office." He leaned over to her. His face was tense. "Hannah Mühlendorff needs privacy, and she needs to get out of Berlin..."

"*What?* Käte, what is he saying?"

"He's saying," Karl told her, "that my mother is Hannah Mühlendorff, and that the whole Stasi net in West Berlin is looking for her."

Ursula shook her head. "My God ... I can't believe it ... Käte, you ... and that general who was killed in the DDR this morning? They showed it all over the country on TV ... you managed *that?* Käte, I've known you since you were twelve, and you, Karl, since you were in diapers. You two aren't capable of—"

"Please, that's enough," Käte said. "Clay told you we have to get out of Berlin. The Stasi followed us to the Wedding Bahnhof. They were on foot but I'm sure they got the limousine license number."

"Ursula," Clay said, "I have a plane waiting for us at Tempelhof. A military transport. I mentioned the possibility of an armored bank truck earlier but I don't think that would be safe. Do any of your rich clients use helicopters?"

"We've got our own," she said.

"Good ... Listen, Ursula, all these Stasi people—I'm not too fond of them. While we're at it we might as well take care of them too—"

"Clayton," Käte said. My God, *enough.*

"Not us, the West Berlin police. All they need to do is find twenty or thirty limousines like the one that delivered us here. Give them license plates with the same number. Make sure they're equipped with bulletproof glass, as I'm sure most of them are. Put three police impostors in each one who vaguely resemble the three of us. Then drive them all toward Tempelhof. It will be like fishing in a hatchery."

Käte's interest stirred in spite of herself. "I suppose it is a good opportunity ... what branch of the police should we contact? Ursula?"

"Well, I've got a client who's a sort of big shot in the department. I'll contact him. Should I tell him Hannah Mühlendorff is here at the bank—?"

"God, no," Clay said. "Tell him your source of information is anonymous. Maybe I've gotten paranoid, but it's possible there could be Stasi informers anywhere—the police, the secret service. At this point we don't need any unnecessary risks."

"I agree, but what do I say if my contact won't listen to me?"

"He will, Ursula. People always listen to their bankers. And seriously, this is a tip they can't afford to pass up."

Ursula went off to make her calls, and was soon back. "All set, the helicopter's on the way. The police too."

Käte looked at her friend. Her new life in the West suddenly loomed as palpable as Clay or Karl. But it was a body without a face or soul. Once again she realized how little she had expected ever to see this day. She looked at Karl. Would he be feeling the same things? He seemed young again, younger than he'd seemed for years, and it struck her that he was happy, at least that some of the terrible burden of being Hannah Mühlendorff's son had been lifted. A young man with a chance to become himself...

"We need to get upstairs right away," Ursula was saying.

Clay, looking at Käte, saw her once again as the beautiful young East German girl he had met in Heinersdorf over twenty years ago. He put his arm around her and kissed her hair.

"Ready to meet some real live American characters?" he asked Karl. "You should get along okay, don't forget you're half-American."

"I'm learning..."

The three of them then made their way toward the elevator while Ursula lingered behind.

The helicopter was perched on the roof of the bank tower. Ursula helped them climb in. "I'll come visit you when you're settled..."

"Where to, Frau vize-präsidentin?" the pilot asked.

"Tempelhof. East end of runway two. There'll be a transport plane waiting. They know you're coming."

"Very well, Frau vize-präsidentin." He closed the door, waited for Ursula to leave the roof and turned to Clay. "Ready?"

"You bet."

The bird whirred upward several hundred feet and tilted forward, joining several other helicopters in the skies above West Berlin. Clay could see the Wall to his left. He looked down at the guards patrolling with dogs, the watchtowers with machine guns, the barren stretch of no-man's-land he knew was sewn with mines. Käte and Karl were holding hands. He wanted to point out to them the noose of police cars already visible around the rapidly approaching airfield but decided they deserved to be left to themselves.

The helicopter touched down minutes later.

The jet transport stood a hundred yards away. Two soldiers in U.S. Air Force uniforms ran toward the helicopter. Clay jumped down and helped Käte to the ground.

"Dr. Clayton Bentley?" asked a black sergeant.

"That's me."

"Well, let's get you on that plane, man. Cap'n Hobart in Frankfurt's been talking all afternoon about some operation you got to do in the morning."

Käte and Karl waited patiently, assuming they would be put through rigorous searches and interrogations. The sergeant nodded at them. "You're coming, too, aren't you?"

"They don't understand much English yet," Clay told the sergeant. "A little school stuff."

"Doesn't make any difference, doc. I'll have your fox speaking English like she's from De-troit time we land in Frankfurt."

Clay nodded, watched the helicopter as it lifted off, then walked with Käte and Karl up the stairs of the transport.

Soon they were airborne. "Are we over the DDR yet?" Karl asked.

"I'm sure we are," said Clay. "Don't worry, this is international airspace. U.S. military passage is guaranteed by—"

The sight of jets interrupted him.

"Your fighter escort," the sergeant said. "That general in Frankfurt, the one whose son you're gonna work on—he's ordered up the whole show. Hey, you must be some kind of doctor, getting all this special treatment."

"Don't know about that." Clay quickly translated the information about the fighters and could see his son's relief. Käte was looking out the window, watching the gray mist dart in nervous tatters past the wing. Clay reached over and took her hand.

"Anyone like a drink?" asked the sergeant. "Not much else to do between here and Frankfurt. Cap'n Hobart's put a bottle of French champagne on board."

Käte glanced at him, not sure she understood.

"*Etwas zu trinken?*" the sergeant said, his accent strongly American. Käte nodded and thanked him.

297

The transport rose above the clouds, and suddenly the world was a place of beauty, pristine and immense. The two F-15s from Tempelhof swept in close. Käte waved.

When the sergeant came back, he brought not only champagne but news from the cockpit that they had just flown over the West German border. The two fighters wagged their wings, banked sharply and disappeared into the blue. The sergeant opened the bottle of champagne and filled four paper cups. "To good people," he said.

They all clicked glasses, but said nothing. Words couldn't fit the moment.

EPILOGUE

East Berlin, February

The blizzard had intensified all day, bringing traffic to a standstill. On Alexanderplatz the drifts looked like Baltic dunes. Vopos huddled in pairs, stomping their feet to keep warm and tapping the ice from their automatic rifles. The crowds moved in silence beneath the steam of a thousand breaths.

The late Wilhelm Jahn's colleague, Erich, stopped briefly in front of the Cafe Warschau, debating whether he should go in. The door looked like a bunker entrance between the high piles of snow shoveled up to either side. Maybe the atmosphere inside would help him. He'd heard it said that just being around poets and writers could get you going with the pen. He wasn't convinced. He was a revolutionary, not a writer—was and always would be, like Wilhelm. These Hannah Mühlendorff stories he'd taken on himself to create were beginning to be an impossible task. One should stick to what one was good at, and that was that.

Discouraged, he trudged on past the shadowy forms of the Vopos, past the great domed S-Bahn station, past the ugly stalk of the television tower. He was five miles from home and determined to walk the whole way. He wasn't worried about being recognized. Wilhelm was the one who'd become recognizable at the end. No, tonight he was worried about other things. He was worried that his debut as Hannah Mühlendorff would fall flat. A lousy story might take the wind out of the sails of the emotional popular movement that had emerged in the wake of Bülow's assassination.

Erich had no doubt that the underground's next victim—the minister of national defense—would eventually fall. But if his story couldn't stir up the same sense of widespread popular anticipation that Hannah Mühlendorff had managed before Bülow's death, he was afraid the impact of the deed would be seriously diminished.

The wind gusted more strongly as darkness fell. He stopped in a noisy bar for hot tea and rum, then hurried along deserted thoroughfares toward Weissensee. Why did the things he put on paper die a sudden death, things that lived so passionately in his mind? What to do? He'd already written twenty drafts, each worse than the last.

He paused in front of old Sacher's cottage. A light burned in the window and a plume of coal smoke hovered about the chimney. He thought about the American, Clayton Bentley, who two months earlier had hidden inside the cottage. A brave man, even if he didn't appreciate *bockwurst*.

He moved through untended thickets, and thought about Käte Frassek. What a marvelous woman ... And especially he thought of his old friend Wilhelm ... Wilhelm Jahn, who had led and inspired them for so many years. He doubted he was the one to bear the responsibility of their legacy ...

He listened to the great leafless oaks creak in the wind, and thought he heard something move in the thicket. He paused for a moment. All he could hear was the snow falling on his jacket and the wind rattling ramshackle trellises—

A hand settled on his shoulder. He spun around, instinctively prepared to strike. In the darkness it was difficult to see. But the faint glow from the cottage window let him make out the gaunt face and ice-caked beard of a tramp.

He wanted to tell the man what he thought of him for startling him, but the night was frigid and the man was in obvious distress. "Hey, for God's sake, haven't you got somewhere to go? It's a bad night to be out and you're sure as hell not dressed for it."

"I had to sell my fur coat outside Magdeburg," the tramp said. "The farmers were going to turn me in for vagrancy if I didn't give it to them."

Erich took the man by the shoulders, looked at him more closely. "*Adelbert?*"

"Yes, Erich, I've come back to help."

Erich embraced him, then led him down an overgrown path. Just then the clouds broke and the moonlight burst on the winter landscape. Together they looked up at a row of birdhouses attached to the low branches of the huge oaks, each wearing a jester's cap of snow. "Nice," Erich said.

"Like a poem...But where are we going?"

"To my new place. From there we'll have to move you around. Want to stay in Berlin?"

"I do, if it's not a burden."

"We need you here, Jürgen...Will you write for us?"

"That's why I came back."

The clouds swallowed up the moon. They smiled at each other in the darkness.

"When do I start?"

"How about tonight?"

"Tonight?"

"Yes. The story must go out soon. Gerlach's assassination has already been planned."

Erich gave a brief description of the bare bones of the story about how the minister of national defense would die. Adelbert could flesh it out, make something real and dramatic out of it. The snow began to fall again and the wind picked up. They walked a stretch in silence.

Adelbert took his friend by the arm. Soon he commenced to speak very quietly, and he told Erich his version of the story of Gerlach's death, the hows and especially the whys. And as they made their way through the night, the snow stinging their faces and the wind groaning in the trees, Erich realized that he was listening not to the poet Adelbert, nor to Hannah Mühlendorff's successor, but to the voice of a people awakening.

Rest easy, Wilhelm.